INSTRUMENT FLYING

INSTRUMENT FLYING

A guide to the instrument rating

—— **DAVID HOY** ——

Airlife
England

Dedication
To Anna and Catherine

Copyright © 1995 by David Hoy

First published in the UK in 1995
by Airlife Publishing Ltd

British Library Cataloguing in Publication Data
A catalogue record for this book
is available from the British Library

ISBN 1 85310 487 6

Printed in England by Livesey Ltd., Shrewsbury.

Airlife Publishing Ltd
101 Longden Road, Shrewsbury SY3 9EB, England

Contents

Typical Twin Engined Trainer Cockpit

Preface

All aircraft have their strengths and weaknesses just as the pilots who fly them. In the United Kingdom it is rare to see two consecutive days when the weather is perfect for VFR flight without reference to instruments. If a pilot wants to operate in the greatest variety of weather conditions, then he must be capable of interpreting the instruments and to know and understand the procedures that have been designed to safely convey an aircraft from one airport to another in even the most exacting weather conditions.

This does not mean of course that a pilot should ignore the limitations of either the aircraft or himself. Irrespective of qualification, a pilot would be foolhardy to consider flight into thunderstorms or into severe icing conditions unless the aircraft is approved for such flight.

This book is principally intended to help prepare a pilot to pass what is regarded as the most exacting flight test in the world, the British Instrument Rating. It will also, I hope, provide some useful tips for instrument flying and will be a handy reference manual for pilots renewing their instrument qualifications.

Subjects covered include:

Instrument Flight
Use of Radio Navigation Aids
Let Down and Approach Procedures
Airways Flight
The Instrument Rating Test.

In my original book, first published in 1981, I said that the Instrument Rating is the final hurdle in the long list of requirements for the airline pilot-to-be. Nothing has changed. The Instrument Rating Test is probably the first test that a pilot will sit that actually tests *captaincy* as well as ability to fly and perform certain tasks. It is not just a test of Instrument Flying or Radio Aid Tracking, it is an examination of the pilot's ability to cope in a high-pressure situation.

I hope that you will find this book both enjoyable and useful.

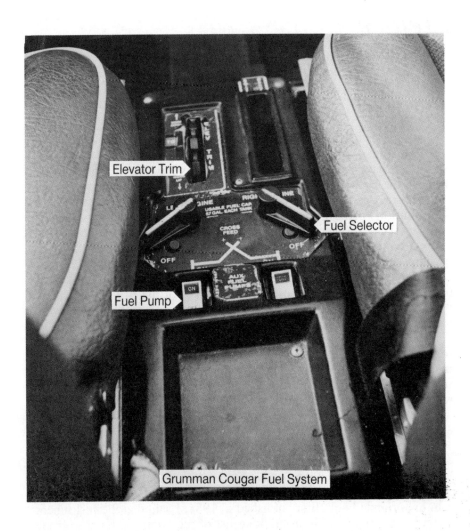

Elevator Trim

Fuel Selector

Fuel Pump

Grumman Cougar Fuel System

Chapter 1

Instrument Flying

Introduction

There are many clichés and truisms written about instrument flying and in the course of this book many will almost certainly be repeated. I make no apologies. This book will hopefully serve many purposes. It should assist not only the low-houred student pilot but also the more experienced aviator about to take his Instrument Rating. It may even help those who are already qualified and simply want a manual to refresh with.

There should be no such thing as a good visual pilot and a poor instrument pilot. Exactly the same principles for accurate instrument flying apply as for accurate 'natural horizon' or visual flying. This is an important principle to grasp. No different tactics are employed for flying straight and level on instruments than for flying straight and level in the local training area without a cloud in the sky or a set of screens to obscure the outside world. Basic technique does not alter. An aircraft is an aircraft whether it's flying in total fog or in eight-eighths blue!

As long as that fact is appreciated the next conclusion is obvious. To have the correct foundations for good IF (instrument flying) your basic general handling skills must be sound. If your basic techniques are faulty, these will run through to the instrument flying . . . so beware. Before you try and impress yourself and your instructor with your ability to stay the right way up, on the correct heading and at the right speed, without at least one eye on that ever-encircling horizon, make sure you can do it properly visually.

In the United Kingdom there are two ratings which are a test of your instrument flying abilities: the IMC (Instrument Meteorological Conditions – shortly to be re-termed the Instrument Weather Rating) Rating and the Instrument Rating. The former is peculiar to the UK and though many will differ, I feel that the amount of training required to obtain this qualification does not sensibly entitle the holder to search out the type of weather it entitles him to fly in. The Instrument Rating does. More on this later. No training is wasted however, and the more that is done the more proficient an instrument pilot you will become. It is also an ability that quenches its thirst on recency. If a pilot has not flown on instruments for several weeks he should not expect to be as accurate as the pilot who flies regularly on instruments. Again beware!

The Instruments and a Working Knowledge

Whilst modern airliner-type aircraft have sought to amalgamate instruments in the glass cockpit philosophy, the basic scan technique and use of these instruments remains the same. Combined with this, a good 'layman's' knowledge of how these instruments work, their occasional faults, problems and their inaccuracies is useful to the proficient pilot.

When flying in IMC conditions the accurate interpretation of the aircraft's flight instruments is essential. To some extent this skill depends upon an understanding of how these instruments work.

The Gyroscopic Flight Instruments

There are principally just three gyroscopically controlled instruments; The Artificial Horizon or Attitude Indicator, the Turn Co-ordinator and the Directional Gyro Indicator. These instruments are driven by a combination of air pressure or suction and electricity. Normally on the smaller aircraft the DGI and the Artificial Horizon are air driven whilst the Turn Co-ordinator is powered electrically. This system offers a back-up should one source of power fail. 'Belt and braces' is a good aviation philosophy.

Gyros have two main attributes: Rigidity and Precession. Rigidity is the property whereby once a gyro is spinning, its axis tends to remain in a fixed position unless an external force is applied to it. This property enables us to measure changes in both the attitude and the direction of our aircraft.

When a force is applied to a gyro's axis, the resultant motion that follows is known as precession. This movement appears as if the pressure had been applied ninety degrees displaced and in the same direction as the rotor is rotating. This principle is used in the 'righting' of the artificial horizon, to be discussed later, and also in the measurement of rate of turn. Precession can sometimes be unwanted as it can cause errors that must be understood.

10

The Attitude Indicator (Artificial Horizon)

Rather like a submarine commander's periscope, the attitude indicator enables the pilot to be given an immediate indication as to what's happening to the aircraft relative to the natural horizon. This is the only instrument that shows both pitch and roll directly. Pitch changes are seen by reference to the displacement of a miniature aircraft to the horizon line. Bank is seen against the same horizon line and also a pointer normally found at the top of the instrument.

This is an earth-tied gyroscope, the axis of the gyro being aligned with the earth's gravity. Initial erection is assisted by the instrument being pendulously weighted and four pendulous vanes which will cause the gyro to return to its correct setting if displaced during flight.

When an attitude indicator is started, the pendulous device senses gravity and causes the gyro to erect vertically by means of the erection force, either an air blast from pendulous vanes or an 'electric torquer'. This alignment with gravity is called the local vertical. In unaccelerated level flight, this pendulous sensor detects the force of gravity and directs the erection mechanisms to align the gyro with the local vertical, removing precession.

When the aircraft is in a co-ordinated turn, the sensor will falsely detect gravity in the same way we humans do, and will try to erect the

11

gyro to an incorrect angle. However the erection force available is very small compared to the rigidity of the gyro in space, so there is little change to the gyro angle during a turn. When again we roll the wings level, the pendulous sensor is accurate and goes to work removing any precession that has developed. *But* the system would not work if we turned the aircraft constantly or flew very shallow angles of bank over long periods of time. However a gyro would be a useless attitude indicator without it being referenced to gravity, because as pilots, we need to determine up from down, and gravity is down.

A gyro remember, remains rigid in space. A gyro free from any precession placed on one's desk now, would in twelve hours time, appear to be upside down. In fact it would be us that was upside down relative to the gyro and not the other way around. The only way we can use gyros therefore, is by constant reference to the local vertical by means of a gravity sensor.

The Errors
We have already discussed how prolonged turns can result in errors although very small. These errors are amplified if a prolonged steep turn is attempted. The error is seen once the aircraft is returned to straight and level flight as a slight climb and a turn in the opposite direction. An unbalanced turn such as a skidding turn will cause the gyro to precess towards the direction of the turn, but again the error is small.

Acceleration and deceleration errors are rarely seen on the smaller singles and twins with little power. However, acceleration can result in the attitude indicator showing a climbing turn to the right and a deceleration as a descending turn to the left.

All attitude indicators need a constant power supply, be it air or electricity. Using principally the property of rigidity they must sustain high rotation speeds for the gyro. Any loss of suction may jeopardise the safe use of this instrument. Include the suction gauge in your scan.

Pilot Interpretation
Mis-interpretation of this instrument though not common can result in dangerous situations developing. Make sure you are fully conversant with all the information the display offers.

The Directional Gyro Indicator (The DGI)
The DGI is normally a vacuum-driven instrument and senses movement about the vertical axis, the gyro having a horizontal axis of rotation. In some light aircraft an electric sensor movement will cause the gyro to remain slaved to Magnetic North. Such a gyro is called a slaved gyro. Normally what is known as a 'magnetic flux detector' is located in a

wing to sense the earth's lines of magnetism. The DGI uses the principle of rigidity to maintain its alignment and just a single gimbal allows the gyro to sense changes in direction.

Errors

The DGI suffers like any gyro from precession and also from the phenomenon of drift – as a result of the earth's rotation, and also from what is known as 'transport wander'. Both of these problems are outside the scope of this book to explain in full. Suffice to say, that an unslaved gyro needs to be checked every fifteen minutes or so, and aligned with Magnetic North.

An error in the air supply to the DGI will of course impair this instrument's accuracy. Again this instrument requires high revolution rates to maintain its rigidity, typically eighteen to twenty thousand RPM.

The Turn Co-Ordinator and Slip Indicator

This instrument enables the pilot to monitor an accurate rate of turn and to determine that it is in balance. A rate one turn is a turn at the rate of three degrees per second, 180 degrees per minute. The required bank is a function of true air-speed. The faster you fly, the larger the bank angle required to achieve a rate one turn.

A useful rule of thumb is to take ten percent of your true air-speed, add seven and that will give you the bank angle required to achieve a rate one turn.

eg   TAS   120 kts

Bank   19 degrees (12 + 7)

The turn co-ordinator displays both yaw and roll by utilising a gyro whose axis of spin is not quite horizontal, thereby being susceptible to both yaw and roll. The older 'Turn and Slip' indicator used a simple gyro with a horizontal axis of spin that detected only yaw and not roll.

It should be understood that turn co-ordinators are set for one particular forward speed and that an aircraft flying at a different speed will mean that the indications are not entirely accurate, although the differences are infinitesimal.

Errors

The main error that the turn co-ordinator suffers from is known as 'Looping Error.' When subject to positive G during a yawing manoeuvre the instrument will over-read. If subject to negative G it will under-read. This is one good reason to level the wings prior to a recovery from an unusual attitude position or negative G. The pilot would otherwise bring

13

his wings level to a false horizon according to the incorrect turn co-ordinator.

The Balance Indicator

The position of the ball of the balance indicator advises the pilot whether the aircraft is 'in balance', neither slipping into the turn nor skidding out of the turn. For a turn to be balanced the aircraft's local centre of gravity will be perpendicular to the plane of the wings. In a way the ball shows you just how well the turn is being flown – Is the correct amount of rudder being applied?

During a turn, the horizontal component of lift acts towards the centre of the turn thus opposing centrifugal force. If this turn is co-ordinated, ie in balance, the horizontal component of the lift is exactly balanced by the centrifugal force and the ball remains centred. If the turn is skidding, the centrifugal force exceeds the horizontal component of lift and the ball becomes displaced away from the direction of turn. This shows that the rate of turn is too large for the angle of bank. More bank is required or less rudder.

In a slipping turn, the opposite applies. Too much bank is being applied for the amount of turn rate and the ball moves towards the centre of the turn. Load factor, the ratio of lift to weight is affected by the co-ordination of the turn. A skid produces a greater centrifugal force leading to an increase in load factor and also an increase in stalling speed. The opposite applies to the slipping turn. Pilots should always seek to keep the ball centred for comfortable co-ordinated flight.

Instrument Checks

Prior to any flight an instrument check is made. If that flight is intended to enter cloud or low visibility it is essential for the pilot to know that his instruments are serviceable. Pilots should not forget that gyroscopes take a certain time to 'wind up.' This is normally a matter of minutes. Flight should not be attempted until they have reached their correct working speed.

During taxi, turns should be accomplished in both directions. It should be noted that the turn co-ordinator should correctly show the direction of turn and the ball should swing out in the opposite direction. The DGI should also show a turn in the same direction and if fitted, the RMI. If the co-ordinator has a 'fail flag' this of course, should not be visible. Check also that the stand-by compass is turning freely and has no trapped bubbles or fluid discoloration. During the start-up, the artificial horizon should erect fairly quickly, within thirty seconds and indicate wings level during turning and a slight pitch down during braking.

After start-up, align the DGI, if unslaved, to the stand-by compass and recheck it prior to departure. Precession should not be more than five degrees per fifteen minutes.

Do not forget the power sources for these instruments. Check for adequate suction and correctly charging ammeters prior to take-off. Some aircraft have warning flags for suction failure or 'dolls' eyes', check that these are not visible also.

The Magnetic Compass

Sometimes known as the E type or stand-by compass, the magnetic compass is a direction-seeking instrument. Whilst this instrument can give relatively accurate information, it is important to have an understanding of its faults and weaknesses.

Deviation

This is the difference between the correct magnetic heading and what the compass actually shows to the pilot. In any cockpit it is almost impossible to completely eradicate spurious magnetic fields which will have an unwanted effect on the compass. It is the job of the engineer to 'swing' the compass and reduce these errors to a minimum and to take note on a compass card of any remaining errors. Deviation is never constant on all headings and can be effected by the introduction of radios or even headsets into the cockpit.

Magnetic Dip

This is due to the vertical component of the earth's magnetic field. There is almost no dip at the earth's magnetic equator and maximum at the magnetic poles. Dip gives rise to acceleration and deceleration errors and also turning errors.

Acceleration/deceleration errors are the observed fluctuation in headings when an aircraft either gains or loses speed. In the northern hemisphere an apparent turn to the north is observed during acceleration and an apparent turn to the south during deceleration. The opposite applies in the southern hemisphere. These errors are worse when changing speed in an east/west direction and are zero when in a north/south direction.

Turning Errors

These errors are at a maximum during turns through south or through north. There are no errors when turning onto east or west. These errors increase towards the magnetic poles and are at a minimum at the magnetic equator. When turning onto a northerly heading using the

15

compass, you should undershoot the required heading and when turning onto a southerly heading you should overshoot.

The question is by how much? This is dependent on latitude. Typically in the United Kingdom an anticipation of thirty degrees will work as the lead or lag figure. For example: if turning to heading 360 degrees from west, bring wings level on indicated heading 330 degrees. If turning to south from east, bring wings level on heading 210 degrees.

In the southern hemisphere turning errors are the opposite.

The Pressure Instruments

The pressure instruments include the Altimeter, the Air-speed Indicator and the Vertical Speed Indicator. Static or ambient pressure is used by all the pressure instruments but pitot or dynamic pressure is used only by the air-speed indicator.

The Air-speed Indicator

The ASI shows the aircraft's speed by making a comparison between dynamic pressure and static pressure. Dynamic pressure is made up of pitot pressure and static pressure. Pitot pressure is the pressure that results from bringing a moving mass of air to a stop within a capsule. However the pressure that is received in the capsule within the ASI is made up of static pressure as well. Since static pressure varies with air density or altitude it is important to separate the static pressure from the calculations. This is achieved by allowing static pressure to also enter the ASI surrounding the capsule which then negates this unwanted effect of varying static pressure. There are a number of different 'speeds' we need to understand:

Vso is our stalling speed in the landing configuration at the maximum landing weight with power off.
Vs1 is the stalling speed at maximum all-up weight in the clean configuration.
Vfe is the maximum flap extension speed.
Vno is the maximum structural cruising speed.
Va is the design manoeuvring speed. This speed allows for gusty or turbulent conditions such that the load factor does not exceed safe limits.
Vle is the maximum speed for the landing gear extended.
Vlo is the maximum speed for the actual operation of the undercarriage.

Indicated Air-speed

This is the air-speed that is actually indicated on the instrument. Normally the ASI dial is colour-coded. Yellow is for the caution range, green for normal and white indicating the flap limiting speed. At the end of the green segment is the maximum normal operating speed Vno. Vne is marked by a red line and is the speed that should never be exceeded.

Calibrated Air-speed

This is indicated air-speed corrected for instrument error, errors in the manufacture or calibration of the ASI. The corrections to apply are normally very small and can be found in the pilot's operating handbook.

Rectified Air-speed

This is calibrated air-speed corrected for 'Position Error'. This is the error in the measurement of pressure, either static or dynamic but normally the former. It may be caused by inaccurate or unbalanced flying or perhaps even the lowering of flaps or undercarriage causing a local disturbance in airflow. Normally the pressure sensors, the pitot head or static vents are located to minimize these errors. Often static vents will be positioned either side of the fuselage to be self-correcting. An excess of pressure on one side will be matched by a low reading of pressure from the other. Again figures from the flight manual will enable the pilot to find RAS.

Equivalent Air-speed

This is RAS corrected for 'Compressibility Error'. The ASI's manufacturers assume that air is not compressible, but in fact it is. At the higher speeds and altitudes the air-speed indicated is in fact an over-reading of the aircraft's true speed due to this compressibility error. This is due to the fact that as the high-velocity air is brought to stagnation at the pitot tube, it is compressed and its density increases. Since the capsule expansion is related to $\frac{1}{2}pV^2$, any increase in density is unwanted for accurate measurements, and a correction has to be applied.

True Air-speed

This is the aircraft's actual speed relative to the ambient air. The ASI is calibrated in accordance with the ISA sea-level density of 1225 grammes per cubic metre. If the actual density is other than this figure then errors will result, and these will be significant. With increasing altitude, air density reduces. As a result, static air pressure reduces and so too will the dynamic pressure which is a function of density. As a consequence, whenever the density is less than ISA, the ASI will under-read.

With increasing altitude the ASI will consequently under-read. This error is called density error. Complications worsen still more when one considers that air density is also a function of temperature and pressure. Warm temperatures reduce density and cold temperatures increase it.

The Dalton Computer can be used to calculate density error, apply it to RAS to obtain TAS.

Serviceability Checks

Prior to taxi, ensure that all holes in the pitot or pressure head are clear. Ensure also that the static vents, if equipped, are clear. Check also that the pitot head is serviceable, but don't leave switched on too long as it is a tremendous drain on the battery and elements are quickly burnt out when there is no cooling air surrounding it.

The Altimeter

The Altimeter advises the pilot what altitude, height or flight level the aircraft is flying at. It also gives an impression of rate of climb and descent and an indirect indication of attitude.

The pressure sensing mechanism of this instrument gives rise to errors, the main one being lag. However once this lag is understood, the altimeter is an extremely useful instrument for not only maintaining level flight, but more importantly recovering back to level flight.

When flying IFR outside controlled airspace, but above 3,000 ft amsl, pilots should set 1013 mbs and fly quadrantal levels. When in controlled airspace pilots should comply with level instructions.

Regional QNH's represent the lowest forecast QNH for that particular area. When set, they will provide the best terrain separation available.

Mis-setting of altimeters is possibly the most common cause of aircraft accident. The presentation of altitude information has undergone very many changes in recent years and it is important for the pilot to become familiar with his aircraft's display. If continuing to fly altitudes either the closest aerodrome QNH may be used, if within twenty-five nms of the aircraft or the Regional QNH . . . which is a forecast QNH for the area.

Quadrantal rules

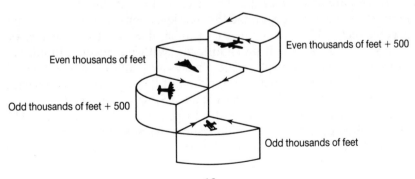

Even thousands of feet

Even thousands of feet + 500

Odd thousands of feet + 500

Odd thousands of feet

The UK and the various regions:

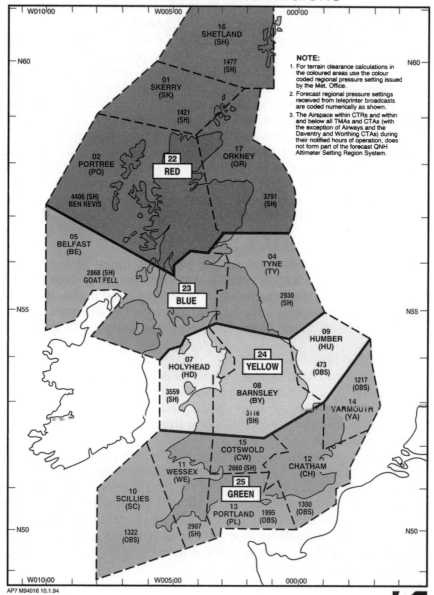

ALTIMETER SETTING REGIONS

NOTE:
1. For terrain clearance calculations in the coloured areas use the colour coded regional pressure setting issued by the Met. Office.
2. Forecast regional pressure settings received from teleprinter broadcasts are coded numerically as shown.
3. The Airspace within CTRs and within and below all TMAs and CTAs (with the exception of Airways and the Daventry and Worthing CTAs) during their notified hours of operation, does not form part of the forecast QNH Altimeter Setting Region System.

AP7 M94016 10.1.94

NATS

19

Errors and the Altimeter

The altimeter sub-scale setting must be correctly set for the area in which one is flying to give accurate information for terrain clearance. Similarly if separation from other traffic is the priority it is important for all the aircraft in the area to have their altimeters correctly set.

Prior to departure check as normal that the static vents are unblocked. Check that when the sub-scale setting is increased the altimeter indication increases and when the sub-scale setting is reduced the indication reduces. This also helps to reduce hysteresis error, which is the unwanted reluctance to movement of the capsules. Check that when the QFE is set that the instrument reads zero to within acceptable limits, typically +50ft to -70ft and if you have two altimeters that the instruments cross check. If both altimeters are set to zero, the sub-scale settings should be within two millibars of each other. When QNH is set, again check that the altimeter indicates airfield or apron elevation to within acceptable limits, and again that if two altimeters are used, that each altimeter is within 100 feet of each other.

Pilot Mis-setting or Mis-reading

Too often, pilots either mis-set sub-scales or simply mis-read their altimeters. This can lead to collision with other aircraft or even with the ground. Either has the same results. When setting the altimeter, check and re-check and cross-check with the other altimeter. The difference between the two altimeters should be sensible. Take time to calculate the difference.

The Vertical Speed Indicator

This instrument gives the pilot not only an indication of rate of climb and descent but more importantly an indication of when the aircraft is flying level. The instrument measures the rate of change of static pressure and air temperature has no effect on this instrument. Therefore there is no correction for density error.

The VSI gives an almost instantaneous indication of a movement away from level flight. As such it is more useful than the altimeter when looking to maintain level flight. Wait for the altimeter to show an error and the error has already been made. After a short period, typically five to ten seconds, the VSI will settle and show the actual rate of climb or descent. Some aircraft are now equipped with IVSIs, Instantaneous Vertical Speed Indicators which utilise accelerometers to reduce the lag suffered by their older counterpart.

Pre-flight Instrument Check

As with all pressure instruments the glass should be unbroken and the readings legible. In addition, check that the display on the ground indicates within a maximum of 200 feet of zero. During strong wind situations or after start-up the local air may result in instrument fluctuations. In flight however these fluctuations should not occur. Check also that the static vents are clear and if heated are switched on during icing conditions. Should the static vent become blocked the VSI will return to a Zero indication and will be of no further use until the blockage is removed.

What is Attitude Instrument Flying?

We've got a problem with our attitude. Over the years a very simple concept of instrument flying has been made unnecessarily complicated. The basic theory was elegant : Put an aircraft in a specific attitude (and configuration), apply a certain amount of power, and it will consistently respond with the same performance. Actually, the problem isn't with our attitude; it's with how we use the instruments to keep the aircraft in the attitude we want, once we get it there. Confused? Hang in there and we'll try to do a little attitude adjustment.

'See where the horizon meets the cowling when you're climbing at seventy knots', my instructor pointed out during one of my very first lessons. 'Keep that attitude and with full power you're always going to climb at seventy knots'.

Once we had the aircraft flying straight and level, he made me memorise where the nose rode in relationship to the horizon. 'With cruise power, if you keep the nose in that position, you'll always fly level', he said. 'See how far above the same distance and you'll fly straight'.

Then we pulled back the throttle and set up a power-off glide at seventy knots. 'Notice how far below the horizon the top of the cowling is? Anytime you want to descend at seventy knots, reduce the power, lower the nose so it's that far below the horizon and you'll glide at seventy knots'.

As students, we're trained initially to establish the attitude of the aircraft by the relationship of features on the aircraft (a row of rivets, the strut, the wingtip, the cowl, a bug on the windscreen) to the horizon or to points on the ground. Want to make a thirty degree bank turn in a Cessna 150 at cruise speed? Simple. Bank the plane until the wing strut is parallel to the ground and keep it there.

Almost without being aware of it, at the same time that we're learning to control the aircraft by referring to outside indicators, we're also beginning to understand how the information presented by the various instruments corresponds to those outside references. We're transferring 'contact' attitude flying (when you have visual contact with the outside world) to instrument attitude flying, which the CAA describes simply as 'the control of an aircraft's spacial position by the use of instruments rather than by outside visual reference'.

During a seventy knot climb with full power, in addition to watching where the nose is in relation to the horizon, we learn how many bar widths the miniature aircraft on the attitude indicator is above the horizon bar. Then, anytime we put the miniature aircraft in that position and apply fully power, we will climb at seventy knots.

During training, when we take away the outside references by flying under a hood or behind screens, we find that everything we were able to deduce about the aircraft's attitude from outside references we can also infer – often more accurately – from the instruments. With experience, we learn to read them and understand what they are telling us.

One instrument, the attitude indicator, quickly becomes a favourite when we are trying to figure out what is going on. It is the one instrument that gives us an instantaneous indication of our pitch and bank, and for that reason it is the one that assumes the centre stage location in the top middle of the instrument panel. As we initiate a level thirty degree bank turn, it is the attitude indicator that lets us set the initial bank angle and adjust the increase in back pressure as the miniature aircraft cants over to one side and moves slightly above the horizon bar. Once the attitude indicator stabilises, we monitor the other instruments, noting the changes indicated by the directional gyro and the compass, and watching to be sure that the altimeter, vertical speed indicator and airspeed indicator remain steady once the turn is established. The turn co-ordinator should show a bank with the ball in the centre – providing, of course, we are not abusing the rudder.

It was all very simple until someone came along and tried to analyse exactly how pilots learn to fly on instruments. Two methods (control and performance – and primary/support) were isolated, defined, and have been picked over ever since.

The control and performance system relies heavily on the attitude indicator, even after the initial attitude is established, to monitor 'howgozit'. The second method concentrates on other instruments to confirm what is happening with the aircraft.

To climb from 2,000 feet to 4,000 feet in a typical trainer, for example, you would raise the nose to the proper attitude for a climb indicated by the attitude indicator and simultaneously increase the power setting for the climb. At that point, your primary focus turns to the altimeter. But the altimeter is not alone in revealing secrets about your upward mobility. The air-speed indicator and the vertical speed indicator also change their stories during an adjustment in altitude. They supplement and support the information from the altimeter. And that is the theory behind the primary/support method.

This method divides the instruments into three groups based on the way they relate to control function and aircraft performance. The instruments for pitch are: attitude indicator, altimeter, air-speed indicator and vertical speed indicator. For bank: attitude indicator, heading indicator and turn co-ordinator. For power: manifold pressure gauge, tachometer/rpm, air-speed indicator and engine pressure ratio (for jets). The attitude indicator, so popular in the control and performance method, is also a standout here, being the only instrument to be included in two of the three groups.

For each particular manoeuvre or portion of a manoeuvre, there is an instrument that is the primary reference and other instruments that supplement and support that primary instrument.

The attitude indicator is initially primary while the climbing turn is established. The air-speed indicator become the primary pitch instrument during the power application until the vertical speed indicator stabilises at the desired rate. The VSI then becomes primary for pitch control and the air-speed indicator becomes primary for power control with the tachometer or manifold pressure gauge for supporting power. The turn co-ordinator becomes the primary bank instrument after the turn is established, with the attitude indicator providing bank as well as pitch information. Got that? You will be tested later.

Trying to distinguish between the two methods is difficult. Not to worry. It is a lot like walking. If you try to analyse what each muscle in the leg is doing, what signals the brain is receiving from its sensors and how it is responding to each input, you will probably trip and fall. Certainly you won't be able to walk and chew gum. Trying to analyse which instrument you look at during a manoeuvre, when, and for how long, is artificially making a science of what should be an art.

Fortunately the two methods of attitude instrument flying are intended only as a launching platform to introduce students to flying on the gauges and to teach them the three skills that are really necessary for instrument flying : cross-check, instrument interpretation and aircraft control.

You learn by doing. After introducing the instruments and demonstrating their strengths and weaknesses, the instructor is really along primarily as a safety pilot when it comes to learning to 'control and manoeuvre an aircraft solely by reference to instruments'. The instructor is there to remind you when you forget something.

If you fixate on one instrument and ignore the story the others are trying to tell you, eventually your instructor will lean over and bring it to your attention. You are in a climbing turn to a heading of 180 degrees and an altitude of 2,500 feet. As you approach 180 degrees you fixate on the directional gyro and forget to watch what is happening with the altimeter. As you pass the assigned altitude, the instructor will tap the altimeter, recommending you to include it in your scan. You quickly learn to cross-check or scan the instrument panel, looking for the information you need from the instrument that is most relevant at the time.

You will know you are beginning to catch-on when your instructor seems to always point to an instrument in that half moment just after you have noticed it but before you have had a chance to react.

Do not get hung-up on which method you are learning – in the end, they are both the same. The trick is knowing what is happening (scanning) so you know what needs to be done (interpreting) and then changing the power setting or control surface positions (to control the aircraft). You just do what you gotta do!

No matter if you subscribe to the control and performance or the primary/support schools of attitude in instrument teaching, it is important to remember that attitude indicators have been known to roll over and play dead, most commonly because the vacuum pump powering the gyro has failed. Anyone flying on instruments must be competent enough to recognise when the gyro instruments have baled out and to be capable of keeping the right side up using partial panel. Without gyros, the supporting instruments that were temporarily primary become primary for real, until you get out of the clouds.

There is something very reassuring about the way attitude instrument flying works in the real world. In a cardinal, when I want to slow down to approach speed, I know that if I reduce the manifold pressure to fourteen inches (just before the gear warning horn begins bleeping) and lower ten degrees of flaps while leaving the rpm set at the 2,300 cruise setting, the aircraft will fly level at ninety-five knots. When the glideslope needle comes alive, all I have to do is drop the gear and the aircraft will settle into a 500 fpm descent and slide down the glideslope at ninety-five knots – every time.

Attitude flying is not just for the little guys. The King Air B200, at 1,700 rpm and 800 pounds of torque, will settle down and fly level at about 160 knots. Lower approach flaps and it slows further to about 140 knots. Now lower the gear and it will maintain 140 knots by descending at about 500 fpm. With little experimentation you can work out the power and configuration combinations that will give you the speeds you want for holding patterns, descent and approach.

Because of its consistency and reliability, attitude flying can alert you to unexpected configurations. If the aircraft is not climbing the way it should, based on the attitude and power settings, it means you have still got some flaps hanging out or you have not raised the gear.

If your descent rate or speed is not what it should be, then something's not set the way you think it is. In the Cardinal, if I have forgotten to lower the gear, with a 500 fpm descent I am going to be going a lot faster than ninety-five knots.

Attitude instrument flying is difficult to explain, hard to teach, and demands hours of practice to master, but it is the core of safe and precise IFR flying. And, in a pinch, it makes a pretty good back-up for the gear warning horn.

Instrument Flying – How is it done?

To say that instrument flying and visual flying are the same is obviously not quite true. If it were there would be no need for instructors or for practice. If there is one thing the competent IF pilot needs, that is practice and lots of it!

However the principles for both are the same. If the pilot sets a POWER and selects an ATTITUDE he will obtain a certain PERFORMANCE. Set 2,200 RPM and the old familiar level flight attitude in most single-engined aircraft will give you a cruising speed of ninety knots. Select a descent attitude of say four degrees pitch down and a power of, say 1,700 RPM and the aircraft will descend at ninety knots and 550 feet per minute. In each case the pilot has selected a power and an attitude and has obtained a certain performance.

Everything so far said can be related to instrument flying as well. In fact, the instruments have been used even when flying visually to confirm that we have been doing things correctly. We can't fly straight and level without the occasional glance at the altimeter for instance. The important thing to appreciate is that, when using the instruments and in particular the artificial horizon, any movement that is seen on this instrument is magnified many times when it comes to flying visually. In consequence make all control movements small and gentle ones.

Remember also that every instrument has a purpose. Don't dwell on one instrument for too long. If you catch yourself looking at one instrument for too long at the expense of the others, mentally chastise yourself and get those eyes moving. Just how you should move the eyes will be dealt with later.

For the sake of good order, we divide the instruments into two: the *Control Instruments* and the *Performance Instruments*.

The control instruments are primarily the attitude indicator or artificial horizon and the power gauge. However we can also include the balance indicator.

The performance instruments include the air-speed indicator, the altimeter and vertical speed indicator, all compass gauges and the turn co-ordinator.

Set the correct power on the control instrument, set the correct attitude on the control instrument and check the correct result on the performance instrument.

To control an aircraft accurately you must be able to hold and to reselect a new attitude. You must also train yourself into noticing a change in attitude that may not be deliberate and to correct it back to where it should be. The performance instruments will of course help you to notice, but the more able pilot should see it on the control instruments first. You must also know when to make a change and by how much.

If having selected a power and attitude combination, you are not achieving the desired result, you have to know what to change in order to correct the problem. However, all changes are made to the attitude or sometimes the balance and to the power. Balance is controlled by rudder position and power by throttle position; attitude is controlled by the control column. The change in position will be reflected on the performance instruments. If the change is not as you require it, be prepared to adjust either the attitude or power or both.

Scanning

This is the word used to describe how the pilot 'looks' at the instruments. It is essential for the pilot to adopt a scheme of scanning that uses all the flight instruments in such a way that they all support and corroborate each other.

The most popular scanning system is known as the 'Selective Radial Scan'. The artificial horizon or attitude indicator is considered the most important instrument and should therefore receive more attention than the other instruments. As such we can think of the A/H as the telephone exchange. All the other instruments are telephones. Before we can phone or look at another subscriber we have to go through the telephone exchange. In other words, our attention should not jump from one instrument to another but always work through the attitude indicator. We are therefore scanning radially away from and back to the attitude indicator.

The scan is also selective. Whilst most scans will involve all the instruments, during specific phases of flight we will give more attention to a certain group of instruments than to others.

For instance, if in straight and level flight, flying on a constant heading and at a constant altitude, our main scan should be on the artificial horizon for pitch and roll, the VSI for height trend and the altimeter and DGI. If the wings are level and a constant direction is being maintained we don't really need to check if the aircraft is in balance. It will be.

Let's now be a little clearer with the phrase *selective and radial*.

Selective simply means that you will be careful in your choice of instruments to scan, to thus minimise time wasting and maximise accuracy. Radial means that we will always treat the A/H as our most important source of information and refer back to it between our checks of the various performance instruments.

Obviously a pilot should not expect to leap from one aircraft type to another and expect to fly either visually or on instruments until a certain experience level has been achieved. I don't know what the visual straight and level attitude is in Concorde for instance and nor do I know by how much to change the attitude in that aircraft to achieve a specific climb performance given a certain power. However, for most light singles and twins the following tips relating to attitude changes and power settings may help.

Set the centre dot of the small aircraft on the A/H to coincide with the horizon line. Thereafter select attitudes using this centre dot. Some aircraft will be fitted with A/H's showing angular displacement from the level flight position. Others will not, and for these think in terms of wing-bar thickness as represented by the small aircraft on the A/H.

For most light singles, if asked to establish a given rate of descent, halve the ROD and subtract that figure from the straight and level power setting. Do maintain the same speed, eg:

Descend at 800 feet per minute

Level flight 2,200 RPM at 90 kts

Descent 1,800 RPM (2,200-400) 90 kts = 800 feet per minute.

During the descent if the speed is incorrect, it can be controlled by the reselection of attitude or power or even a combination of both. If the ROD is wrong the same parameters can be altered to achieve the final aim. *It is the mark of the good instrument pilot who can correctly interpret what changes need to be made to achieve that final aim.*

Only when you can maintain speed to within five knots, height to within fifty feet and heading to within five degrees are we really talking about accurate flying. By using the correct scanning technique you will achieve these levels of accuracy and even better.

If descending in an aircraft fitted with a constant speed propeller and power set by manifold pressure, one inch of MAP represents 100 feet per minute in descent. If you wish to descend at 500 feet per minute reduce power by five inches.

If levelling from a climb or a descent sufficient anticipation must be applied. For a climb, normally ten percent of the rate of climb will suffice. For descent, try twenty percent. For example, climbing at 400 feet per minute, anticipate your level-off altitude by forty feet. If descending at the same rate, use eighty feet. Remember, in a climb gravity is trying to stop you climbing; in a descent it wants you to keep going!

Anticipation on turning also varies between aircraft to some extent, but typically, take half your bank angle and use that as a lead to your new heading. Bank twenty degrees, anticipate heading and start to bring your wings level when within ten degrees of your new heading. Remember that most instrument turns will be rate one, ie three degrees per second. To calculate the bank angle required for rate one, take ten percent of your TAS and add the figure seven. An aircraft travelling at 120 kts will require a bank angle of nineteen degrees to achieve a rate one turn.

Let us now turn our attention to the various recommended scans for the various stages of flight.

Scanning During Straight and Level Flight

During visual flying we divide this exercise into two. For level flight we say that we should firstly select the correct power followed by the correct selection of pitch attitude. No different for instrument flying! Once the power has been correctly chosen place the centre dot of the aircraft on the artificial horizon against the horizon line of this instrument. We must now check a performance instrument to confirm that the aircraft is maintaining level flight. The instrument chosen for this checking is the vertical speed indicator. The scan for level flight is therefore A/H to VSI back to A/H. This also incidentally applies to level turns.

From time to time the pilot should glance to the altimeter to confirm that the correct altitude is being maintained, but this is a secondary scan. The primary scan is to the vertical speed indicator.

In visual straight flight, we say that we have to keep the wings level and the aircraft in balance. In addition we need to select a reference point in the distance to aim at. In IMC conditions this reference point is replaced by the DGI and a heading is chosen or perhaps a track as displayed by the ADF or a VOR. Again we keep the wings level by reference to the artificial horizon and we check to the balance indicator that we are keeping the aircraft in balance by use of the rudder. We check the DGI (or compass) to see that the aircraft is maintaining direction as demanded.

For straight and level flight we have to combine the aforesaid scans and find ourselves checking VSI and DGI for the performance we need against the attitude we've chosen. If we are not maintaining height or heading then something has to be done. For height errors of less than 100 feet then simply readjust attitude to recover to the correct height. Errors greater than this will require a change in power as well as attitude. Directional errors of less than five degrees may well be corrected by very gentle rudder application or very small bank whilst errors of five degrees or more will require gentle bank. Halve the heading error and use that figure as the maximum bank angle you would apply during correction . . . up to a maximum of Rate One.

Remember that during level flight the VSI will indicate a movement away before the altimeter. Don't wait for the altimeter to tell you that an error has already been made.

Consider also that if both speed and height are wrong on the same side, namely too fast and too high or too low and too slow, a power alteration as well as an attitude change will always be necessary.

Scanning During Climb Entry

Visually, prior to each climb we have our preliminary checks. Mixture set, carb. heat cold and engine gauges check. The same applies to pre-climb checks on the instruments. Check also that you are not climbing into a sub-zero layer by reference to the outside air temperature (if your aircraft is not cleared for icing) and ensure that the radar controller is aware of your intentions to change level.

The same entry procedure applies, namely Power/Attitude/Trim.
1. Apply the correct climb power.
2. Simultaneous rudder to maintain balance and direction.
3. Select known climb attitude, and coarse trim if required.
4. Allow air-speed to settle.
5. Adjust attitude to compensate for small speed errors.
6. Maintain attitude and fine trim as necessary.
Select – Hold – Trim – Check – Trim.

In terms of scanning, as always the scan starts at the attitude indicator, for the attitude selection. Whilst the air-speed is reducing a short glance to the turn co-ordinator to confirm the correct rudder has been applied (this is a secondary scan) and then to the air-speed indicator. We then check to the DGI to confirm that the direction is being maintained. As the aircraft approaches its assigned altitude the altimeter is then brought into the scan. The primary scan is therefore the attitude indicator, the air-speed indicator and the direction indicator.

Scanning at the Level-off

Approximately ten percent of your rate of climb should be the figure used to anticipate the level-off. Climbing at 800 feet per minute will therefore require an eighty foot anticipation of your level-off. At this point, smoothly squeeze forward on the control column, reselecting the straight and level attitude. First scanning point therefore is the attitude indicator. Remember, as the air-speed increases a lower nose attitude will be needed to maintain level flight. Scan across to the altimeter to confirm that you have stopped the climb at the correct position. As the air-speed increases coarse trim as required to prevent the aircraft climbing further. Just before the aircraft reaches its required cruising speed, reduce power to the required setting and settle back into the normal straight and level scan, as described earlier. To complete apply fine trimming to a hands-off situation.

Scanning During Descent Entry

Normal visual pre-descent checks apply. Mixture set, carb. heat to requirement. In addition, ensure that radar has been informed and if flying in true IMC conditions consider very carefully the terrain and your 'Minimum Safety Altitude'. Do not descend below it. If your airframe is cold, consider also the possibility of airframe icing as you descend into moister air.

Power, attitude, trim applies again, just as for visual descents. If flying a fixed-pitch propeller, a useful tip is to halve the requested rate of descent and deduct this figure from your RPM gauge. Descent at 800 feet per minute requires a 400 RPM power reduction. This works as long as you remember to maintain the same speed.

All descents in IMC conditions should be 'cruise descents' in order to maintain engine warming and adequate suction for driving the gyro instruments. This also reduces the risk of carburettor icing.

Select the required power and simultaneously adjust the rudder to maintain balance and direction. Simultaneously select your anticipated pitch down attitude to enter the required rate of descent. The scan still centres upon the attitude indicator. From the AI scan to the VSI to confirm the required rate of descent has been achieved. Scan also to the ASI to confirm the required speed has been achieved. A combination of power and attitude changes will be needed to achieve the required result. Slightly too high a rate of descent but at the correct speed will need an increase in power as well as a raised nose attitude. Too low a rate of descent and a low speed may be a situation recoverable by simply selecting a lower nose attitude.

It is unlikely that the changes needed will come naturally even to an experienced pilot. One has to think about it!

Scanning for a Level Turn

When turning in IMC conditions we aim to limit the bank angle such that a Rate One turn is not exceeded . . . three degrees per second. This has several advantages. Less anticipation is required on the level-off and less back-pressure or change in attitude is needed to maintain level flight. The reduced bank angle also reduces any disorientation that may result.

Scan again centres on the attitude indicator. Having advised the radar controller of your intention to turn, select the requisite bank angle on the A/I and simultaneously apply the requisite amount of rudder to remain in balance. In some aircraft very little, if any, rudder will be required.

Scan immediately to the VSI and confirm that the new banked attitude and pitch attitude are maintaining level flight. Adjust if necessary. Scan across to the ASI and determine if any extra power is needed to maintain required speed. Short turns may require no additional power, longer turns will require extra power.

From time to time glance at the altimeter to confirm that no change in attitude is required to re-acquire lost or gained height. As the heading is approached include the DGI in your secondary scan. Allow approximately half your bank angle in degrees anticipation of level-off. Twenty degrees of bank will need ten degrees anticipation.

Scanning During the Climbing Turn and the Descending Turn
Remember that when climbing, you will be inevitably flying at a lower air-speed and closer to the stalling speed. When turning, the stalling speed increases. In order to avoid crossing the line and running the risk of stalling, limit your climbing bank angle to fifteen degrees. In this way an adequate climb performance will also be maintained as well as avoiding a possible stall.

Remember that during a climbing turn, a close inspection of pitch and roll attitude must be maintained to avoid either diverging from the original setting. During both climbing and descending turns maintain a close watch on the air-speed indicator.

Limited Panel
In the event that the aircraft suffers a loss of the suction pump, the pilot may be left without the artificial horizon/attitude indicator and the directional gyro indicator. This situation is tested during GFT 3 of the commercial flight test and also during an Instrument Rating for issue on a Private Pilot's Licence. In the UK it will also be examined during the IMC rating or Instrument Weather Rating, a qualification peculiar to the UK.

Control of pitch will now be related to control column position and scanning to the VSI and the altimeter. Indirect pitch information can be derived from the ASI and the power gauge. Given a certain power, level flight will be determined by a given speed. Again knowledge of the aircraft is a prerequisite. All control column movements fore and aft should be gentle and of a small magnitude. Roll information is derived from the turn co-ordinator and the magnetic compass. Pilots should endeavour at all times to keep the aircraft in balance by reference to the balance ball.

Scan will therefore centre on the VSI for level flight and the turn co-ordinator for straight flight. Turns may be accomplished again using the VSI for level flight and the turn co-ordinator for ensuring the correct bank angle and therefore rate have been achieved. The stopwatch and your knowledge of compass errors can be used for turning with reasonable accuracy onto required headings.

For timed turns, remember 'rate one' means three degrees per second. A turn of thirty degrees will take ten seconds. The VOR rose on most aircraft is divided into thirty degree segments. Use the rose for orientation and for calculating how many seconds a turn will take. Always turn the shortest way unless otherwise instructed. Again the VOR rose will help in this respect.

Start the stopwatch prior to rolling into the turn and commence roll out at the end of the timing and not before. Don't anticipate the time. A turn of 180 degrees will take sixty seconds. Start the stopwatch, roll into the turn and only bring the wings level once the minute has elapsed, paying close attention to rolling out at the same rate as you rolled in.

Recovery from Unusual Attitudes.

At some stage of your flying career you will be expected to show a recovery from various unusual attitudes and when flying with a limited panel of instruments, no attitude indicator and no DGI. This can prove surprisingly difficult if ill-prepared.

Such recoveries can be divided into high speed and low speed recoveries. For each recovery type, avoid combining control movements. If pitch and roll are required, do them separately. Since the pilot is relying upon the turn co-ordinator for roll information, any 'g' applied to this instrument whilst rolling will cause the instrument to read incorrectly.

High Speed Recovery
1. Close throttle completely.
2. Level wings by reference to the turn co-ordinator.
3. Apply rudder to maintain aircraft in balance.
4. Apply back elevator to arrest descent, scanning from turn co-ordinator to altimeter. The second the altimeter shows that the descent has stopped, check forward on the control column to maintain height and prevent the aircraft entering a climb.
5. As the air-speed approaches (as it reduces) your manoeuvring speed re-apply power to maintain it.

Low Speed Recovery
1. Apply full power with co-ordinated rudder to maintain balance.
2. *If air-speed signifies an approaching stall* move the control column gently forward to avert risk of a stall, and then gently level the wings by reference to the turn co-ordinator.

3. *If no risk of stall* roll wings level by reference to the turn co-ordinator and then move control column gently forward, maintaining wings level, until the altimeter indicates the climb has been arrested.
4. Maintain full power until the air-speed arrives at required manoeuvring speed at which time reduce power to correct setting.

Confirm that the recovery has been achieved above the minimum safety altitude. Reconfirm heading by reference to the stand-by compass. But what could cause an unusual attitude to develop, full or limited panel . . . spatial disorientation:

The examiner will be looking for prompt recovery without excessive loss of height.

Sensory Illusion and Spatial Disorientation

In the first few lines of this book it was emphasised that as long as they appeared serviceable, the instruments should be believed over and above what the body's senses are trying to tell the pilot. Disorientation is a condition in which the pilot believes something is happening that in fact isn't. This may relate to the aircraft's geographical position, its attitude in space relative to the real horizon or even its motion, acceleration or deceleration.

In normal visual conditions the pilot has ample visual information available from the earth's horizon. The cues that are seen visually confirm what the pilot interprets via the balance mechanism of the inner ear, and from pressures felt via the control column and rudder pedals. To some extent attitude is also being confirmed by sound, again detected by ear. It is possible to be fooled by some of these signals and misinterpret one situation for another.

In a level co-ordinated turn, the local gravity should be working through the centre of the pilot's body. In a rate one turn, where little change in attitude is needed to maintain level flight it would be easy to think that the wings were in fact level. Recovery back to straight and level flight may be interpreted as a turn into the opposite direction.

Other situations may lead the pilot into spatial disorientation include the following:

> Turbulence.
> Strobe lights reflecting from cloud.
> Navigation lights reflecting from cloud.
> Hazy conditions.
> Night flying/complete lack of horizon.
> Autokinesis.
> Flying above sloping cloud layers.
> Scanning too quickly from one side of cockpit to the other.
> Rapid head movements.
> Rapid control movements.
> Pressure vertigo (disorientation during ascent and descent).

Also contributing to the above factors: ill-health, pilot under medication, blocked respiratory tracts, pilot fatigue/hangover from excessive alcohol, out of practice.

The problem with spatial disorientation is that one may not be aware of it until very late. Its approach is insidious. Believe your eyes, and not your senses unless you have good cause to believe your instruments are not telling you the truth. It's highly improbable they are all not working!

INSTRUMENT FLYING (Basic Manouevres)
STRAIGHT AND LEVEL

AIM: To fly the aircraft by sole reference to instruments.

AIRMANSHIP: LOOKOUT (Safety pilot) — Physiological considerations; Engine checks.

AIREX: Note: Smooth control movement — relax grip on control column.

◀▶ Primary Scan ◀─► Occasional to Frequent Scan ◀───► Occasional Scan

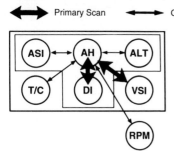

Control Instruments : Power — Ball — A/H
Attitude Instruments: A/H (Master Instrument)
Performance
Instruments: ASI — ALT — T/C —
D.I. — VSI

Note: Power + Attitude = Performance

Technique: Selective Radial Scan — SRS

1) CONSTANT HEIGHT

Power as required

Select attitude: A/H — VSI — A/H

Hold

TRIM

Adjust — A/H
and re-trim if necessary

Check correct speed

2) CONSTANT DIRECTION AND BALANCE

Check wings level — A/H

T/C — Ball in middle — A/H

D.I. check correct and constant
direction — A/H

Selective Radial Scan (SRS): A/H — VSI — A/H — D.I. — A/H — ALT

Occasional: A/H — ASI — A/H — T/C — A/H — RPM — A/H

CLIMBING

AIM: To climb and level-off the aircraft under sole reference to instruments.

AIRMANSHIP: LOOKOUT (Safety Pilot); Engine checks

AIREX: From Straight & Level

ENTRY

Pre-entry checks

Full power/BALL

A/H — Select attitude
Check
Hold
Settle

TRIM

Check ASI

Adjust attitude — A/H
if necessary

D.I. check constant
direction — Adjust if necessary

IN THE CLIMB

S.R.S.:—
A/H — ASI — A/H — D.I. —
A/H

Occasional:
A/H — T/C — A/H
A/H — ALT — A/H
A/H — Ts & Ps — A/H

Frequently:
A/H — ALT — A/H as
required height approaches

LEVEL-OFF

Anticipate

A/H — Progressively select
S & L attitude

ALT check

Speed increases

Set cruise power/BALL

TRIM

Then as per S & L S.R.S.

DESCENDING (Rate of Descent)

AIM: To descend the aircraft at various Rates of Descent, speeds and with flaps, under sole reference to instruments.

AIRMANSHIP: LOOKOUT (Safety Pilot); Engine checks.

AIREX: Revision of part 1.

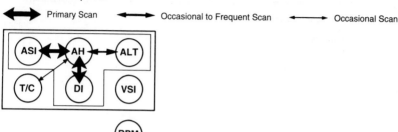

⟷ Primary Scan   **◄━━** Occasional to Frequent Scan   **◄━━►** Occasional Scan

1) RATE OF DESCENT AT CRUISE IAS

a) **Entry from Straight & Level**

Adjust power — BALL
A/H — Attitude

Hold

ASI — Check
Aircraft settled
ASI — Check Rate of
Descent

Adjust RPM — A/H if
necessary

TRIM!

D.I. check for constant
direction

b) **S.R.S.:—**
A/H — ASI — A/H — D.I. —
A/H — VSI — A/H
Ts & Ps check

c) **Level-Off**
As per gliding

2) RATE OF DESCENT AT VARIOUS SPEEDS

a) **Entry from Straight & Level**

Adjust power for required
IAS at S & L — then as
per 1a

b) **S.R.S.:—**
As per 1b

c) **Level-Off**
As per 1c

Note: If Rate of Descent changes:— 1) Check IAS correct
If IAS not correct, then a change in attitude is required to maintain Rate of Descent.

If IAS correct, then Power — Attitude is required to maintain Rate of Descent.

37

RATE 1 & MEDIUM LEVEL TURNS

AIM: To execute level turns at 15° bank (rate 1) and 30° bank (medium turn) under sole reference to instruments and to roll out onto specific headings.

AIRMANSHIP: LOOKOUT (Safety Pilot); Engine checks.

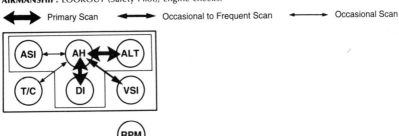

RATE 1 TURN

ENTRY	IN THE TURN	ROLL OUT
A/H — Select attitude 15° bank Hold	S.R.S.:— A/H — ALT — A/H — D.I. — A/H	Anticipate A/H — Level wings Hold
T/C — Rate 1 Ball — Balance	Occasional:— A/H — ASI — A/H — T/C	Adjust if necessary S & L scan
Adjust if necessary		

MEDIUM LEVEL TURN

ENTRY	IN THE TRUN	ROLL OUT
A/H — Select attitude to 30° bank BALL - to balance	S.R.S.:— A/H — BALL — A/H — ALT — A/H	A/H — Level wings BALL — to balance Hold
Hold	Then as per above	D.I. — Check
ALT — Check		Adjust if necessary
Adjust if necessary		S & L scan

CLIMBING & DESCENDING TURNS

RATE 1 TURN ONLY!

S.R.S.:—
A/H — ASI — A/H — BALL —
A/H

Then as per above.

GLIDING

AIM: To glide and level-off the aircraft under sole reference to instruments.
AIRMANSHIP: LOOKOUT (Safety Pilot); Engine checks
AIREX: From Straight & Level

←→ Primary Scan   ←→ Occasional to Frequent Scan   ←→ Occasional Scan

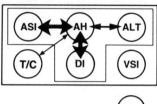

ENTRY

Pre-entry checks

Close throttle — BALL
Maintain height

At 72 kts:—
A/H — Select glide attitude
Hold

ASI Check

A/H — Adjust if necessary

TRIM!

D.I. check for correct heading

IN THE GLIDE

S.R.S.:—
A/H — ASI — A/H — D.I. —
A/H

Occasional:
A/H — T/C — A/H
A/H — ALT — A/H
A/H — Ts & Ps — A/H

Frequently:
A/H — ALT — A/H as height
approaches

Note:
Clear engine regularly

LEVEL-OFF

Anticipate

Cruise power — BALL

A/H — S & L attitude

ALT check

Hold

TRIM!

Then as per S & L S.R.S.

NB: Gliding is not normally used in IMC conditions.

39

INSTRUMENT FLYING (Advanced Manoeuvres)

LIMITED PANEL

AIM: To fly the basic manoeuvres accurately on instruments without the use of the Direction Indicator and the Artificial Horizon.

AIRMANSHIP: LOOKOUT (Safety Pilot); Engine checks.

AIREX: Straight & Level flight. Rate 1 turns onto specific headings using timed turns and the Magnetic Compass.

Pitch Control in Level Flight — Indirect information from ASI, ALT, VSI.

Lateral Control in Level Flight — T/C — BALL, Magnetic Compass.

STRAIGHT & LEVEL

Check correct power set

T/C — Wings level
BALL — Balance
ALT — Correct pitch attitude
VSI — Trend

TRIM!

ASI — Check

Magnetic Compass correct and
constant direction

SCANNING TECHNIQUE

From T/C — BALL scan clockwise

T/C — BALL — ASI — T/C — BALL — ALT
T/C — BALL — VSI — T/C — BALL
Magnetic Compasss — T/C — BALL

LEVEL TURNS

ENTRY

T/C — BALL — Select Rate 1 turn

Hold

ALT/VSI — Check constant height

Scan technique

ROLL OUT

Check watch or Magnetic Compass

Anticipate

T/C — Level wings
BALL — Balance

Hold

Magnetic Compass settled

Adjust if necessary

COMPASS ERRORS

0° on EAST or WEST
30° on NORTH or SOUTH

Undershoot required in Northerly sector

Overshoot required in Southerly sector

TIMED TURNS

Rate 1 turn = 3° per second

40

LIMITED PANEL

AIM: To fly accurately the basic manoeuvres on instruments without the use of the Direction Indicator and the Artificial Horizon.

AIRMANSHIP: LOOKOUT (Safety Pilot); Engine checks.

AIREX: Revision as necessary. Demonstration and practise of Climbing and Gliding.

    Control Technique: Select — Check — Hold — Adjust — TRIM!

CLIMBING

ENTRY	IN THE CLIMB	LEVEL OFF
Pre-entry checks	Scan from:—	Anticipate
Smoothly apply full power BALL — T/C — Wings level	T/C — BALL — IAS — T/C — BALL to Magnetic Compass Back to T/C — BALL	ALT — Select correct pitch attitude
EASE control column back to achieve correct IAS	Ts & Ps check	Check Hold
Check Hold Settle	ALT — Frequently scanned as required height approaches	T/C — BALL check
		IAS — Check
TRIM! Adjust if necessary		Adjust power/BALL
		TRIM
		Check for Straight & Level

GLIDING

ENTRY	IN THE CLIMB	LEVEL OFF
Pre-entry checks	Scan as per climb	Anticipate
Close throttle — BALL T/C — Wings level	Clear engine	Smoothly set cruise power — BALL T/C — Wings level
ALT — Maintain height		
IAS — At 72 kts. select glide attitude		ALT — Correct pitch attitude
Check Hold		Check Hold
TRIM! Adjust if necessary		TRIM!
		Check for Straight & Level

Practise Climbing and Gliding Turns and Rates of Descent.

LIMITED PANEL — RECOVERY FROM UNUSUAL ATTITUDES

AIM: To recover the aircraft from unusual attitudes to Straight & Level.

AIRMANSHIP: LOOKOUT (Safety Pilot); Engine checks.

AIREX: Recovery from Steep Climbing Turns, Spiral Dives, Stalls and Steep Turns.

STEEP CLIMBING TURN
Recovery:—

Full power
Level wings — T/C
Balance — BALL
Select level attitude — ALT
Check
Hold
IAS check cruise
Check for Straight & Level

STALL
At stall warner/buffet

Recovery:—

T/C — BALL — Wings level & balance

ALT/ASI for pitch

At cruise speed:— Adjust power

Check for Straight & Level

SPIRAL DIVE
Recovery:—

Throttle closed
T/C — Level wings
BALL — Balance

ALT — Select level attitude

Check
Hold

IAS check cruise
Set cruise power

Check for Straight & Level

STEEP LEVEL TURN
Recovery:—

T/C — Level wings
BALL — Balance

ALT — Check for correct pitch

Hold

Adjust power

Check for Straight & Level

42

STEEP LEVEL TURNS

AIM: To execute a level turn at 45° bank under sole reference to instruments and to roll out onto specific headings.

AIRMANSHIP: LOOKOUT (Safety Pilot); Engine checks.

AIREX: Revision as necessary.

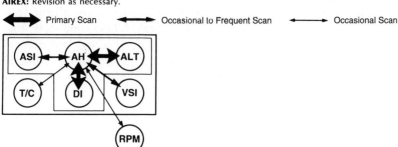

ENTRY

A/H — Smoothly apply bank
BALL to balance

At 30° bank:
Increase power to maintain IAS
ALT — Increase back pressure
Centre dot above horizon

Hold

Adjust if necessary

IN THE TURN

S.R.S.:—
As per medium level turns

ROLL OUT

Anticipate

A/H — Level wings
BALL — to balance
IAS — power adjust
ALT — Release pressure

Hold

D.I. — Check

Adjust if necessary

Straight & Level scan

(grateful thanks to PRIMO LONZARDI for diagrams).

Navigation by Instruments

As the regulations presently stand, the Instrument Rating Test does not allow the use of such luxuries as satellite navigation or any other aids other than the basic minimum equipment required for flight into controlled airspace. Such equipment includes two VORs, one ADF, one transponder with height read-out, one DME, one ILS and two comms boxes. It is clearly important for the student and qualified pilot, come to that, to have a correct understanding as to how these aids work and of course their limitations.

Let's review these limitations here:

Comms Boxes

RT communication is normally achieved using VHF transmissions. These are line of sight. Range is therefore affected by altitude. Don't attempt to call agencies outside of the recommended range.

On some occasions you may be able to hear the ATC controller but he may not be able to hear you or vice versa. Be prepared to change comms box. Normally each comms box will have its own aerial. One aerial may be better positioned to receive or transmit than the other. Consider this.

When flying in icing conditions it is not unusual for the aerials to be sufficiently covered in ice to cause the VHF signal to deteriorate.

Often airways' controllers talk exceptionally quickly and often abbreviate call-signs somewhat more than you would wish. Keep your ears open for your call-sign. Keep your RT brief and to the point. Reports in the airway should be kept to a minimum. Only make a position report when requested to do so or if you feel you need to trigger a further clearance.

On a single crew operation establish the habit of always changing the radio box that is not in use. In this way you can always return to the previous frequency if you have no joy in raising the next frequency. Always copy down frequencies and transponder codes. Don't rely on your memory.

Most ATIS frequencies work on separate ATIS VHF frequencies these days, although some are still paired with VORs. If copying the weather never turn the volume down so much on your working frequency that you cannot respond to instructions given.

Always check your radio boxes prior to flight. The Instrument Rating examiner will expect, if possible a check on two frequencies per radio box. A check on the ATIS frequency is considered satisfactory for one of these checks.

The ADF

NDBs non-directional radio beacons, utilise the medium frequency band principally. As such their emissions are ground waves and as long as the aircraft is within their promulgated range, irrespective of height, the signal can be received irrespective of altitude. Again, the examiner would expect to see the ADF checked on two frequencies. Tune, identify the signal and check for sensible QDM. If fitted, check antenna and see how rapidly the needle returns to the correct QDM.

The VOR

The VOR's range is limited to 'line of sight' as it works on the VHF band. Not all airfields will therefore have a VOR beacon sufficiently close for a check to be made. If there is however, check that a sensible QDM can be achieved by each VOR to that station.

Check also that five degrees movement of the OBS results in half-scale deflection on the display and that ten degrees results in full-scale deflection. Check also the function of the to/from flag by rotating the OBS through ninety degrees and that when selected to the reciprocal the needle re-centres with a from indication.

If there is one available check on an ILS frequency. Ensure that the indications seen tie in with the aircraft's position on the ground.

The Transponder

Select the VFR squawk (UK 7000), rotate to TST and check that the light illuminates. Whenever changing transponder codes, it is good airmanship to select stand-by first. This avoids the risk of transponding an incorrect code. Note the similarity and proximity of the VFR code to the emergency codes.

The DME

The DME works on the UHF band. It is normally the most accurate navigation aid in the cockpit. As such this is very much a line of sight aid. If there is a DME located on the field, simply tune and identify and check that the range is sensible. Many ILS installations have co-located DMEs. These are clearly ideal for this check. If there is no local DME, all that you can check is that when you select ident a noise can be heard albeit without the ident.

In flight DMEs ident every thirty seconds and Murphy's Law states that you will have to wait the full thirty seconds.

The principle with all radio aids is simple. Before their use all steps must be taken to ensure that they are serviceable and can offer you reliable information. They must all be checked if possible, before flight and before their immediate use. Under no circumstances commence a let down on an aid that has not been just identified. Continue to check aids during use, in particular aids that do not give a clear indication of failure, such as the ADF.

Markers

As more and more airfields are being equipped with DMEs associated with the ILS, fewer and fewer airfields are retaining their marker facilities. Pilots no longer need markers to confirm that they are at the correct height and therefore on the correct glide slope! Markers in the form of middle and inner marker also served as a warning of runway or 'Decision Height' approach. Again with a DME, indicating exactly how many miles left to the threshold, this is not necessary.

However markers are still mandatory kit for an aircraft wishing to fly IFR in controlled airspace and should therefore be checked before flight. There are many different makes of marker. Generally they all work in a similar fashion. The outer marker is a blue light, the middle marker an amber light and the airways marker, a white light. The markers all work on the 75 mhz frequency (VHF) and are simply checked by selecting 'test' which should illuminate the lights and on some types actually sound a tone in your headset.

For flight at levels below approximately 14,000ft set the markers to 'high sensitivity' and to headset. For higher altitude flying set the markers to 'low' sensitivity. The higher the aircraft flies, the wider is the marker beam and therefore the less sensitive the receiver has to be to receive it.

Air Traffic Control and Clearance

A pilot who is flying under Instrument Flight Rules in controlled (Class A) airspace is required to comply with the instructions given him by an

Air Traffic Controller. The only exception to this is when the pilot feels compliance jeopardises the safety of the aircraft and its occupants.

It is the controller's responsibility to provide adequate separation for all traffic under his control and to expedite the flow of traffic within his airspace. It is the pilot's responsibility to receive and correctly acknowledge all instructions given and to carry them out expeditiously and correctly.

During the Instrument Rating Flight Test, the candidate's RT and ability to correctly comply with instructions is very closely examined. The Pilot's RT is the examiner's window to the pilot's state of mind. Confident and correct RT implies the flight is going well and normally will engender respect from the controllers. In this way, controllers will be more likely to give the candidate the clearance he is looking for. Poor, sloppy RT helps nobody and will normally result in the controller feeling less than amenable to your special requests.

Apart from the individual airfields handling their own airspace, the United Kingdom has its own Air Traffic Control Centres which control primarily the airway systems. Each centre is divided into sectors that are manned by one or more controllers depending upon the size of the sector. The controllers can take responsibility for en route traffic and also for traffic arriving and departing from the major . . . and not so major airports.

Flight Plan
For aircraft wishing to use controlled airspace, a flight plan must be filed. The form CA48 is completed in triplicate at least thirty minutes, ideally one hour, before start-up or taxi is requested. Normally one copy is retained by the local Air Traffic Control, the middle copy is given to the teleprinter or fax operator and the final copy is retained by the pilot. Flight plans must be filed within all Class A airspace if the flight is to be conducted in accordance with Instrument Flight Rules.

Chapter 2

The Instrument Rating

The Instrument Rating is the qualification required of a professional pilot who wishes to act as pilot in command or as co-pilot in controlled airspace in circumstances requiring compliance with the Instrument Flight Rules. A valid Instrument Rating is also needed for a pilot who wishes to act as Captain on a scheduled journey and for any flight where the aircraft exceeds the weight of 2,300kgs for the purposes of public transport except for a flight beginning and ending at the same aerodrome and not extending more than twenty-five nautical miles from that aerodrome.

The flight test for the Commercial Instrument Rating is normally carried out in a multi-engined aircraft, other than a centre line thrust aeroplane. The candidate for the flight test should either hold a multi-engine type rating or have passed the test for such a rating in the preceding six months.

Details of training requirements and flying experience requirements can be obtained from the Civil Aviation Publication CAP 54.

The Instrument Rating initial flight test is conducted by a CAA flight examiner. The test comprises four main sections:
Section 1: Departure Procedures.
Section 2: Airways Procedures.
Section 3: ILS instrument approach procedure.
Section 4: NDB or VOR instrument approach procedure.
(flown in a simulated asymmetric condition)

There are also three sub-sections:
Sub-section A: Preliminary and external checks.
Sub-section B: Holding Procedures.
Sub-section C: Engine Failure Procedures.

48

United Kingdom Civil Aviation Authority

INSTRUMENT RATING (AEROPLANES) — CERTIFICATE OF TEST

Name: David Thomas HOY   Licence No: 238608J/A

I, the undersigned, being a person authorised by the Civil Aviation Authority to sign Certificates of Test in respect of an Instrument Rating, certify that I am satisfied that on the date specified below, the holder of this certificate passed an Instrument Rating flight test.

Aircraft Type or Simulator Code	Date of Test	Signature and Date of Signing	Name in BLOCK CAPITALS Licence No.
GA7	19.12.90	*Mululum* 19.12.90	P R DALLOSSO 3/733
GA7	6.12.91	6.12.91	D.K. DAVIES AT23162114/1
GA7	19.1.93	19-1.93	D K DAVIES AT23162114/A.
GA7	4.11.93	4-11.93	D.K. DAVIES AT23162114/A.

FCL 150/J 160689   *All entries to be made in ink*

The flight examiner will choose a route for the test which may or may not start and end at the same aerodrome but will not normally exceed a distance of 150 nautical miles.

The significance of sections as opposed to sub-sections is important to understand. On the first attempt at the IR a candidate may not fail any more than one section in order to avoid retaking all four sections at his next attempt. All four sections and three sub-sections should be taken at the first attempt. A candidate may fail any number of sub-sections and will only be re-examined on the sub-sections that he has failed. Whilst no one wishes to fail anything, failure of two sub-sections does not cause the candidate to resit sections that he had previously passed.

From this, you should gather that the most important Approach or Section is the last one. Suppose for instance that the candidate fails his departure yet flies a good Airways, Hold, ILS and Asymmetric. If he were then to fly a poor NDB Approach he would be required to resit all four sections again. It is on the last Approach or Section that the result of the complete test could hang!

Candidates are allowed three attempts to complete all sections and sub-sections of the flight test. Failure to complete within these three attempts will incur mandatory additional flight training as determined by the Senior Flight Examiner at the CAA.

A maximum of nine attempts are allowed to achieve an Instrument Rating. After nine attempts it is unlikely that the CAA will allow you to continue and probably unlikely that your bank manager will either. It is also a good time to reconsider your career options!

The Test in Detail

Let us now look at the test in more detail. Tests for the Instrument Rating will normally occupy a full morning or afternoon. There are historically two report times: 0845 hrs and 1245 hrs.

The candidate's flying instructor should ensure that prior to this report time all the necessary paperwork is in order. The candidate should be in possession of the Form FCL 170A. This form states that in the opinion of the person who has signed it, the candidate is now ready and able to pass the flight test. The 170A flight is normally one of the last flights the candidates will do prior to sitting the actual Instrument Rating. It is simply a mock flight test.

The examinee should hold a current medical certificate (a licence is not necessary) and proof of either holding a multi-rating test/1179 or of having recently passed such a test for the issue of a type rating on a multi-engined aircraft.

The aircraft which has been chosen for the flight test should have been specifically approved by the authority. This involves having a CAA examiner inspecting the aircraft, its paperwork and its blind-flying screens in order that an Approval Form may be issued. Such forms are valid for twelve months and must be renewed again by a flight examiner.

The candidate should normally be introduced to the examiner by his flight instructor. The examiner will at this stage discuss briefly the weather situation and give the candidate the route he wishes to be flown and various key times that are needed for the flight plan.

The approximate time then allowed for planning is one hour. During this time, the candidate will be expected to file the flight plan, obtain all the necessary weather (departure, destination and en route) and to compute headings, timings etc for the various procedures that he will be expected to carry out during the flight. A weight and balance calculation and a fuel plan should also be completed and a copy given to the examiner at your next meeting when the main briefing will be given. Consideration of take-off distance calculations should also be made.

Chapter 3

The Examiner's Briefing

'Good Afternoon, my name is Nigel Ashley.
First of all, the preliminaries.

Have you checked the weather for today? Are you happy that we can complete the flight in today's conditions and have you confirmed the weather as being satisfactory at both destination and planned diversion?

Can you confirm that there are no Notams or Royal Flights that are going to affect us today?

Were the facilities adequate for your planning and have you had a chance for a cup of coffee?

Good
First of all let me say, that if you have any questions at all, do ask me as we proceed through this briefing. Don't save the questions up to the end lest you forget one or two.

Charts
Please lay your charts out facing towards you. Let me check that we are both using the same charts and that they are in date.

Documentation
I would like to first check the aircraft's documentation and, if I may, I would like to check your licence and medical.
As you know, the purpose of this flight is to assess your suitability for holding a British Instrument Rating. The flight, which is considered Public Transport, is assumed to take place entirely within controlled airspace under

Instrument Flight Rules. All procedures should be in accordance with your company operations or training manuals and all checks and drills where appropriate should be as per your company check-lists. All such checks should be called out loud.

Responsibilities
Although technically I will be the aircraft commander, for the purposes of this flight I would like you to assume that you are the captain of a single crew public transport flight from here to Birmingham. The flight should therefore be flown in a safe but commercially expeditious manner. I will simply act as a qualified observer and unless I consider it necessary for the purpose of flight safety, I will not assist you or interfere in the conduct of the flight in any way, excepting during the simulated engine failure that we shall discuss later.

ATC Liaison
All communication to air traffic control is your responsibility and you should comply with their instructions unless you feel that compliance jeopardizes the safe conduct of the flight. Air Traffic Control's instructions will, of course, take priority over what we are trying to plan.

Radio Aid Identification and Use
As you will appreciate, it is a requirement that a radio aid must be confirmed serviceable before its use. In flight, if you plan to use a radio aid, please indicate to me at the time, that you have identified it. In the event that this is not indicated to me, I will assume that the aid has not been identified.
You are responsible for all of the equipment of the aircraft and for its correct use throughout the flight. This includes use of the De-icing equipment of the aircraft, if fitted, and the correct setting of the altimeters in accordance with the operations manual.

The Simulated Weather
I know you've checked the weather, but irrespective of the weather conditions pertaining, I would like you to assume the following:

1. Your aircraft was parked outside last night in sub-zero conditions and that today's flight is the first flight of the day.
2. The "O" isotherm degree is on the surface and light to moderate icing conditions are forecast at all levels.
3. Cloud entry will occur between 150 feet and 200 feet and you will remain in cloud until the final part of the last approach. This is simulated by the closing of the visor.

Aircraft Control
This is a hand-flown exercise with no use of the auto-pilot or flight director, if fitted. All turns should be limited to rate one with a maximum bank angle of twenty-five degrees.

Speed Agreement
Can we now go through the speeds that you will be using for this flight?

Vr
Take-off Safety Speed
Normal Climb Speed
Airways Cruise Speed
Holding Speed
Intermediate Approach Speed
Final Speed (Normal and Single-Engined if different)
Blue Line Speed (Vyse)

I will assume that you are trying to achieve these speeds unless you advise me differently during the flight. For instance, it would be quite in order for you to elect a different speed for an interim cruise climb if required.

Do you have any questions, so far?

Let us now go through today's flight . . .

The flight today comprises four sections and three sub-sections. We will go through the trip in the order that we should encounter each part.

The Departure
The departure that we are anticipating is the Daventry 1W which calls for a maintenance of runway heading to 1500 feet followed by a left turn back to the CIT climbing as cleared. Follow the departure in both the horizontal and the

vertical; pattern unless directed otherwise by Air Traffic Control.

Following arrival at the CIT NDB, leave the beacon on the QDR of 310 degrees climbing as cleared. You will then intercept the QDM of 260 degrees into the Daventry VOR. In the event that you are asked to hold on the airway, then please take up the hold in the appropriate manner. On reaching Daventry, the plan is to follow the standard Birch 2A arrival unless directed otherwise by ATC.

At some stage we hope to be directed to the BIR NDB in order to take up the hold. Please join the hold in the appropriate manner and demonstrate to me an ICAO one minute race-track pattern. This will be using the ADF and the stopwatch only. If you have, by this time, tuned in the ILS, I will detune it, so that it neither confuses or assists you. If deselected, I will return the aid to you in the same condition that I deselected it at the commencement of the ILS procedure.

Only one full hold is required, but should Air Traffic require you to do more than one hold, then each hold will be assessed. If an Expected Approach Time is given, please arrange for your last hold to leave the beacon as close as possible to that EAT.

From the holding pattern, when cleared, leave the beacon to commence the first approach, which should be the ILS. Please follow both the vertical and horizontal pattern of the procedure as adjusted by the editorial below (pointing to the Let Down plate) or as directed by Air Traffic Control.

The ILS should be flown in your minima. What are these minima please?'

> '*Decision Height: 250 feet*
> *RVR: 900 metres*'

'Upon reaching Decision Height, you are to assume that the runway is not visible and carry out the standard missed approach or again, as directed by Air Traffic.

During this go-round, at some stage normally above 500 feet, I will cover the throttles with my flight board and retard one of the two throttles for a simulated engine failure. Please identify which engine has failed, at which point I will reveal and release the throttles to you. You should then continue with the Standard Engine Failure After Take Off checks. I should stress that these are *Touch Drills Only*. Navigation and Air Traffic Liaison remain your responsibility during the Asymmetric.

In the event that we are given a protracted climb, I may return the "dead" engine to you to assist with the climb. When we reach our cleared altitude, I shall then return you back to the Asymmetric condition. You will not be expected to carry out any further checks or drills.

We will then return "single-engined" back to the beacon for the final procedure, the Asymmetric NDB approach.

On reaching the beacon, I would ask you to follow the published procedure, in both the horizontal and vertical pattern as adjusted by the editorial below (pointing to the let down plate). Upon reaching the minimum descent height, assume that the runway again is not immediately visible and please advise me how much longer we have in time or distance to run to the threshold.

What are the minima for the NDB Procedure'?

> *'Decision Height: 340 feet*
> *RVR: 1100 metres'*

'I should point out that whilst we plan to carry out both approaches procedurally, in the event that radar vectors are offered for one of the approaches, it is quite in order for you to accept. I should stress that one of the two approaches must be flown by the full procedure.

Emergencies

Other than the simulated engine failure after take-off there are no planned emergencies. In the event that something unusual does occur and I consider it necessary to intervene I will advise you accordingly. If I feel the need to take control, I will advise you that I have control.

Finally, I should point out that, during the flight, I will from time to time be taking notes. These do not necessarily indicate a criticism of your flight and please do not be put off. I may simply be taking a note of a pressure setting or a clearance of some kind.

In Conclusion

That completes the briefing. Do you have any questions or points that you would like to make before we go out to

check the aircraft. Are you fully sure of your role in this
flight?
What time have you filed for taxi?
Good, we'll now walk out to the aircraft for the walk-
round.'

The Walk round/Check A and Internal Checks

Though it is not essential that a check-list is used when doing the
external checks, it is certainly advisable. As you walk out to the aircraft,
indicate to the examiner that you are aware of the location of the external
fire extinguishers. Advise him that you are checking that the aircraft is
standing correctly and not leaning unduly to one side. Check also that
there are no signs of any leakage beneath the aircraft such as hydraulic
fluid, oil or even fuel. Check that the aircraft can be taxied without
obstruction and that the slipstream from your aircraft will cause no harm
to aircraft parked behind it.

Advise the examiner that you would check that the aircraft was
completely clear of ice before you attempted to move any control
surfaces. The examiner may ask you how you would de-ice the aircraft.
Various options are available in terms of de-icing fluid and more simply
the aircraft could be parked inside a warm hangar. Under no
circumstances would you be prepared to accept the aircraft with ice on it!

During the walk round the one theme that you should continue to
remember is ice. Check all the hinge lines, undercarriage bays, pressure
heads and static vents for any sign of ice. Don't forget to come equipped
to drain the tanks and to check the pitot heat's serviceability. Ensure
visual checks are made for the fuel state and oil levels. If the aircraft is
de-iced check that the system is serviceable and, if it uses de-icing fluid
check that there is sufficient fluid for the flight. This, by the way, is not
the time to discover that the aircraft needs fuel or oil. This should have
been confirmed earlier of course.

Once the external check has been completed, climb on board the
aircraft. Before the internal checks are commenced, go through the basic
safety checks with the examiner. Ensure that he is familiar with the
emergency exits and how to use them. Point out the position of the
aircraft's internal fire extinguisher and first-aid kit. Indicate to him how
he may adjust his seat position and the temperature within the aircraft.

Commence the internal checks.

Again follow the check-list to the letter. Typical areas receiving
criticism include the checking of the radio navigation aids, releasing the
parking brake before the power has been reduced, starting the engines
without clearing the propeller area and lowering flap without ensuring

56

personnel are clear of the flap area. Don't attempt to start your engines when wearing a headset. If someone shouts to you that it is not clear, you need to be able to hear them.

Checking the Navigation Aids

The Markers
Select Test; check the lights illuminate and set switch to headset and to high sensitivity.

The ADF
Check on two frequencies. Ensure that on each, the correct QDM is seen. Select antenna on each and ensure that the needle slews away from the QDM and swings nice and sharply back to the correct QDM.

The VOR
This can only be checked if there is a VOR close by, if not even on the field. Centre the beam bar and check that this is a sensible QDM/QDR. Move the OBS by five degrees and check for half-scale deflection on the beam bar. Move, then, the OBS by ten degrees and check for full-scale deflection of the beam bar. Finally move the OBS through ninety and then through 180 degrees. Check that the to/from flag changes and that on the reciprocal the beam bar re-centres.

For both the VOR and the ADF, remember to identify the incoming signal.

The ILS
If you are at an airfield where there is an ILS, identify the signal and check that you have a full-scale deflection on the localiser to the correct side. The OBS movement should have no effect on the indication of the localiser.

The DME
If there is a local DME, identify it and check for a sensible indication in terms of known distance from the transmitter.

The Transponder
Set to 7,000 and select Test. The light should illuminate. Return the selector to Stand-by.

The COMMS Boxes
Check each communications box, if possible, on two frequencies. The ATIS is acceptable for one check per box but remember this does not test your transmissions.

Chapter 4

The day comes . . .

After several weeks of training, at last, the day arrives for your Instrument Rating Flight Test. As with most things associated with the Civil Aviation Authority, if your paperwork is not in order, forget it! What paper work?

Personal Paperwork

It is a requirement that you have a current medical certificate. This is for your own protection. You do not need a current licence. If this medical requires you to carry two pairs of specs. make sure you do. If the test is to be in a multi-engined aircraft, you must have proof of having passed a multi-engined 1179 (day only is acceptable) or to be the proud holder of a Group B rating on your PPL. The 1179 Form should be duly completed by an appropriate Type Rating Examiner.

If you are taking a PPL or a BCPL Instrument Rating there is still a requirement for you to have a *Letter of Authority* from the Civil Aviation Authority which effectively is their permission for you to take the test.

Perhaps the most important piece of paper, however, is the Form 170A. This is a form signed by an instructor/examiner who has flown with you and has convinced himself that you are capable of passing the flight test. The 170A was designed to stop wasting examiners' time and to reduce the number of first-time failures that were so prevalent in years gone by.

Aircraft Paperwork

It is a requirement of the flight test that all the appropriate and original documentation is available for inspection by the examiner. The examiner is entitled to ask you questions relating to the certificates. They are as follows:

Certificate of Airworthiness (Valid three years)
Flight Manual for Aircraft
Certificate of Registration (not reqd. on internal flights)
Certificate of Insurance
Certificate of Maintenance Review
Certificate of Release to Service
Wireless Telegraphy Licence
Certificate of Approval of Radio Installation
Aircraft Technical Log and Deferred Defects Sheet
Certificate of CAA approval for CAA flight tests

Let's have a brief look at these various documents to hopefully answer any questions you may be asked.

The *Certificate of Airworthiness* confirms that the aircraft has been considered airworthy by the authority and that the aircraft is in the Public or Private Transport category. The Certificate will normally state that the Flight Manual also forms part of the certificate. This is normally valid for a maximum of three years.

The *Certificate of Registration* confirms ownership to the name that falls on the certificate. This document is not required for internal flights within the United Kingdom.

The *Certificate of Insurance* confirms that the aircraft is covered for third party liability in respect of accident. Normally the maximum amount is noted on this document.

There are two maintenance documents for an aircraft on a Public Transport C of A: The *Certificate of Maintenance Review* and the *Release to Service*. The Review is a confirmation that the preceding year's maintenance has been checked and found satisfactory. This document is issued annually. The Release is issued each time the aircraft undergoes a scheduled Maintenance Check. Such a check may occur every fifty hours or sixty-two days as in the case of the LAMS Schedule. Such frequency of checks is typical for most light aircraft. However the authority, may, from time to time authorise different frequency of check cycles.

The *WT Licence* is rather like 'car tax'. It is a document confirming that the appropriate fee has been paid for the use of the 'radio waves', which of course are government owned! This certificate is issued annually upon receipt of the necessary fee.

The *Certificate of Approval of Radio Installation* confirms that the radios in the aircraft were, at the time of inspection, working within their necessary tolerances and were considered fit for use. There is also an annual Radio Check (also associated with a form) that confirms the radios are continuing to function correctly.

59

The *Technical Log* is a diary of the aircraft's previous flights and defects. It is also a record of the aircraft's remaining hours to its next check. Associated with it is the *Deferred Defects Log*. This is a record of those defects that are not considered sufficiently serious to ground the aircraft but are nonetheless required to be rectified, if not immediately, sometime in the near future.

Finally we have the *Certificate of Approval for Flight Test*. This is sometimes overlooked. It is however very important and must be valid. It is the CAA's recognition of your aircraft as being fit for Flight Test. An examiner will issue this only if he is happy with the state of the aircraft and its radio aids and documentation. Most importantly, he will check the standard of the blind flying screens. If you are planning to use an unapproved aircraft for the training and to have it approved once the training is complete, think again. Make sure your aircraft is approved at the beginning. Never ever leave the approval to the day of the test. The examiner may not be prepared to approve it for you, left so late.

United Kingdom
Civil Aviation Authority

Certificate No: 007005/001

CERTIFICATE OF AIRWORTHINESS

Nationality and Registration Marks	Constructor and Constructor's Designation of Aircraft	Aircraft Serial Number
G-BNAB	**GULFSTREAM AMERICAN CORP** **GULFSTREAM AMERICAN GA-7**	**GA7-0114**

TRANSPORT CATEGORY (PASSENGER)

This Certificate of Airworthiness is issued pursuant to the Convention on International Civil Aviation dated 7 December 1944, and to the Civil Aviation Act 1982, and the Orders and Regulations made thereunder, in respect of the above-mentioned aircraft which is considered to be airworthy when maintained and operated in accordance with the foregoing and the pertinent operating limitations. The CAA Approved Flight Manual forms part of this Certificate.

Condition(s): This Aircraft must be maintained to the CAA Approved Maintenance Schedule.

Date: **25 JULY 1991**

for the Civil Aviation Authority

This Certificate is valid for the period(s) shown below			Official Stamp and Date
From: **25 JULY 1991**	To: **31 OCTOBER 1991**		**C.A.A.**
From: 4 November 1991	To: 3 November 1994		
From:	To:		
From:	To:		
From:	To:		

No entries or endorsements may be made on this Certificate except by an authorised person. If this Certificate is lost, the Civil Aviation Authority should be informed at once. Any person finding this Certificate should forward it immediately to the Civil Aviation Authority, Safety Regulation Group, Aviation House, South Area, Gatwick Airport, West Sussex, RH6 0YR.

CA358C
051190

UNITED KINGDOM
CIVIL AVIATION AUTHORITY

CERTIFICATE OF REGISTRATION OF AIRCRAFT

CERTIFICATE NUMBER G-BNAB/R4

1 Nationality and Registration Marks	2 Constructor and Constructor's Designation of Aircraft	3 Aircraft Serial Number
G-BNAB	GULFSTREAM AMERICAN CORP GULFSTREAM AMERICAN GA-7	GA7-0114

4 Name and Address of Registered Owner or Charterer

CHALREY LTD
11 CLONARD WAY
PINNER
MIDDLESEX
HA5 4BT

5 It is hereby certified that the above described aircraft has been duly entered on the United Kingdom Register in accordance with the Convention on International Civil Aviation dated 7 December 1944, and with the Air Navigation Order 1989.

For the Civil Aviation Authority
Aircraft Registration
CAA House
45-59 Kingsway
London WC2B 6TE
Tel 071-832 6299
Fax 071-832 6262
Telex 94028422 CAA G

DATE OF ISSUE   14 JANUARY 1993

NOTES (a) The person in whose name an aircraft is registered may or may not be its legal owner. Prospective purchasers are warned, therefore, that this Certificate of Registration is not proof of legal ownership.
(b) No entries or endorsements may be made in this Certificate except by the Civil Aviation Authority.

SEE FURTHER NOTES OVERLEAF

United Kingdom
Civil Aviation Authority

Certificate of Approval
of Aircraft Radio Installation

Ref: 9/23/ G-BNAB   Date   2nd October 1989

Registration Marks   G-BNAB

Type   GULFSTREAM AMERICAN GA-7

NOTE: (i)   This Certificate supersedes Certificate dated   Pre October 1989

    (ii)   This Certicate must be passed to subsequent Operators

    (iii) The Operator must be in possession of a current Department of Trade Aircraft Licence, which is validated by this Certificate. Any modification to the Radio Installation will necessitate the re-issue of this Certificate.

~~ISSUE~~   REPLACEMENT

The above named aircraft's radio apparatus, details of which are listed below, and its installation is approved as complying with all relevant requirements of British Civil Airworthiness Requirements.

DME	960 to 1215 Mhz
ATC TRANSPONDER	1090 Mhz
VHF COMMUNICATION	118 to 137 Mhz
WEATHER RADAR	9300 to 9500 Mhz

The Airborne Radio Apparatus installed on the aircraft is approved to transmit within the frequency bands listed above.

The equipment that comprises the radio station is recorded by the Civil Aviation Authority and conforms to the performance and operational classifications of CAP 208.

For the Civil Aviation Authority.

No entries or endorsements may be made on this Certificate except by an authorised person. If this Certificate is lost, the Civil Aviation Authority should be informed at once. Any person finding this Certificate should forward it immediately to the Civil Aviation Authority, Safety Regulation Group, Aviation House, South Area, Gatwick Airport, Gatwick, West Sussex RH6 0YR.

AD 917A
111188

RADIOCOMMUNICATIONS
AGENCY

BLS AVIATION
ELSTREE AERODROME
BOREHAMWOOD
HERTS
WD6 3AW

Department of Trade and Industry Radiocommunications Agency

Wireless Telegraphy Act 1949 Section 1

Aircraft Radio Licence

Validation Document

Date for Renewal: 31-OCT-94

This licence (the "Licence") granted under section 1 of The Wireless Telegraphy Act 1949. on 24-SEP-84 (the "Date of Issue") by The Secretary of State for Trade and Industry ("The Secretary of State") to the Licensee ("Licensee") (which expression includes all persons from time to time owning any share in the aircraft referred to above) named in column 5 below ("the Licensee") authorises the establishment of the station described in clause 1 **subject to the provisions contained in the Aircraft Radio Licence Clause Booklet.**

1 Aircraft Reg	G - BNAB
2 Call Sign	G - BNAB
3 Aircraft Make	GULFSTREAM AMERICAN GA7
4 Tier Code (See Attached Form)	C
5 Licensee Name	CHALREY LTD
6 Licensee Address	11 CLONARD WAY HATCH END MIDDLESEX

The Radiocommunications Agency is an Executive Agency of the Department of Trade and Industry
The Agency Enquiry Point and Switchboard is ☎ 071 215 2150

United Kingdom
Civil Aviation Authority

Noise Certificate

Number _____ 1508 _____

1 Nationality and Registration Marks	2 Constructor and Constructor's Type and Model Designation of Aircraft	3 Constructor's Aircraft Serial No.
G-BNAB	Gulfstream American Corporation GA-7/Cougar	GA7-0114

Statement of additional modifications incorporated for the purpose of compliance .... None ....

....

Maximum weights approved.

Take-off ... 1724 kg .... Landing .... 1724 kg ....

This aircraft conforms to Noise Type Certificate No XXXXXXXXXXXXXX with the modifications (if any) specified above.

This Noise Certificate is issued pursuant to the Air Navigation (Noise Certification) Order 1970 as amended, in respect of the above-mentioned aircraft, which is considered to comply with the relevant noise requirements when maintained, overhauled and repaired in accordance with the Civil Aviation Acts 1949–1971 and the Orders and Regulations made thereunder.

The relevant noise requirements are those of BCAR Section N. The level of severity of these noise requirements is equal to the standards of Annex 16 to the Convention on International Civil Aviation; thus any aeroplane which complies with them will also comply with Annex 16.

Date ... 30th May, 1984 ....
                                                for the Civil Aviation Authority

CA 1790   *See overleaf*

64

The day comes . . .

Gibbs Hartley Cooper Limited

Bishops Court, 27-33 Artillery Lane, London E1 7LP

Incorporating

Richards, Longstaff (Insurance)

TO WHOM IT MAY CONCERN   2nd December 1993

CERTIFICATE OF INSURANCE

THIS IS TO CERTIFY that   Grumman GA-7   G-BNAB

is INSURED by   Insurance Companies in London

Policy No: WAV9300830

in the name(s) of   Cabair Group Limited &/or Associated &/or
                                     Subsidiary Companies &/or Agents &/or
                                     Employees for their respective rights and interests

for the period to   30th November 1994

against all risks in flight or on the ground anywhere in EUROPE, THE MEDITERRANEAN
AND CANARY ISLANDS, COUNTRIES BORDERING THE MEDITERRANEAN AND
THE MIDDLE EAST

and coverage includes LEGAL LIABILITY to THIRD PARTIES and PASSENGERS up to
the following Limit of Indemnity:-

COMBINED SINGLE LIMIT
(THIRD PARTY/PASSENGER
AND FREIGHT LIABILITY):   £2,000,000   any one accident unlimited in all
                                               during the policy period

Subject to the policy terms, conditions and limitations

GIBBS HARTLEY COOPER LIMITED

Member of the British Insurance & Investment Brokers' A... 33 ... ex 895079 ... uccit o Facsimile:071-782 9032/071-377 2139
Registered Office:Bishops Court, 27-33 Artillery Lane, London E1 ... P Registered No 149013 England *member* HSBC group   GHCA2

Cabair Maintenance Limited

**MAINTENANCE STATEMENT
AND
SCHEDULED MAINTENANCE INSPECTION CERTIFICATE OF RELEASE TO SERVICE**

Aircraft type: *GA-7 Cougar*   Registration Mark: *G-BNAB*

SCHEDULED MAINTENANCE INSPECTION: *50 Hour*   was completed

on: *22-4-94*   at: *4630.2*   airframe hours:

Category	Lic/Auth/App No:	Signature
A Airframe		
C Engines	*18694*	*Hewell*
R Radio		
X ——— Electrics		
X ——— Instruments		
X ——— Autopilots		
X ——— Compasses		

The work recorded above has been carried out in accordance with the requirements of the Air Navigation Order for the time being in force and in that respect the aircraft equipment is considered fit for release to service.

The next SCHEDULED MAINTENANCE INSPECTION is due at: *4680.2* hrs

150 Hour   on: *22-6-94*

The following out of phase inspections/components changes are due before the next Scheduled Maintenance Inspection specified above:

Item	Due		Sector Log Reference on Completion
	hrs	Date	
Nil			

This maintenance statement is not complete unless a valid Certificate of Maintenance Review is attached.

C0821

66

Cabair Maintenance Limited

MAINTENANCE STATEMENT
AND
SCHEDULED MAINTENANCE INSPECTION CERTIFICATE OF RELEASE TO SERVICE

Aircraft type: *G A -7 Cougar*   Registration Mark: *G-BNAB*

SCHEDULED MAINTENANCE INSPECTION: *'R' Annual* was completed

on: at: ——   airframe hours:

Category	Lic/Auth/App No:	Signature
A̶ A̶i̶r̶f̶r̶a̶m̶e̶		
C̶ E̶n̶g̶i̶n̶e̶s̶		
R Radio	!7350	
X̶ E̶l̶e̶c̶t̶r̶i̶c̶s̶		
X̶ I̶n̶s̶t̶r̶u̶m̶e̶n̶t̶s̶		
X̶ A̶u̶t̶o̶p̶i̶l̶o̶t̶s̶		
X̶ C̶o̶m̶p̶a̶s̶s̶e̶s̶		

The work recorded above has been carried out in accordance with the requirements of the Air Navigation Order for the time being in force and in that respect the aircraft equipment is considered fit for release to service.

The next SCHEDULED MAINTENANCE INSPECTION is due at: ——   hrs

'R' Annual.   on: 3 . 11 . 94

The following out of phase inspections/components changes are due before the next Scheduled Maintenance Inspection specified above:

Item	Due		Sector Log Reference on Completion
	hrs	Date	

This maintenance statement is not complete unless a valid Certificate of Maintenance Review is attached.

00672

Cabair Maintenance Limited

CERTIFICATE OF MAINTENANCE REVIEW

NATIONALITY AND REGISTRATION MARKS	CONSTRUCTOR AND CONSTRUCTORS DESIGNATION OF AIRCRAFT	AIRCRAFT SERIAL NO. (CONSTRUCTORS NO.)
G BNAB	GA7 COUGAR	GA7 - 0114

CATEGORY   TRANSPORT CATEGORY (PASSENGER)

CERTIFIED THAT A MAINTENANCE REVIEW OF THIS AIRCRAFT AND SUCH OF ITS EQUIPMENT AS IS NECESSARY FOR ITS AIRWORTHINESS HAS BEEN CARRIED OUT IN ACCORDANCE WITH THE REQUIREMENTS OF THE AIR NAVIGATION ORDER FOR THE TIME BEING IN FORCE

THIS CERTIFICATE IS VALID FOR THE PERIODS SHOWN BELOW	AUTHORISED SIGNATORY AND DATE
FROM 4-11-91 TO 3-11-92	19341 4-11-91
FROM 5-12-92 TO 4-12-93	Hewell 18694 5-12-92
FROM 16.12.93 TO 15.12.94 3.11.	T.S. Wilson 24920 16.12.93
FROM TO	
FROM TO	
FROM TO	

Fig 17   0326

68

The day comes . . .

Cabair Maintenance Limited

WEIGHT AND CENTRE OF GRAVITY SCHEDULE

AIRCRAFT TYPE __GA-7 Cougar__   REGISTRATION __G-BNAB__   SERIAL No. __GA7-0114__

JOB REFERENCE __AB/63-13637__   DATE __09/12/1992__

MAXIMUM AUTHORISED WEIGHT __3800__   lbs/kgs.

PART 'A' BASIC WEIGHT

The basic weight of the Aircraft as calculated from Weighing Report Number __ATS-110-3291__   Dated __04/12/1992__   Is __2796.5__   lbs/kgs.
The Centre of Gravity of the Aircraft in the same condition at this weight and with the landing gear extended is __95.09__ inches forward/aft of the datum.
The total moment about the datum in this condition is __265,925.0__   lb/in.
The Datum referred is the one to which the limits in the Certificate of Airworthiness relates and is defined as __A point 50" forward__ of front face __of engine firewall.__
The basic weight includes the weight of unusable fuel and unusable oil and the weight of the following items which comprise the list of basic equipment:-

ITEM   WEIGHT   LEVER ARM (in)

As listed in Equipment list dated 10/07/1979.
+ T.K.S De-ice System.

PART 'B' VARIABLE LOAD

The weight and level arms of the variable loads are shown below. The variable load depends upon the equipment carried for a particulat role.,

ITEM	WEIGHT		LEVER ARM (in)	MOMENT (lb/in)
Pilot	Use Actual		91.0	
Passenger (Row 1)	"	"	91.0	
Passenger (Row 2)	"	"	128.0	
Fwd Baggage	"	"	26.0	
Aft Baggage	"	"	160.0	
Cargo Area	"	"	125.4	

69

PART 'C' LOADING INFORMATION (Disposable Load)

Information is given below to enable the disposable load (Fuel & Payload) to be distributed so that the Maximum Weight and Centre of Gravity limits given in the Flight Manual/Certificate of Airworthiness are not exceeded. The total moment change when landing gear is retracted _____N/A_____ lb/in.

The appropriate lever arms are:-

ITEM		LEVER ARM (in)
Fuel in main tanks		112.0
Fuel in Aux. tanks		-----
Oil in engine/s		64.4
De-Ice fluid in tank		160.0
Passengers Row 1		91.0
Passengers Row 2		128.0
Row 3		-----
in Row 4		-----
Cargo Area ~~Row 5~~	Rear Seat Folded down (Max 340Lbs)	125.4
Seats Row 6		-----
Baggage Holds No. 1	Front (Max 75Lb)	26.0
No. 2	Rear (Max 175Lb)	160.0
175Lb Rear includes ----	T.K.S. De-Icing Fluid	160.0
Wing lockers		

FUEL, OIL AND DE-ICING FLUID

Maximum usable capacity of fuel in main tanks	95	Imp. Gall
Maximum usable capacity of fuel in Aux. tanks	---	Imp. Gall
Weight of this quantity of fuel @ 7.2 lb/Imp. gall	684	lbs.
Maximum usable capacity of engine oil	3.333	Imp. Gall
Weight of this quantity of oil @ 9 lb/Imp. Gall	30	lbs.
Maximum usable capacity of De-Ice fluid in tank	9.5	Imp. Gall
Weight of this quantity of fluid @ 11 lb/Imp. Gall.	104.5	lbs.

NOTE: The total loading weight of the Aircraft is the sum of the operating weight and the weights of variable and disposable loads.

This Schedule was prepared on _____09/12/1992_____ and supercedes all previous issues.

Signed _____ Authority _C.Tyler 25708 A+C_

or C.A.A. Approval No. _____ Date _09/12/1992_

CAA

APPLICATION/CERTIFICATE OF APPROVAL OF AEROPLANES FOR USE ON FLIGHT TESTS CONDUCTED BY CAA

Name and Address of Applicant/Owner CABAIR COLLEGE OF AIR   Aeroplane Type GA7

TRAINING LTD. CRANFIELD AIRFIELD BEDFORD   Registration G-BGAG

Tel No.

Purpose for which required | GFT | IR | CPL | PPL | SERIES | ~~ONE TEST ONLY~~ | Candidate's Name

APPROVAL DETAILS

(Item 1-8 to be completed by Applicant)

1. Controls ☑
2. Brakes (See Note 1)

For Official Use Only   YES/~~NO~~

3. Screening (See App. 1 Para 3.2 & 3.3)
    Material PLASTIC   No. of Parts 5 + 2 LIMPNEL
    Screens Identification (See Note 2) 1-7
    CAA/AWD Approval (if req'd) Mod. No. 9/211/811

4. Flying Clearance Aeroplane Certified for Light/Moderate/~~Aerobatic~~ Servicing* (See App. 1 Para 4)   SAT/~~DSAT~~   YES/~~NO~~

5. Minimum Demonstrated Cross-wind Component 25 KTS.   SAT/~~NO~~

6. Compass Installation (Types) KNS 55 / AIRPATH   SAT/~~DSAT~~

7. Radio Installation (Class 1 or 3. For scale see App. 1 Paras 1 & 6)

Equipment	Make/Model	Class	G/S	Loc	(tick as appropriate)
VHF 1	KY195	1			
NAV 1	KN580	1	✓	✓	
or VHF/NAV 1					
VHF 2		1			
NAV 2		1		✓	
or VHF/NAV 2	KN60				
ADF 1	KR87	1			
ADF 2					
DME	KN580				
Transponder	KY75A	Mode A+C	Codes 4016		
75 MHz Mkr.	KMA20	ON/OFF switch YES/~~NO~~ (See Note 3)			

Intercom: Separate/~~from VHF 1/From VHF 2*~~   SAT/~~DSAT~~ (Applicant)

8. Other Equipment: First Aid Kit ☑ Fire Extinguisher ☑ Life Jackets (ANO Sched 4 (2)(b))(iii) ☑
    Spare Fuses ☒ Safety Harness ☑ Anti-Col Light (see ANO Sect 2 Rules 9, 10 & 11) ☑
    Dipstick ☑   Signed: Date: 17/11/93

I certify that the information given above is correct.

* Delete as applicable

NOTES
1. A central handbrake may be accepted in exceptional circumstances and then only on a single-engine Aeroplane
2. Screens are to have: A/C registration; be numbered left to right or in the order that they are to be erected; and TOP in the appropriate position printed on each screen
3. Where no ON/OFF switch is fitted, suitable blanks for the marker lights must be provided

(Items 9 to 13 to be completed by Examiner)

			SAT	UNSAT
9	(a)	C of A Category TRANSIT(A) Expiry Date 31/10/94	✓	
	(b)	C of R Owner's Name CHALLEY LTD	✓	
	(c)	Technical Log (if applicable)	✓	
	(d)	Record of Hours & Defects	✓	
	(e)	CRS	✓	
	(f)	Certificate of Approval of Aircraft Radio Installation	✓	
	(g)	Aircraft Radio Licence	✓	
	(h)	Weight Schedule	✓	
	(i)	CMR (except Private)	✓	
	(j)	Check Lists (Doc 7 App. 1 para 9)	✓	
	(k)	Insurance Certificate	✓	
	(l)	Noise Certificate	✓	
	(m)	Aeroplane Manual/Pilot's Handbook	✓	
10		With screens fitted check:		
	(a)	Candidate's view (see App 1 para 3) 31(a) ☑ 32(a) ☑ 33(a) ☑	✓	
	(b)	Examiner's view (see App 1 para 3) 31(a) ☑ 32(a) ☑ 33 ☑		
11		For GFT/PPL/IR check covers for A/H ☑	✓	
12		HSI (if fitted) ☑ Heading Indicator ☑		
13		Examiner's Access (see App 1 para 2.2)	✓	
		Owner's Nameplate	✓	

Date of Approval or Re-Approval	FEE PAID	Examiner's	Expiry
	Amount	Signature/Name	Date
G. ARMOUR 17·11·93	To be invoiced £40	N.J. ASHLEY	16·11·94

FCL FORM 176 (3rd ISSUE)

All checks must be as per check list .....
The examiner is at liberty to refer to his check list
during the flight to ensure compliance with it.

Where possible make sure that you have a good night's sleep the day before the test. Of course pre-exam nerves affect everybody to a greater or lesser extent. As you have been training towards the test you will probably have come to the realisation that it is not so much how many hours that count, more how many good nights' sleep you have had in-between training days.

Make sure on the day of the test you give yourself plenty of time prior to the official report time. This time should be used to completely check the aircraft, drain the tanks, check the oil levels and de-icing systems. Make a close examination of the weather system affecting your part of the country and check all the TAFs and Actuals pertaining to the most likely destinations. Check the upper winds and the freezing levels and examine the Notams and Royal Flight Bulletins. Is there anything to affect you? Check all the aircraft's documentation and double check that all your personal equipment is to hand, in particular your medical, 1179 form and duly signed Form 170A.

Remember it is unprofessional to be late. Much of the result of your test is determined by the first impressions you give. As with any interview or first meeting, the examiner will subconsciously if not consciously form an impression of you, his candidate, probably before you've even opened your mouth. Pilots are generally well-groomed, short-haired and well presented individuals. If you want to join that club you've got to look the part. When the examiner asks for your impression of the weather . . . imagine he is your Captain and expects a brief but sensible summary of the weather situation.

Having agreed, between you, that the weather is fit for the test, the examiner will give you the destination and probably the route that he would like you to follow. It is normally the examiner who will contact the destination and arrange a booking for your procedures. But it is your responsibility to file the flight plan and this I would suggest is the first thing you should do following your initial meeting with the examiner.

Chapter 5

Mistakes That You Could Make!

The Departure

Poor heading control
Poor maintenance of balance
Poor synchronisation of propellers
Generally inaccurate speed control
Inadvertent disobedience of clearance
Turned the wrong way after departure
Levels at incorrect altitude or flight level
Wrong pressure setting selected
Failure to cross-check altimeters during climb
Failure to set 1013 mbs when cleared to a flight level
Mis-setting of Omni Bearing Selector/s prior to departure
Failure to use the Set Heading Bug
Inaccurate setting of altimeter
Poor knowledge of aircraft documents
Poor planning
Failure to tighten friction nut
Failure to sign technical log
Missing of radio call and general poor RT procedures
Lack of icing checks during the climb

The Airways

Poor initial level-off
Forgetting to set cowl flaps prior to the top of climb
Generally poor height control
Failure to maintain heading within five degrees

Failure to adjust to hold speed prior to arriving at the holding fix
Forgetting to adjust mixture levers in the cruise or for the descent
Mis-setting of Omni Bearing Selectors
The use of aids prior to their correct identification
The use of aids outside of promulgated range
Failure to note in writing all clearances offered
Poor use of available aids
Failure to anticipate turning points (commercial turns)
Failure to understand or follow routeing offered by ATC
Failure to maintain radio aid tracking within five degrees.
   (VOR +/- half-scale)
Poor heading control on airway
Misinterpretation of ATC routeing instructions

The ILS Approach and Missed Approach

Failure to satisfactorily complete pre-landing checks
Failure to identify aid prior to let down
Mis-selection of/forgetting to set runway QDM to the OBS
Forgetting to report beacon outbound
Poor outbound timing
Failure to monitor gate angle outbound
Failure to monitor glide-slope position outbound
No Captain's brief
Poor ATC liaison to arrange necessary descent
Poor rate of descent control and attitude maintenance
No go-around briefing given or prepared for
Poor choice of intercept angle (too much or too little)
Doing too much in the turn onto final
Selection of QFE during the descent and levelling at incorrect level
Late on Final Approach Checks
Inability to maintain Localiser or Glide-slope within one half-scale
Poor speed control on approach
Failure to monitor VSI during the descent
Excessive heading and power adjustments
Poor interception of glide-slope/late/too early initiation of descent
Failure to use trim sufficiently
Poor check procedure through marker
No checks through 1,000 feet
Inadequate calls approaching Decision Height
Forgetting correct Decision Height with obvious consequences
Descending excessively below Decision Height
New Decision Height advised by ATC (Overshoot not below . . .) not noted

Anticipating Decision Height too early
Missing ATC instructions
Inadequate icing checks
Poor RT liaison
No cruise checks
Lack of icing checks
Failure to obtain ATIS at destination airfield
Poor speed control in cruise and/or cruise descent

The Hold

Failure to regain inbound axis
Failure to maintain inbound axis
Failure to adjust outbound heading correctly
Poor calculation of outbound timing
Failure to start stop-watch on the abeam QDM
Failure to monitor ADF needle on the outbound leg of the hold
Poor height control during hold
Poor speed control during hold
Lack of icing checks during hold
Failure to use DME if available during hold to warn of approaching
  beacon.
Inaccurate bank angles maintained during hold turns
Poor liaison with ATC leading to unnecessary and excessive delays
Poor transition from ILS descent to go-around attitude
Late application of power during go-around
Failure to maintain runway QDM during the go-around
Failure to comply with go-around instructions
Failure to copy abnormal go-around instructions
Forgetting to set QNH (if applicable) during the go-around
Overshooting cleared altitude/flight level
Forgetting to select either gear up or flap up on the go-around
Forgetting to reduce the climb power on go-around
Failure to set aids correctly for the missed approach
Failure to identify those aids
Excessive icing checks

The Asymmetric

Poor speed control during the symmetrical part of the go-around
Failure to adjust attitude (normally lower) as engine is failed
Poor aircraft control after failure
Inadequate use of rudder

Failure to maintain heading and balance as engine is failed
Excessive delay in engine identification
Inability to maintain climb profile
Poor initial checks
Initial checks out of order
Forgetting to feather failed engine
Calling the wrong engine
'Feathering' the wrong engine
Forgetting to check for fire on the appropriate engine
Slow ancillary checks
Forgetting key points of ancillary checks
Failure to achieve and maintain blue line speed following failure
Touch drilling the wrong engine's switches
Incorrect setting of cowl flaps following failure
Poor subsequent monitoring of live engine gauges
Forgetting any of the following: suction/load shedding/cross-feed
Failure to maintain icing checks during the asymmetric

The Asymmetric NDB Approach

Poor entry to and subsequent control of descent
Poor use of rudder to compensate for power changes
Generally poor anticipation of rudder during all power changes
Premature lowering of gear and/or flaps
Poor appreciation of power available
Late anticipation of power need during level off from a descent
Failure to monitor gate angle on extended procedure if applicable
Poor speed/attitude control during descent
Misinterpretation of ADF during the approach
Disobeying ADF needle indications
Excessive/inadequate drift corrections
Poor procedure for beacon passage
Maintaining attack heading through beacon
Forgetting to start stop-watch at correct position
Poor descent profile before or after the beacon
Failure to utilize available information on plate
Descent whilst outside of five degrees of track
Descending without clearance
Failure to maintain balance
Forgetting to descend!
Forgetting Final Approach Checks
Subsequently forgetting to lower gear
Inadequate knowledge of the up-to-date Wind Velocity at approach to MDH

Failure to maintain MDH minus nothing/ plus one hundred feet
Poor speed control during descent
Poor power control during descent
Letting down without having first identified the aid
No captain's brief prior to approach
Stop-watch not wound or set correctly
Stop-watch not running
Failure to advise examiner time or distance to run to threshold
Failure to reduce from attack heading to single drift having regained
  final approach track.
Failure to initiate descent at the correct position

For the next 3 hours....He has your flying future in his hands

Chapter 6

The Departure

The Departure is the name given to that section of the test which takes the aircraft from the commencement of the pre-take-off checks to the first reporting point in the airway.

This is a difficult time for the Instrument Rating candidate as he will have had little time to settle down and calm those familiar nerves. It's important to therefore be well prepared before advising the ATC controller that the aircraft is ready for departure. Do a complete scan of all the aircraft's instruments to confirm that everything is in the correct position and in particular the navigation aids. Make doubly certain that not only are the aids correctly tuned and if possible identified but that also the OBS settings on the VORs are correctly set. There is nothing worse than getting airborne only to find that an aid needs to be reset or to follow the wrong indications from an incorrectly set VOR.

In order to avoid this situation, it would do no harm to give a 'departure brief' to the examiner prior to departure. Involve the aids that you will be using in this brief and at the same time confirm that everything is set correctly. This will also be a good time to remind yourself of cleared altitudes that you will not be flying through and to set your heading bug for the intended climb out.

During the initial climb out ensure that the extended runway track is maintained by taking due allowance for wind. If there is an NDB on the climb out to assist centre line tracking, consider using it, although sensible drift assessment may be just as good as tracking an NDB from some distance.

Take care to settle into the correct climbing attitude as early as possible with accurate speed control and in balance. Try to synchronise the engines during the early stages of climb out but don't be put off if you see the examiner doing the finer touches himself. It's probably more annoying to him!

79

The second the visor is shut on the blind-flying screens check for 'ice'. Thereafter, every 1,000 feet ask the examiner to check for external ice formation. Call the after take-off checks out aloud but not so loudly that you fail to hear Air Traffic instructing you to change frequency or continue the climb etc.

The departure can be a worrying time but try not to let a small mistake upset you. The examiner may not have noticed the mistake himself or may not view it quite as seriously as perhaps your instructor might.

During the initial part of the climb out up to about 150 to 200 feet the examiner will allow you to establish the climbing attitude and direction visually. Don't spend too much time looking at the visual horizon but *as early as possible* establish for yourself the *instrument picture*. You're immediately into the 'climbing scan'.

Make full use of the Set Heading Bug if fitted. Do not turn unless the bug has been set to your next intended heading. This should prevent you inadvertently overshooting that heading. Consciously warn yourself of approaching cleared altitudes or flight levels and *if in doubt, ask the controller for clarification.*

Dont spill his Gin+Tonic on the brake check

Prepare yourself for any frequency changes. The next frequency should be in the second box awaiting its selection. Make certain that your RT is to the point, succinct and gives the information that the controller needs to know. Brief RT is normally the best RT, but not so brief that you miss the key elements of the call!

If a mistake is made on the departure try to put it out of your mind; remember there's a lot of test left to do.

(STANSTED) LONDON
CLACTON SID

Trans alt **6000**

1. Initial Climb: Ahead to 850. **2.** A/C unable to comply with SID's or non standard clearance must inform ATC prior to take-off. **3.** Max 250kt below FL100 unless otherwise authorised. **4.** On initial contact with London Control, include callsign, SID designator and current altitude/flight level. **5.** En-route cruising level will be given by London Control after take-off. **6.** See B1 for Noise Procedures. **7.** Climb gradients in excess of 3.3% are necessary to meet Noise Abatement requirements and for ATC separation purposes. **8. Comm Failure**: Climb to flight planned level after last specified altitude.

G2	Z9

22 JUL 93

EGSS

NOT TO SCALE

25nm

Barkway
BKY 116·25

BKY 14d

2500 or above

CLN 1S

120R
126R
152R

BKY 17d

3000 or above

CLN 16d

at 5000

BPK
13d

120°

CLN 271R

091°

CLACTON
'CLN' 114·55/429
N51 50 9
E001 09 0

CLN
33d

CLN 28d

3000 or above

CLN 21d

4000 or above

CLN 12d

at FL60

Brookmans Park
BPK 117·5

CLN 3R

2₁	1₉
2₂	2₂

SSA 25nm

SID	R/W	ROUTEING (including Min Noise Routeing)	ALTITUDES
CLN 3R	23	Ahead to BPK 13d then left on Tr 091M (CLN 271R) by CLN 33d to CLN.	CLN 28d 3000 or above CLN 21d 4000 or above CLN 16d at 5000 CLN 12d at FL60
CLN 1S	05	Ahead until crossing BKY 126R then right on BKY 120R to intercept Tr 091M (CLN 271R) to CLN.	BKY 14d 2500 or above BKY 17d 3000 or above CLN 21d 4000 or above CLN 16d at 5000 CLN 12d at FL60

© BRITISH AIRWAYS *AERAD*

Rev: Nil

On page 81 is shown a typical departure plate, in this instance for Stansted Airport in Essex. At the top of the plate is the 'editorial' which gives detailed notes of the departure not included in the plan-view seen in the middle of the plate. At the bottom of the plate, the pilot can see that this is a plate for two named departures: the Clacton 3R (Three Romeo) and the Clacton 1S (One Sierra).

We can see that this plate was updated on 22 July, 1993 and if you look at the bottom of the plate there were no revisions to the previous one. The Transition Altitude is 6,000 feet. Whilst most of the editorial is self explanatory let's go through the two departures:

CLN 3R

This is the SID applicable to runway 23. From the editorial we can see that the aircraft may not turn until above 850ft (QNH). This represents 500ft above ground level. The aircraft is expected to maintain runway track until 13 DME from Brookmans Park, coinciding with the 152 Radial from Barkway and then commence a left turn in order to intercept track 091 degrees to Clacton. Assuming this departure clearance is given the aircraft is expected to reach at least 3,000ft by CLN 28 DME, 4,000ft by 21 DME and to be level at 5,000ft by CLN 16 DME and FL 60 by Clacton 12 DME.

CLN 1S

This is the SID applicable to runway 05. Again pilots may not commence the turn until 850ft amsl. Runway QDM is maintained until crossing the Barkway 126 radial at which point (assuming above 850 ft) a right turn is carried out in order to establish the track 120 degrees from Barkway. This track is maintained until Track 091 degrees is established into Clacton. As for the 3R departure, various passing altitudes are given for the departure

Consider how you would set up your navigation boxes for the departure:

CLN 3R

Nav 1	Clacton 114.55 OBS: 091 degrees
Nav 2	Barkway 116.25 OBS: 152 degrees
DME	Brookmans Park 117.5 till 13 D the CLN.
ADF	SAN 339 khz (for maintaining runway QDM)

CLN 1S

Nav 1	Clacton 114.55 OBS: 091 degrees
Nav 2	BKY 126 degrees and then 120 degrees
DME	BKY till 17 D then to Clacton
ADF	SAN 339

(STANSTED) **LONDON**
BUZAD & WESTCOTT **SID**

Trans alt **6000**		

1. Initial Climb: Ahead to 850. **2.** A/C unable to comply with SID's or non standard clearance must inform ATC prior to take-off. **3.** Max 250kt below FL100 unless otherwise authorised. **4.** On initial contact with London Control, include callsign, SID designator and current altitude/flight level. **5.** En-route cruising level will be given by London Control after take-off. **6.** See B1 for Noise Procedures. **7.** Climb gradients in excess of 3.3% are necessary to meet Noise Abatement requirements and for ATC separation purposes. **8. Comm Failure:** Climb to flight planned level after last specified altitude. **9.** WESTCOTT SID's at ATC discretion.

G1	L9

EFF
22 JUL 93

EGSS

NOT TO SCALE

2₁	19
2₂	19

SSA 25nm

BARKWAY
BKY 116·25
N51 59·4
E000 03·8

BUZAD 3R, 1S

BUZAD 1S
WCO 1S
at **5000**

BKY 5d

3000 or above

BUZAD
BKY 23d
N51 56·5
W000 33·0

BKY 7d

WESTCOTT
'WCO' 335
N51 51·1
W000 57·6

39
262°

267°

BKY 2d
BUZAD 3R
WCO 3R
at **5000**

285°

BKY 2d
355°

BKY 105R

BKY 120R

WCO 3R, 1S

BKY 5d

3000 or above

BKY 8d

BPK 11·5d

BUZAD 1S
WCO 1S

24
208°

Brookmans Park
BPK 117·5

BKY 175R

BKY 160R

BUZAD 3R
WCO 3R

COMPTON
CPT 114·35
N51 29·5
W001 13·1

25nm

SID	R/W	ROUTING (including Min Noise Routeing)	ALTITUDES
BUZAD 3R	23	Ahead to BPK 11·5d then right on Tr 355M (BKY 175R) by BKY 8d to BKY 2d. At BKY 2d left on BKY 267R to BUZAD.	BKY 175R/5d 3000 or above BKY 267R/2d at 5000.
BUZAD 1S	05	Ahead until crossing BKY 120R then left on Tr 285M (BKY 105R) by BKY 7d to BKY. At BKY left on BKY 267R to BUZAD.	BKY 105R/5d 3000 or above BKY at 5000.
WCO 3R	23	Ahead to BPK 11·5d then right on Tr 355M(BKY 175R) by BKY 8d to BKY 2d. At BKY 2d left on BKY 262R to 'WCO' then left on Tr 208M (CPT 029R) to CPT.	BKY 175R/5d 3000 or above BKY 262R/2d at 5000.
WCO 1S	05	Ahead until crossing BKY 120R then left on Tr 285M (BKY 105R) by BKY 7d to BKY. At BKY left on BKY 262R to 'WCO' then left on Tr 208M (CPT 028R) to CPT.	BKY 105R/5d 3000 or above BKY at 5000

© Rev: Tracks

BRITISH AIRWAYS AERAD

Now let's examine the Buzad and Westcott SID from Stansted. Again the plate is full of information. Note and read all the editorial. The transition altitude is 6,000 feet. Standard setting may therefore be set as the aircraft passes 4,000 feet in the climb to a flight level.

No turns are allowed below 850 feet QNH ie 500 feet above ground level. First call to London to include Aircraft Call-sign, name of SID and passing level/altitude. This enables the controller to check the serviceability of your transponder's height read-out.

Look at the departure: BUZAD THREE ROMEO.

This applies to runway 23. Aircraft are expected to maintain Runway QDM until 11.5 DME from Brookmans Park and to then turn right to establish the 355 QDM to Barkway. Aircraft should be established on this track by 8 DME from Barkway and remain on this track until 2 DME from Barkway.

At 2 DME from Barkway aircraft should make a left turn to establish the 267 degree track from Barkway to BUZAD and thence en route to the airway. Aircraft should be at 3,000' or above at 5 DME BKY and be level at 5,000' by BKY 2 DME

So how would you set your navigation aids?

DME: BPK 117.5 and after use to BKY 116.25
VOR 1: BKY 116.25 with 355 set on the OBS
VOR 1: BKY 116.25 with 160 set (X cut for 11.5 DME BPK) then 267 set
ADF: SAN for maintaining runway QDM after take-off.

Transponder as directed.

Have a look now at the Buzad 1S Departure and work out for yourself how you would set up your radio aids.

Chapter 7

Flight on the Airways

The airways are defined as Category A airspace. One is therefore not entitled to enter this airspace unless you are the holder of a valid Instrument Rating. It is in this airspace that a positive *Radar Control Service* is provided and pilots are expected to comply with all instructions given. The airways are designed to offer a safe separation from other traffic, both horizontally and vertically and to provide safe terrain separation at the base.

Airways are ten miles wide, five miles either side of centre line. Their vertical extent varies from airway to airway. They are constructed about a matrix of VORs and NDBs although the latter are becoming scarcer and scarcer. These VORs and NDBs are usually the reporting points for aircraft travelling from beacon to beacon. Reporting points are most normally non-compulsory, in other words pilots do not have to report as they overfly them. There are some reporting points, most often found at the end of the airways that are compulsory but the trend now is not to report unless requested to do so. (For the purposes of the Instrument Rating Test, the examiner expects the candidate to make 'mock reports' to him even if ATC have not requested reports to be made to them.)

If asked to make a report, the call should be in the following order:

Position
Time
Level
Estimate

London Control, Cabair 03 was Daventry 22, Flight Level 60, Brookmans Park 34.

Upon first contact with the airways controller, pilots should notify the Departure Type, their passing level and their Squawk. The controller needs to verify that you are the aircraft he is looking at and that your reported passing level agrees with the transponder read-out. The controller will normally require the pilot to 'squawk ident'. This will cause the code to start flashing and confirm that the correct aircraft has responded to the instruction and to make the aircraft more conspicuous on the radar screen.

Selection of Flight Level

This normally follows the semi-circular rule: Eastbound fly ODD level, and Westbound fly EVEN levels. Plan for an odd flight level if flying on a track between 000 and 179 degrees and at an even flight level if flying on a track between 180 and 359 degrees.

Airway Nomenclature

Airways are known by a letter and a number (it used to be colours). For instance: *Bravo 3* or *Alpha 1*.
The only airway still referred by colour is the 'Purple Airway'.*

* General Note
A *Purple Airway* is an area of controlled airspace reserved for the purposes of a Royal Flight.
In the United Kingdom separation is controlled by either London Control or by Scottish Airways.
The lowest usable flight level on an airway will provide a minimum of 1,500 feet separation from the highest obstacle on the ground.
When joining or leaving an airway, aim to join/leave as close as possible to ninety degrees to the airway centre line.
Flight plans must be filed for flight on airways normally before take-off with a minimum of thirty minutes notice. It is possible to file an 'in flight' flight plan, in which case at least ten minutes notice is required.

Communication Failure

In the event of communication failure, change your squawk to 7,600, transmit blind your intention to leave controlled airspace if VMC and the land as soon as possible. In the event that you have recently been given a specific instruction, comply with it until such time as you consider it safe to leave the airspace. This is best done by exiting the airspace at right angles to the airway centre line. There may be specific procedures related to certain airspace which should be followed, the details of which may be obtained from your Aerad Charts.

Should the aircraft be in IMC, then continue as per your flight plan to the holding point of the aircraft's destination. Thereafter comply with the local procedures. Do not climb or descend but maintain your last instructed level until that point is reached. On reaching the holding point, commence descent as per local instructions.

In the event that comms failure occurs after the hold has been established and you have been advised that a delay is not determined and no 'Expected Approach Time' has been given, *DO NOT LAND AT THAT AIRFIELD*. Endeavour to find an area where VMC may be established and land at another suitable airfield.

Navigation Aid Failure

There is a minimum equipment list for flight into controlled airspace under Instrument Flight Rules. Failure of part of this equipment requires the pilot to normally leave that airspace and if VMC land as soon as possible. Practically, subject to ATC's permission, flight may be continued to destination and a landing made. A typical example of this would be failure of the 'mode C' of the transponder.

Wherever a problem occurs seek help from Air Traffic Control . . . they are there to help.

Joining and Leaving

Airways are normally joined or left at a specified reporting point. Often aircraft are expected to be level at their cruising altitude/flight level prior to entry into that airspace. Sometimes controllers will allow aircraft to join controlled airspace in the ascent or even leave 'in the descent' subject to no confliction with other traffic.

VOR Tracking

Most pilots will tell you that there is nothing simpler than tracking a VOR with the regular beam bar display and most pilots would be right. There are, however, many pilots who do not do it correctly and so a few paragraphs spent discussing it can do no harm.

The cockpit display will show the pilot what is his QDM to the station if a 'to' flag is showing and his QDR from the station if a 'from' flag is showing. A radial is always a track from the station. If, for instance, an aircraft is on the 180 degree radial it is due south of the station.

If tracking to a facility, ensure that the 'to' flag is visible and if tracking away, ensure that the 'from' flag is showing. Take great care to ensure that an accurate setting is achieved with the Omni Bearing Selector, the OBS.

Let's assume that we're tracking along the airway B3 towards Daventry on the 130 degree radial and heading 310 degrees. The aircraft is on track. Should the heading fail to maintain this track, it is up to the pilot to firstly regain track and to secondly and subsequently find a heading that will maintain the track. Pilots should avoid over attacking the track only to find the aircraft passing from one side to the other. Instead, make sensible and judicious changes in heading to ensure that the track is held.

Aircraft on track:

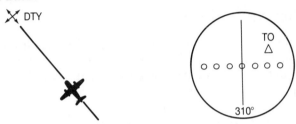

Aircraft to the left of track with Fly Right Indication:

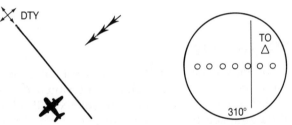

Aircraft alters course to right by thirty degrees (into wind):

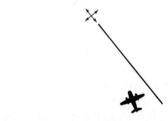

Aircraft regains track and makes allowance for W/V:

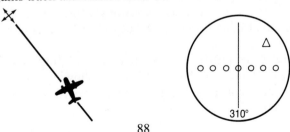

As the aircraft approaches the facility, the indications will change more quickly. The DME can be used to good effect here, but remember that the DME will be indicating your height the closer you are to your station. An aircraft at Flight Level 60 for instance, may well be some one mile above ground level. Typically about two or three miles from the VOR station the pilot should concentrate more on heading control rather than maintaining a track.

The Commercial Turn

Assuming a VOR is associated with a DME or perhaps a cross-cut from another VOR, a pilot need not fly directly overhead the VOR unless requested by ATC. It is quite in order to 'cut the corner' as long as the aircraft remains within the confines of the airway. Depending on the wind effect, it would be quite in order for the aircraft to anticipate the corner by say, three to four miles and to turn onto the next track early.

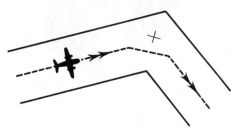

Cross-Cuts

Occasionally, along an airway, a pilot may wish to check or advise his position by use of a cross-cut. The most commonly used method in general aviation is to always set the radial from the cross-cut and in this way the presentation on the VOR will be such that the beam bar will always come in from the side that the station is located. Once the beam bar has moved to the other side, the pilot will know that the position has been passed.

Some operators prefer to set cross-cuts such that the beam bar always comes in from the same side, normally the left. In this way, if ever a beam bar is sitting in the right hand side of the VOR display, the pilot will know that the position has been crossed.

En Route Holding

For a myriad of reasons including weather, traffic congestion, it could be possible for ATC to require your aircraft to hold at an unscheduled location. Where practicable ATC will arrange for this to happen at a VOR or even at an en route NDB. Holds on an Airway should be assumed to be normally right-handed unless stipulated otherwise on the airways chart.

If you feel your ETA, which you previously informed your examiner, is incorrect, advise him of your revision DONT GIVE UP!

Altimeter Settings

The one rule that holds good for all cockpits is that at least one altimeter should be set to a relevant QNH assuming more than one altimeter is available. In this way terrain separation information is always available.

For take-off, the aerodrome QNH is the normal setting. When cleared to a flight level, the standard setting 1013mbs may be set when passing an altitude that is within 2,000ft of the transition altitude. Once above transition altitude the number one altimeter will normally remain on the 'standard setting' and the other altimeter to the regional QNH.

Once cleared for a descent to an altitude, the QNH should be set, unless a flight level vacating report has been requested. The aircraft should then remain on QNH until established upon final approach when QFE or any other desired setting may be used. More and more operators are now using QNH for final approach.

The Weather

It is a requirement for the aircraft commander to confirm that his flight may be made safely. One of his concerns therefore should be the weather that the aircraft is flying in and will be flying to. Weather information can be obtained from the communications frequency in use or from London Volmet and in some cases from the ATIS of the destination aerodrome (Aerodrome Terminal Information Service). More and more airports are now providing an ATIS. This weather should be obtained normally prior to first contact with the approach controller. The weather must be obtained prior to making an approach.

The Approach Ban

An approach to an airfield where there is a recognised Instrument Approach Procedure may not be made below 1,000ft above ground level unless the visibility is above the minima for that approach. If after having passed 1,000ft, should the visibility drop, the approach may continue to decision/minimum descent height. Continuation below Decision/Minimum descent height may only be continued if there is *sufficient visual reference element*. For a precision approach at least six lead-in lights must be visible. For a non-precision approach this is increased to seven and/or the touch-down zone visible.

Planning the Flight

Ensure that all charts are available and are in date.

Know the taxi route to the holding point for the runway in use.

Look up and study the most likely departure routes (SIDS) and likely cleared altitudes.

Study the airways route, noting all appropriate tracks and possible re-routeings. Note possible holding points and hold directions.

Note regional QNHs on route.

Note, if possible en route frequencies.

Check Notams and Royal Flights.

Check weather for departure/en route, destination and diversion fields.

Check serviceability of radio aids that are intended for use.

Note Radio failure procedures for departure and destination.

Chapter 8

The Arrival

Most major airports will have a standard terminal arrival procedure that is published on a STAR plate or chart. This will show the preferred inbound routeings, tracks and distances to the airport or final holding location. Information on arrival beacons and frequencies will be given and speed limit points.

For the student and qualified pilot alike it is important to understand the chart correctly and to be able to glean its information relatively quickly. It's particularly important to know when to slow down to holding speed and how much distance the pilot will need in order to commence a descent.

At a typical training aircraft speed of three miles a minute and a rate of descent of 750 ft per minute, an aircraft will need four miles per 1,000ft for height loss. If descending from 8,000ft to 3,000ft the descent should be started no later than twenty miles from the point where the level must be reached. If your aircraft travels at a different speed, work out the distance per 1,000ft for yourself.

For training aircraft a reduction of speed too early can be a problem for air traffic control, so it is advised to maintain the airway speed until at least five miles from the holding facility. For larger aircraft, pilots must observe speed limit points by which their aircraft should have reduced to the appropriate speed.

The chart shown is the 'STAR' for London Luton Airport. Note that these are the Westcott Stars for aircraft routeing inbound to Luton from the West. The chart is not drawn to scale.

In the bottom left-hand section the reader sees what revisions have been made to this chart since the last one. Transition Altitude for Luton is 6,000ft. Speed Limit points are marked by the letter 'S' in a circle. Holds are shown at Lorel, Askey, Westcott, Daventry and Honiley. An

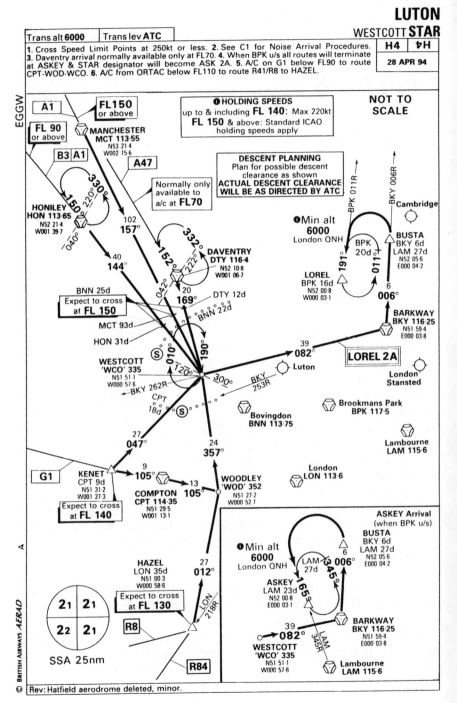

LUTON
WESTCOTT **STAR**

SSA 25nm

© BRITISH AIRWAYS *AERAD*

Rev: Hatfield aerodrome deleted, minor.

94

aircraft routeing in from Manchester, for example, may very well expect direct track Westcott (NDB) followed by a left turn towards Barkway before being picked up on radar for a vectored approach into Luton.

Arrivals are normally given a name and pilots advised by Air Traffic Control prior to their commencement.

'Good Afternoon, Cabair 03, expect a LOREL 2A arrival, Luton Information Sierra is current. Commence descent to be level at Westcott 5,000 ft on the Luton QNH 1012mbs.

It is common in arrival situations for the radar controller to take over the aircraft's arrival with radar headings taking the aircraft a long way from the originally intended track. This will normally be more expeditious but sometimes can be further. Don't forget when you are on a radar heading, you must stay on it until released.

To be honest, they are normally a godsend as the controller is taking over the responsibility for your navigation thus considerably reducing your workload. However, remain aware of your location, reference the airfield and associated beacons. Don't go to sleep!

Chapter 9

The Hold

The hold is a necessary evil! It is a delaying procedure that enables a pilot to keep an aircraft within a specified area whilst awaiting onward clearance. This clearance could be perhaps to commence an approach or to continue en route. In a way it represents a failure of the airway or procedural system. The ideal situation is one in which we don't have to hold.

Occasionally a hold can be utilised by the pilot rather than instructed by ATC as perhaps a weather avoidance facility or perhaps instructions from company to delay arrival.

Aircraft can hold now almost anywhere as aircrafts' navigation equipment becomes more and more sophisticated. More traditionally the hold is set up about an NDB or a VOR or even on a VOR radial at a specific DME distance from the VOR installation. It could also be at the intersection of two VOR radials. Insofar as the Instrument Rating Test, the candidate is expected most normally to hold using a needle presentation, most commonly an ADF needle homing to an NDB. If the aircraft is equipped with an RMI needle that can slave on a VOR, it is permissible to be tested using this equipment.

Most holding patterns are right-handed. This is not always the case however. Local conflicting terrain or conurbation areas could cause the hold designer to make the hold left-handed. A left-handed hold may suit a particular procedure better than a right-handed hold.

The ICAO one minute racetrack pattern calls for the aircraft to approach the facility along a predescribed track (the 'Inbound Axis') to then turn right onto the outbound leg and to fly on this heading for a period of one minute from the abeam position before turning right, once again to reintercept the inbound axis. All turns are assumed to be rate one with a maximum allowable bank angle of twenty-five degrees should the aircraft require that angle to achieve a rate one turn.

As mentioned the timing starts the second the aircraft passes abeam the beacon. This of course could occur during the turn. Both the timing outbound and the heading should be adjusted to take into account the wind effect on the hold.

The Hold Entry

The join to a hold is dependent upon the heading that the aircraft is steering at the time of beacon passage and not its track.

The hold is divided principally into three sectors: Sectors 1, 2 and 3. This is achieved by drawing a line, inclined towards the inbound axis at an angle of 70 degrees. The inbound axis is then extended through the beacon. See figures below.

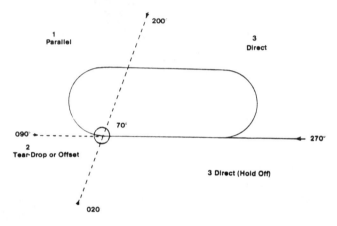

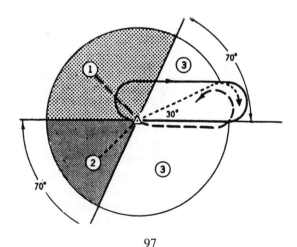

The Sector 1 is called the Parallel Entry, the Sector 2 is for the Teardrop or Offset Entry and the Sector 3 is reserved for the Direct Entry.

Let's firstly look at the Sector 1.

Sector 1

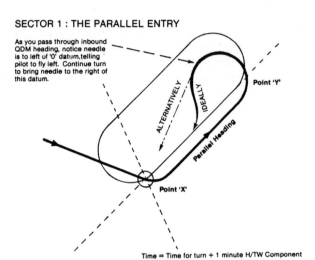

Fly parallel to inbound QDM, do not backtrack on it.

Time X – Y one minute in still air – add time if necessary to allow for turn at X. After turn inbound, take a large cut to establish on inbound QDM – tracking direct to beacon is permissible, but opportunity to find out drift on inbound QDM would be lost.

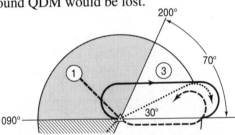

In the case of the hold above (270 IB axis right hand), for aircraft approaching on headings between 090° and 200° the parallel entry is the correct one. The aircraft should be turned on to a heading to parallel the inbound axis. Note that there is no back-tracking required. At the completion of this turn the aircraft should maintain its parallel heading for a period of one minute, plus/minus the wind (one second per knot). The aircraft is then turned towards the holding side to either route straight back to the beacon or preferably reintercept the inbound axis, assuming the intercept angle is less than 50°.

Sector 2

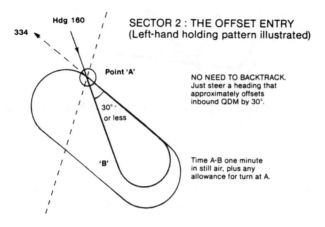

Head outbound 30° off reciprocal of inbound QDM ± allowance for wind in order to complete inbound turn on inbound QDM.

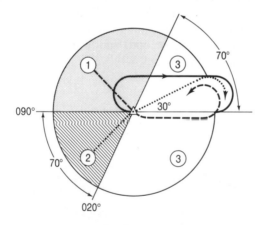

Again for the hold described, if the aircraft's heading is between 090° and 020° the Tear-drop or Offset join applies. As the aircraft flies over the beacon it is turned onto a heading to make good a track of 30° or less from the inbound axis. This heading is maintained for one minute, plus/minus the wind and the aircraft is then turned back to reintercept the inbound track. Again, in this join, the pilot is not required to back-track the beacon.

Sector 3

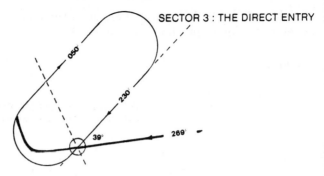

This entry can be divided into two: entry from the holding side and entry from the non-holding side.

From the holding side
Immediately the aircraft passes over the beacon the aircraft should be turned onto the outbound heading for the hold. Note from the diagram that the probability is that the aircraft will overshoot the inbound axis unless the first turn rate is reduced or even stopped. (Figure above)

From the non-holding side
In this case, the aircraft has effectively already turned through a number of degrees towards its outbound heading. Pilots are advised to take the difference between their actual heading and the inbound axis, divide this figure by three (3 degrees per second) and to maintain their heading for that number of seconds. (Figure below)

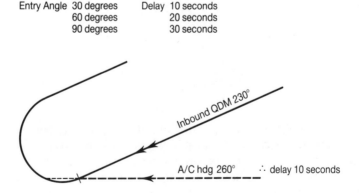

The Hold and your calculations

The Heading

Imagine a hold with an inbound QDM of 270 degrees. The hold is right-handed. If a wind is present from the north-west, the first turn over the beacon will be squashed. This would cause the aircraft to be too close to the inbound axis when on the outbound leg. The outbound heading therefore needs to be adjusted.

A good rule of thumb is as follows:
If the wind to track angle is more than forty-five degrees apply three times drift to the outbound heading. If the wind-track angle is less than forty-five degrees allow double drift. The drift referred to is the single drift needed to maintain the inbound axis.

By allowing this increased drift, it should allow the aircraft to be turned reasonably easily onto track. Occasionally the three times drift applied may be too much drift causing the outbound heading to arrive on the wrong side of the wind. Should this happen, then reduce the three times drift to two.

How to Plan the Hold

1. Calculate the inbound heading based on single drift. Note this drift amount (x degrees).
2. Calculate the wind/track angle (y degrees).
3. If y is more than 45° apply three times x to the track reciprocal. If less than 45° apply two times x. If around 45° use two and a half times x.
4. Calculate the outbound heading based on the above calculation.
5. Work out the wind 'head or tail-wind' component.
6. Add or subtract this figure from the one minute.
7. If using an RBI calculate your 90/60/30 headings. (More on this later).

The Timing

There is no laid down figure for total timing for the hold. Since the timing should run from abeam the beacon it is normally accepted that the total time aimed for is approximately three minutes (from the abeam to beacon passage). All that the CAA examiner is concerned with, is that a sensible adjustment is made to the outbound timing to compensate for the effect of the wind.

This is quite simple. Using a computer, calculate your outbound ground-speed based on the new calculated heading. Decide how much head or tail-wind the aircraft is going to experience. Assuming a tail-wind subtract one second per knot of tail-wind from the standard one minute leg. If it's a head-wind add this time to the outbound one minute leg.

A twenty knot tail-wind would require an outbound timing of forty seconds from the abeam position. A ten knot head-wind would require a timing of one minute and ten seconds. Simply add or subtract the time as necessary. The adjustment, remember is one second per knot per minute.

I should point out that the holding pattern above Flight Level 140 requires a basic outbound timing of one minute thirty seconds, not one minute. We therefore add or subtract one and a half seconds per knot of head or tail-wind.

The 90/60/30 Check Headings

When using a Relative Bearing Indicator (an ADF needle against a fixed card), it is important to pre-calculate the headings that the aircraft will pass through on the inbound turn of the hold which are at ninety degrees, sixty degrees and thirty degrees to the inbound axis. The pilot should know that at ninety degrees the approximate relative bearing should be seventy-five relative (285 for a left-handed hold) and at sixty degrees the relative bearing should be fifty degrees on the RBI. When at thirty degrees to the inbound axis the relative bearing should be approximately twenty-five degrees (335 degrees for a left-handed hold).

If the relative bearings are not as expected this indicates that the aircraft will either overshoot or undershoot the inbound turn. For a right-handed hold if the observed relative bearings are greater than expected, the aircraft is overshooting the inbound axis. Solution: maintain the rate one turn and reintercept the inbound axis from the non-holding side. If the relative bearings are less than you would expect to see this indicates an undershooting situation.

Put more simply:

Over-reading Over-shooting (Continue the turn)
Under-reading Under-shooting (Slow the turn or hold off)

If the hold takes too long or is too short for your requirements, divide the error by two and add or subtract this time from your next out-bound timing.

Hold Adjustment

If you are required to hold for a period of time that requires more than the one hold then you will have the opportunity to adjust and improve the outbound heading and/or timing. If the aircraft is tending to overshoot the inbound axis adjust the drift on the outbound leg by five degrees for a small error and ten degrees for a large error. If late or early over the beacon halve the error in time and adjust the outbound time by the same amount.

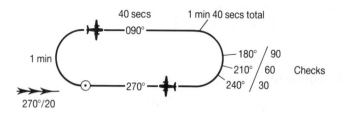

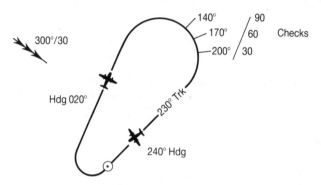

Monitoring the ADF Needle on the Outbound Leg

As the aircraft travels down the outbound leg of the hold, monitor the position of the ADF needle in relation to the inbound axis QDR/QDM. At the end of the outbound leg the needle should be approximately thirty degrees off the inbound axis. This angle is called the *gate angle*. Should the aircraft reach this angle prematurely it is an indication that the aircraft is too close to the axis and an overshoot may be likely. Consider the value of 'flying up the gate' to the required time.

If the gate angle is not reached at the end of the outbound leg this points to the possibility of an impending undershoot and given sufficient time the outbound heading should be adjusted towards the inbound axis. *Always monitor the gate angle on the outbound leg of the hold.*

The Expected Approach Time/Onward Clearance Time

An EAT is given normally as a precaution against radio failure so that the pilot knows when to leave the holding beacon to commence his approach to land. An onward clearance time is a similar time used to allow aircraft to leave one position on an airway, for instance, to continue its journey having been previously held. Such times are of interest to the pilot as he wants to know what, if any, his expected delay will be.

It is the pilot's responsibility to adjust the timing in the hold in order to meet the expected EAT or OCT. At the same time the pilot must remain within the designated holding area.

VOR Holding

If your aircraft is equipped with an RMI needle that can slave to a VOR, VOR holding is very little different to ADF holding. There is, however, no dip error. That is the tendency of the ADF needle to dip towards the lower wing during a turn, thus giving an apparent overshoot indication during inbound turns.

In the hold – **head** outbound as required so that you will be on the inbound QDM on completion of the inbound turn. ALLOW 3 x DRIFT OUTBOUND.

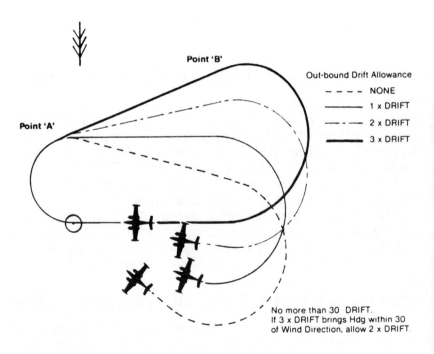

Point 'B'

Point 'A'

Out-bound Drift Allowance

- – – – NONE
- ———— 1 x DRIFT
- —·—— 2 x DRIFT
- ▬▬▬▬ 3 x DRIFT

No more than 30 DRIFT.
If 3 x DRIFT brings Hdg within 30
of Wind Direction, allow 2 x DRIFT.

If a slaving RMI needle is not available and what is available is only the basic VOR/OBS/Beam bar type display different techniques must be used.

1. Set the OBS to VOR 1 to the Inbound Axis. Track inbound on this VOR.
2. Set No. 2 VOR to the abeam radial for the initial timing and then to the gate angle radial.
3. During the inbound turn set the No 2 VOR to a QDM ten degrees offset towards the holding side as a warning of the approach of the inbound axis. Note that the moment the No 2 VOR beam bar passes through the middle, No 1 VOR will become active.
4. The stop-watch is started in the overhead (when the to/from flag changes to from).
5. The stop-watch is restarted in the abeam using the OBS setting from (2) above.

Please note that the adjustments to outbound headings and timings are as for the ADF hold. A hold is a hold, be it on an ADF or on a VOR.

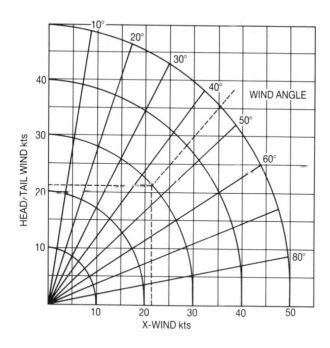

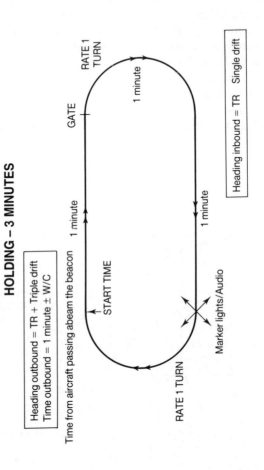

HOLDING – 3 MINUTES

Heading outbound = TR + Triple drift
Time outbound = 1 minute ± W/C

Time from aircraft passing abeam the beacon

GATE

RATE 1 TURN

1 minute

START TIME

1 minute

1 minute

1 minute

RATE 1 TURN

Marker lights/Audio

Heading inbound = TR   Single drift

Holding Entry Procedure:

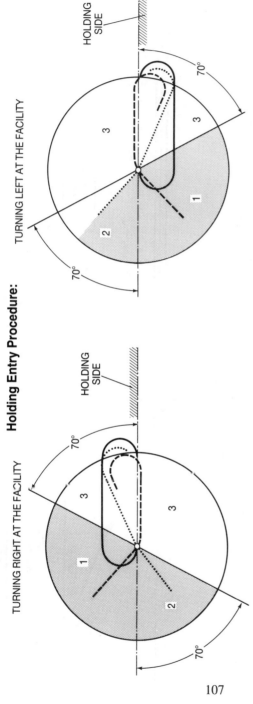

1. Sector 1 procedures (parallel).
   Having reached the fix, turn onto outbound heading for the appropriate period of time.
   Turn towards the holding side to intercept the inbound track or to return to the fix.
   On second arrival over the fix, turn to follow the holding pattern.
2. Sector 2 procedure (offset).
   Having reached the fix, turn onto a heading to make good a track making an angle of 30° or less from the inbound track on the holding side.
   Continue for the appropriate period of time.
   Turn to intercept the inbound track and follow the holding pattern.
3. Sector 3 procedures (direct).
   Having reached the fix, turn in the same direction as that specified for the holding pattern to be followed.

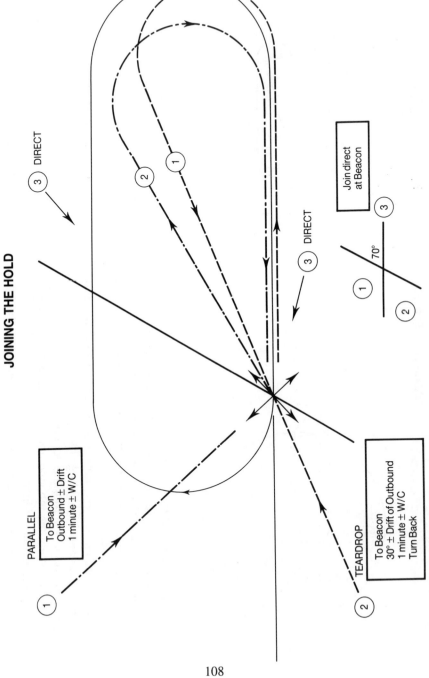

JOINING THE HOLD

③ DIRECT

③ DIRECT

PARALLEL

To Beacon
Outbound ± Drift
1 minute ± W/C

TEARDROP

To Beacon
30° ± Drift of Outbound
1 minute ± W/C
Turn Back

Join direct
at Beacon

70°

Chapter 10

Flying the ILS

ILS is the abbreviation for the Instrument Landing System, which is the most commonly used precision approach aid in the world. It is known as a precision aid as it offers electronic guidance in both height in relation to the ideal approach path and also in azimuth in relation to the final approach track of the runway.

The ILS installation comprises two transmitters: the localiser transmitter for centre-line control and the glide-slope transmitter for height control.

The localiser provides azimuth guidance normally along the runway's extended centre line and transmits on a VHF band of frequencies 108 — 112 Mhz at normally 200 Khz spacings eg 108.9, 109.1. Some military installations may differ.

The glide-path transmits on the UHF band of frequencies between 329 and 335 Mhz with 300 Khz spacings.

The localiser and glide-path transmissions are what is described as frequency paired. When the localiser frequency is selected it will automatically select the correct glide-path frequency. For instance the localiser frequency 110.3 Mhz will always be paired with the 335 Mhz glide-path frequency.

In addition to the basic localiser and glide-path transmissions many ILS installations will also have a system of marker beacons. These are slowly being withdrawn as more and more airfields become equipped with DME's (Distance Measuring Equipment). When installed they are used to confirm the aircraft's correct position in the procedure. Markers operate again on VHF but on the one frequency of 75 Mhz. In order to differentiate between different types of markers, they are amplitude modulated to give different colours and sounds within the cockpit.

Intercepting the localiser (Runway QDM 003°)

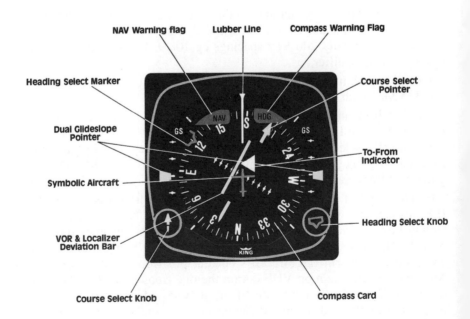

Outer Marker	Flashing Blue Light	Low Pitched Dashes
Middle Marker	Amber light	Ident Dots & Dashes
Inner or		
Airways Marker	White Light	High Pitched Dots

Markers should be set to 'Audio' and to 'High' sensitivity for low altitude flight where the width of the beam is small. For high altitude flight the sensitivity should be set to 'Low' where the beam width is wide.

Most approach let down procedures will have associated *Non Directional Beacons* known as Locator NDBs. These assist the pilot in maintaining good spatial awareness within the procedure and give accurate overhead passage, unlike markers which indicate for lengthy periods.

Radar
Most, but not all, airfields that offer ILS will also offer Radar. Radar is a useful tool to the controller to expedite traffic onto an ILS approach with vectors.

The Limitations of the ILS

An ILS allows a pilot to fly an approach down to specified minima. Such minima are dependent upon the category of ILS that the airfield is offering and which the aircraft can accept. These categories are as follows:

CAT 1   Guidance to 200 feet above the ILS reference point.
CAT 2   Guidance to 50 feet
CAT 3A/B/C Guidance to the surface of the runway subject to visibility minima.

Flying The ILS Approach

An ILS approach, flown well, is one of the most satisfying aspects of all instrument flying, for it combines so many different skills: control of pitch attitude, accurate control and adjustment of heading and speed. If a student has not flown for some while, it is most often his ILS which deteriorates more than any other separate section of the test. The ILS involves true skill and good interpretation of what is actually happening to the aircraft.

The ISL Approach

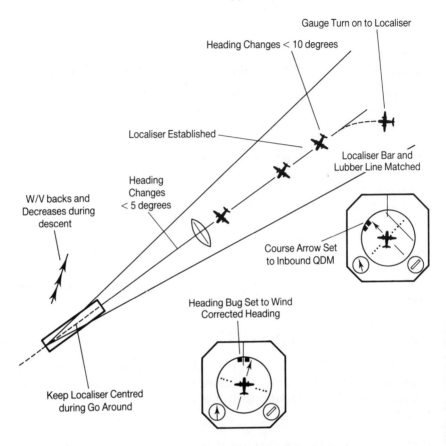

Prior to commencing and even to turning onto the ILS localiser it is essential that the aid has been correctly identified, checked and set. Ensure that you are receiving the correct ident. Most Ilss in the UK are prefixed with the letter 'I'. Check that there are no fail flags showing and that you are receiving or have received a Fly up indication before establishing the localiser. Whether you have an HSI type display or the older fashioned VOR display, ensure that the Runway QDM is accurately set against the lubber line.

Before flying the approach make a mental approximation of the wind effect both on the Rate of Descent and therefore power required and also on the average or datum heading for the approach. This will be the first heading that you turn onto having captured the ILS localiser.

Do not be under the illusion that you should be able to fly either a constant heading approach or a constant powered approach. The wind effect will change during a descent and quite probably so will the power output from your engines for a given height. Let's look at the control of the localiser first:

The Localiser

The localiser is simply a track in the sky. The closer the aircraft becomes to the point of transmission, the more sensitive the localiser becomes and the quicker it displays a divergence from the centre line.

As the aircraft is placed upon an intercept heading for the localiser the pilot should again consider the effect of the wind. Is the aircraft ploughing into a head-wind when perhaps a slightly greater intercept angle should be used or is there a tail-wind present. In this instance, a lessor intercept angle may be more advisable. The typical intercept angle is forty-five degrees. This gives sufficient time for the aircraft to be turned in order to capture the localiser.

The second the localiser starts moving, call out aloud —'Localiser Alive' or 'Localiser Active' to notify both fellow crew members' and yourself the aircraft is shortly about to turn. Advise Air Traffic once the aircraft is established. To be established, the aircraft needs to be within one half-scale deflection and heading in the appropriate direction. Remember firstly that any heading changes made should be made promptly and be as small as possible.

Remember also that any heading that causes the localiser to return to the centre will not be a heading to remain on. Typically four or more miles from the runway centre line use heading alterations of no more than ten degrees at a time. Once closer than four miles, restrict heading changes to five degrees or less. Be patient!

If the error is not getting worse and is showing only a slow improvement do not be tempted to over pursue an errant localiser. Select a heading, hold the heading and check to see if it is working for you. *If not* then and *only* then reselect.

You may wish to have the heading bug selected on your heading as the approach progresses. I would recommend against this for two reasons: every time the heading is changed your right hand will be taken away from the throttles or column control and part of your mind will be diverted from the 'job in hand', and . . . the heading bug can obscure the indications of heading at the top of an already 'cluttered' dial.

As an alternative I would suggest one of the following:
1. Set the bug on the wind direction.
2. Set the bug directly behind the aircraft (no confusion).
3. Set the bug on the next major heading should an overshoot be required.

As mentioned earlier, as the aircraft flies further down the cone, the localiser is becoming more and more sensitive. It's essential that any small deviation is seen and normally reacted to. Don't however underestimate the wind's effect. A backing wind during the descent could be either assisting or hindering you as you approach decision height. Consider its effect prior to sliding down the approach.

The best wind for the localiser control is a wind that is coming positively from one side of the approach all the way down. The worst wind is the fifteen knot headwind that will be on your left if you alter heading to the right and on your right if you alter heading to the left!

Be systematic with all heading alterations and try to remember the resulting effects of the various headings you have used. Since all heading changes will be small, use small bank angles to achieve these changes. If the aircraft suffers from adverse yaw, then remember to back up all bank with sympathetic rudder. If the heading changes are of the magnitude of two degrees or less and the weather conditions are smooth you may consider simply to adjust heading with rudder alone. It's a thought!

Remember also that as the aircraft descends the likelihood of windshear and turbulence increases and this will also have an effect on the aircraft's track across the ground and increase the difficulty in maintaining both the localiser and the glide-slope.

The Glide-path

'Controlling the glide-path is like flying straight and level down-hill'. The glide-path is again a line in the sky to be followed, a line that becomes increasingly more sensitive the lower the aircraft becomes as the aircraft flies into the ever narrowing cone.

Prior to intercepting the glide-path, the pilot should consider the head-wind/tail-wind effect on the aircraft's anticipated rate of descent and power requirement. A strong head-wind will require a higher power setting. A slack wind or even a tail-wind will require the aircraft to have a much higher rate of descent and therefore a much lower power setting.

Whilst I appear to be equating power settings to rates of descent, this is not how the ILS should ideally be flown. Glide-slope position should be principally controlled by gentle pitch attitude changes. Aircraft low, select a higher nose attitude. Aircraft high, select a lower nose attitude. Once the new attitude has been selected, the attitude should be rigidly maintained and the effect of the new attitude monitored.

Airspeed is in the control of the power levers. Too slow, be prepared to add power. Too fast and be prepared to reduce power. Remind yourself that during the descent a normally aspirated constant speed engine will develop more power and it may be necessary to therefore reduce the

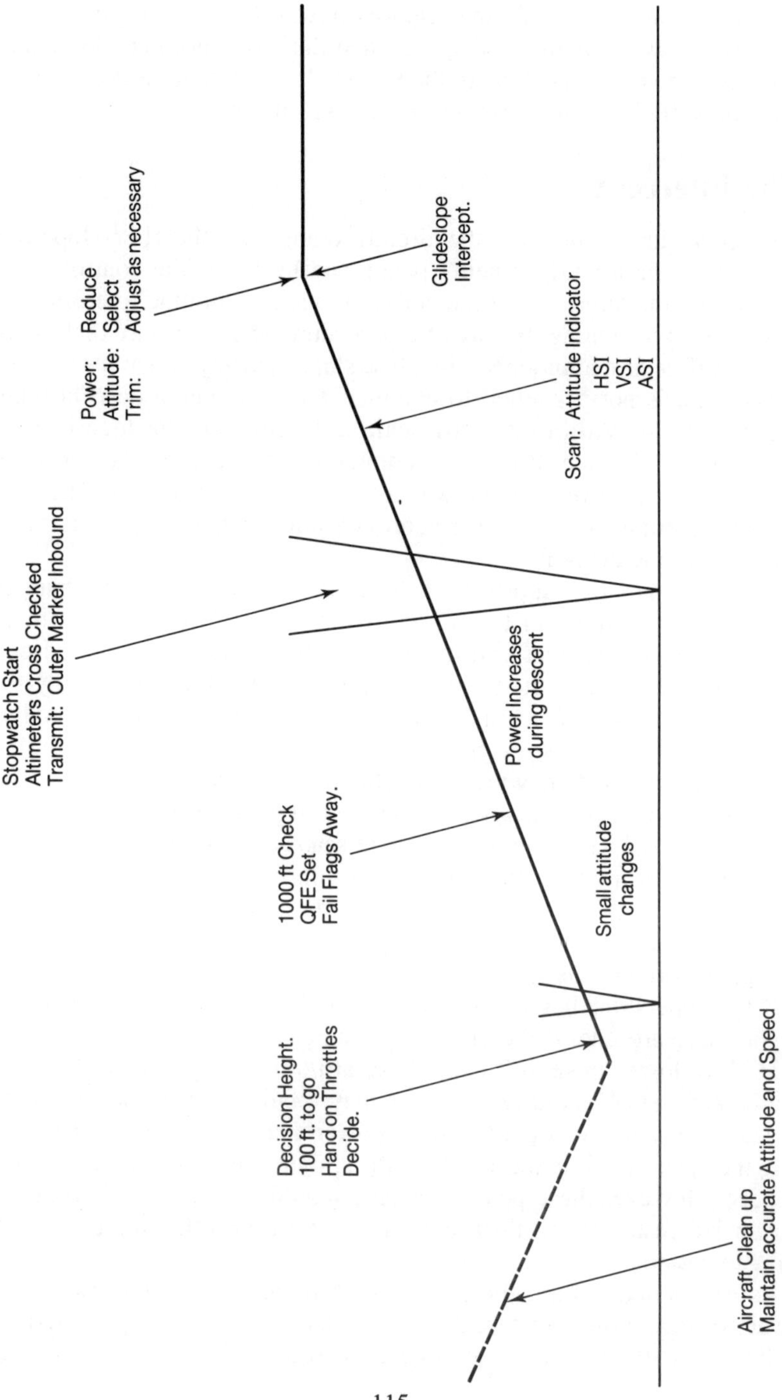

Stopwatch Start
Altimeters Cross Checked
Transmit: Outer Marker Inbound

Glideslope
Intercept.

Power: Reduce
Attitude: Select
Trim: Adjust as necessary

Scan: Attitude Indicator
       HSI
       VSI
       ASI

1000 ft Check
QFE Set
Fail Flags Away.

Power Increases
during descent

Small attitude
changes

Decision Height.
100 ft. to go
Hand on Throttles
Decide.

Aircraft Clean up
Maintain accurate Attitude and Speed

throttle setting to maintain the required power. If however the aircraft is slightly below the nominated speed, then the wise pilot may do better to leave the power levers alone in the knowledge that the power output may increase sufficiently to offset the speed loss suffered.

The Intercept

Most procedures will cause the aircraft to approach the glide-slope from beneath. If the aircraft is being positioned by radar, the controller will ensure that the aircraft is at the correct range and altitude to ensure this. Pilots, self-positioning by way of a procedure, should ensure that, before the aircraft is turned inbound, the glide-slope is safely above the aircraft.

The pilot is not permitted to commence or continue a descent unless the aircraft is within one half-scale deflection of the localiser. An indication of the rate of descent required can be seen by the speed that the glide-slope moves down towards the centre of the display. The faster the glide-slope moves, the greater the anticipation required for the initiation of the descent.

As the glide-slope approaches the centre of the display, prepare the aircraft for the descent to follow. Slowly retard the throttles to the approximate setting that you had previously calculated for the descent. Simultaneously select the anticipated pitch down attitude (typically four degrees for most light twins). Finally trim to requirement. Normally a slight trim forward is the best action even if you feel the aircraft is reasonably trimmed anyway. This deliberate nose down trim is designed to offset the effect of the power increase during the descent.

As the aircraft settles into the descent scan across to the Vertical Speed Indicator. The rate of descent should approximate to five times the aircraft's ground-speed. Check again to the glide-slope position and if captured, you now have a good indication of the rate of descent required for the majority of the approach.

If the glide-slope begins to indicate a slight fly up . . . select a slightly higher nose attitude. If the glide-slope indicates a slight fly down, select a slightly lower nose attitude. These attitude changes should be kept deliberately small. Attitude changes may require power changes. If the speed is low and the aircraft is low a power increase will be needed.

If the speed is high and the aircraft is high, a power decrease will be needed. However these power changes should be kept low. Too large a power increase may result in too rapid a correction that the pilot is too slow to correct.

As mentioned before, the power is changing during the descent. Be aware of this. Note also that the wind velocity is also changing and this will have an effect on the rate of descent required. The closer the aircraft comes to Decision Height, the more sensitive becomes the glide-slope and the quicker the pilot must respond to any pitch changes needed. Make no bones about it, the ILS requires a lot of concentration.

All attitude changes, as with the heading changes, should be accurate and systematic. Be careful to select and hold attitudes before selecting the new attitude or power setting. *Do keep the VSI in the scan* as this will indicate a divergence away from the glide-slope some three to five seconds before that divergence actually occurs.

Maintain a close scan on the air-speed and in particular the *trend* of the speed. If the speed is temporarily low but increasing there may be no problem. A speed that is low and becoming lower must be reacted to!

Typical ILS Profile

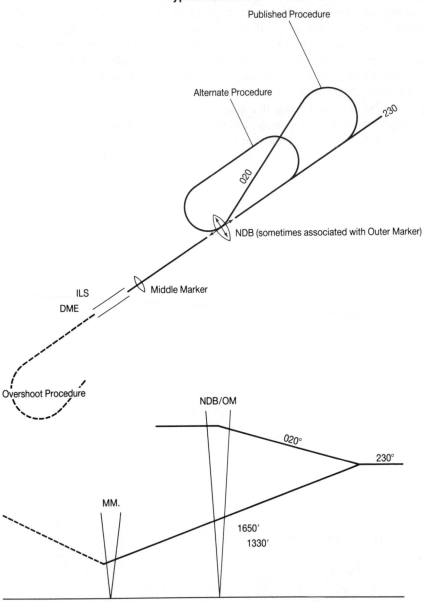

Published Procedure

Alternate Procedure

230

020

NDB (sometimes associated with Outer Marker)

ILS
DME

Middle Marker

Overshoot Procedure

NDB/OM

020°

230°

MM.

1650'
1330'

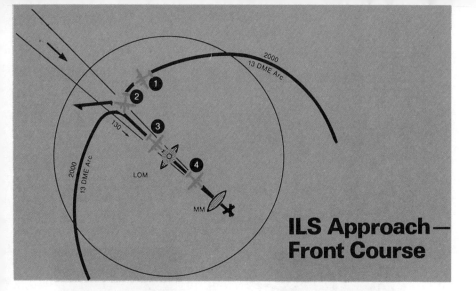

ILS Approach—Front Course

1. You are vectored from the holding pattern to the 13-mile DME arc. The aircraft is turning, with the Heading Bug set on 170° to intercept the Localizer. You have already set the Selected Course Pointer on the inbound ILS course 130° and the KI 525A shows the Localizer course is directly ahead. The Glideslope pointers came into view when the ILS frequency was tuned, since a usable Glideslope signal is being received.

2. Capturing the ILS course can be accomplished without overshooting or bracketing with the same technique you used in intercepting an enroute course: simply keep the top of the Deviation Bar on the Lubber Line and coordinate your turn until the bottom of the bar is aligned with the Course Arrow. Each dot on the LOC Deviation Scale represents 1/2° deviation when tuned to an ILS frequency.

3. The KI 525A shows you that you have intercepted the Localizer course. The Glideslope pointers have started to center, although the display indicates your aircraft is still below the glidepath at this point.

4. You are now centered on the Localizer and the Glideslope. Once again, the KI 525A shows your aircraft is crabbed about 5° to the right to maintain the Localizer course.

119

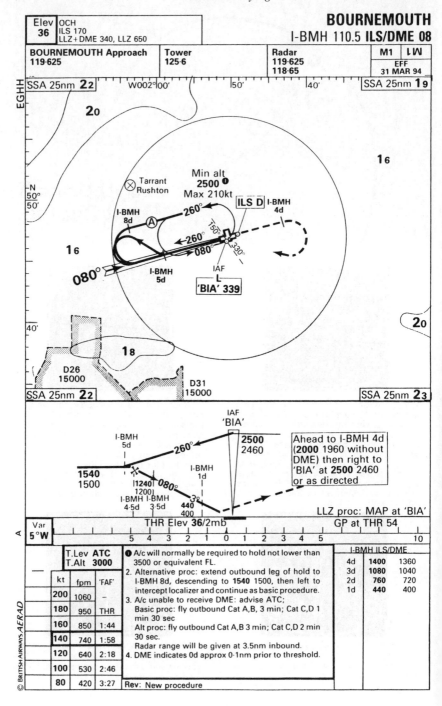

| Elev | OCH | | BOURNEMOUTH |
| 36 | ILS 170 LLZ+DME 340, LLZ 650 | | I-BMH 110.5 **ILS/DME 08** |

| BOURNEMOUTH Approach 119·625 | Tower 125·6 | Radar 119·625 118·65 | M1 | LW |
| | | | EFF 31 MAR 94 | |

SSA 25nm **22**   W002°00'   50'   40'   SSA 25nm **19**

20

EGHH

16

⊗ Tarrant Rushton

Min alt **2500** ❶ Max 210kt

ILS D I-BMH 4d

I-BMH 8d ⒶA

260°

150°

330°

I-BMH 5d

IAF **L** 'BIA' 339

080°

260°

080°

16

20

40'

18

D26 15000

D31 15000

SSA 25nm **22**

SSA 25nm **23**

IAF 'BIA'

I-BMH 5d

260° **2500** 2460

I-BMH 1d

I-BMH 4·5d

I-BMH 3·5d

1540 1500

|1240| 1200|

080°

440 400

Ahead to I-BMH 4d (**2000** 1960 without DME) then right to 'BIA' at **2500** 2460 or as directed

LLZ proc: MAP at 'BIA'

GP at THR 54

THR Elev **36**/2mb

| Var 5°W | 5 | 4 | 3 | 2 | 1 | 0 | 1 | 2 | 3 | 4 | 5 | 10 |

	T.Lev **ATC** T.Alt **3000**	❶ A/c will normally be required to hold not lower than 3500 or equivalent FL.	I-BMH ILS/DME
		2. Alternative proc: extend outbound leg of hold to I-BMH 8d, descending to **1540** 1500, then left to intercept localizer and continue as basic procedure.	4d **1400** 1360
—			3d **1080** 1040
			2d **760** 720
	kt	fpm	'FAF'		1d **440** 400
	200	1060	–	3. A/c unable to receive DME: advise ATC;
	180	950	THR	Basic proc: fly outbound Cat A,B, 3 min; Cat C,D 1 min 30 sec
	160	850	1:44	Alt proc: fly outbound Cat A,B 3 min; Cat C,D 2 min 30 sec.
	140	740	1:58	Radar range will be given at 3.5nm inbound.
	120	640	2:18	4. DME indicates 0d approx 0·1nm prior to threshold.
	100	530	2:46	
	80	420	3:27	Rev: New procedure

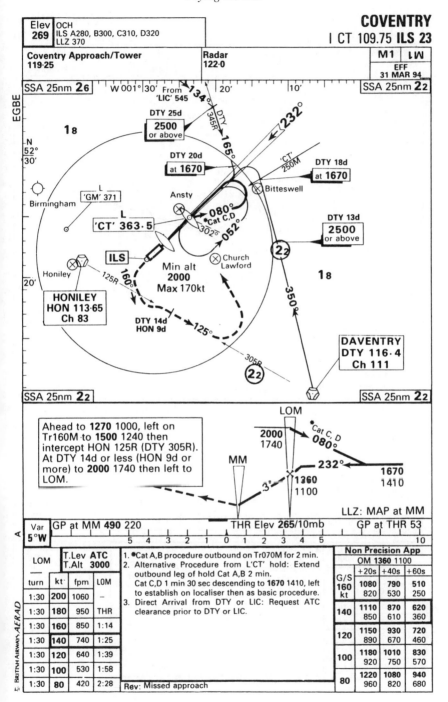

Elev	OCH
269	ILS A280, B300, C310, D320
	LLZ 370

COVENTRY

I CT 109.75 ILS 23

Coventry Approach/Tower	Radar	M1	LW
119·25	122·0	EFF 31 MAR 94	

SSA 25nm **26**   W 001° 30' From 'LIC' 545   20'   10'   SSA 25nm **22**

EGBE

1 8

DTY 25d
2500 or above

232°

DTY 20d
at 1670

165°

345R

DTY

134°

'CT' 250M

DTY 18d
at 1670

N 52° 30'

'GM' 371 L

Ansty

080° *Cat C,D

Bitteswell

DTY 13d
2500 or above

Birmingham

'CT' 363·5 L

302°   052°

2₂

ILS

Min alt **2000** Max 170kt

Church Lawford

1 8

Honiley

160°   125R

350°

HONILEY HON 113·65 Ch 83

DTY 14d HON 9d   125°

305R

DAVENTRY DTY 116·4 Ch 111

2₂

SSA 25nm **22**   SSA 25nm **22**

LOM

Ahead to **1270** 1000, left on Tr160M to **1500** 1240 then intercept HON 125R (DTY 305R). At DTY 14d or less (HON 9d or more) to **2000** 1740 then left to LOM.

2000 1740

*Cat C, D 080°

MM

232°

1670 1410

3°   **1360** 1100

LLZ: MAP at MM

Var 5°W	GP at MM **490** 220						THR Elev **265**/10mb				GP at THR 53

5   4   3   2   1   0   1   2   3   4   5   10

LOM	T.Lev ATC					Non Precision App

	T.Lev **ATC**
LOM	T.Alt **3000**

1. *Cat A,B procedure outbound on Tr070M for 2 min.
2. Alternative Procedure from L'CT' hold: Extend outbound leg of hold Cat A,B 2 min. Cat C,D 1 min 30 sec descending to **1670** 1410, left to establish on localiser then as basic procedure.
3. Direct Arrival from DTY or LIC: Request ATC clearance prior to DTY or LIC.

				OM **1360** 1100		
turn	kt	fpm	LOM	G/S 160 kt	+20s	+40s	+60s
1:30	200	1060	–		1080	790	510
					820	530	250
1:30	180	950	THR	140	1110	870	620
					850	610	360
1:30	160	850	1:14	120	1150	930	720
					890	670	460
1:30	140	740	1:25	100	1180	1010	830
					920	750	570
1:30	120	640	1:39	80	1220	1080	940
1:30	100	530	1:58		960	820	680
1:30	80	420	2:28	Rev: Missed approach			

A

© BRITISH AIRWAYS AERAD

121

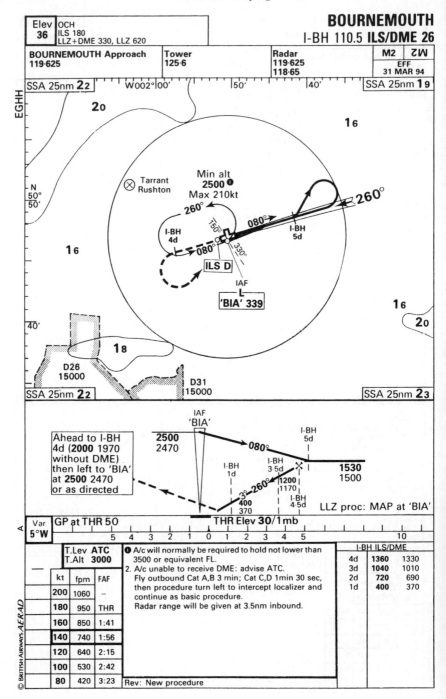

Elev	OCH		**BOURNEMOUTH**
36	ILS 180		**I-BH 110.5 ILS/DME 26**
	LLZ+DME 330, LLZ 620		

BOURNEMOUTH Approach 119·625	Tower 125·6	Radar 119·625 118·65	M2 ZW
			EFF 31 MAR 94

SSA 25nm **22**   W002°00' |50' |40'   SSA 25nm **19**

EGHH

2o

1 6

16

⊗ Tarrant Rushton

Min alt **2500 ❶** Max 210kt

260°

260°

I-BH 4d

080°

750'

080°

I-BH 5d

330°

080°

ILS D

16

IAF **L** 'BIA' 339

1 6

2o

40'

1 8

D26 15000

D31 15000

SSA 25nm **22**   SSA 25nm **23**

IAF 'BIA'

Ahead to I-BH 4d (**2000** 1970 without DME) then left to 'BIA' at **2500** 2470 or as directed

2500 2470

080°

I-BH 5d

I-BH 1d

I-BH 3·5d

✕

1530 1500

1200 1170

260°

3°

400 370

I-BH 4·5d

LLZ proc: MAP at 'BIA'

| Var **5°W** | GP at THR **50** | | THR Elev **30/1**mb | | | |

5   4   3   2   1   0   1   2   3   4   5   10

	T.Lev **ATC** T.Alt **3000**	❶ A/c will normally be required to hold not lower than 3500 or equivalent FL.	I-BH ILS/DME
—		2. A/c unable to receive DME: advise ATC.	4d **1360** 1330

	kt	fpm	FAF	
	200	1060	–	
	180	950	THR	
	160	850	1:41	
	140	740	1:56	
	120	640	2:15	
	100	530	2:42	
	80	420	3:23	

Fly outbound Cat A,B 3 min; Cat C,D 1min 30 sec, then procedure turn left to intercept localizer and continue as basic procedure.
Radar range will be given at 3.5nm inbound.

	I-BH ILS/DME
4d	**1360** 1330
3d	**1040** 1010
2d	**720** 690
1d	**400** 370

Rev: New procedure

Chapter 11

Decision Heights

A Decision Height is the height at which a decision is made as to whether or not it is safe to continue the approach to a landing. Decision heights are used on Precision Approaches where electronic guidance is available in both azimuth and height. Such approaches include ILS, MLS and PAR.

The Decision Height is calculated by taking the highest of the following: the System Minima, the State Minima and the OCH (Obstacle Clearance Height) and then adding a Position Error Correction (PEC) of fifty feet. The Precision Approach OCH includes an aircraft height loss allowance to cover the initiation of a missed approach.

There are five categories of aircraft (A to E) depending upon the aircraft's threshold speed defined as 1.3 times the stalling speed in the landing configuration. The OCH for your particular category aircraft should be chosen when calculating Decision Heights.

At RAF aerodromes in the United Kingdom and overseas, Decision Heights are calculated by adding a *height increment* to the given *procedural minimum*. For a three degree glide-slope this increment is thirty feet for a category A aircraft. Again the figure should be compared with the system/state minimum.

The system minima are as follows:

ILS   200 feet
PAR   200 feet (Precision Radar Approach)
MLS   200 feet

Decision Heights are related to runway threshold elevation unless otherwise stated.

With offset localiser the specified Decision Height should not be less than the height of the normal glide-path at the point where the localiser intercepts the runway extended centre-line.

Minimum Descent Heights

The MDH is the height at which a pilot may not fly below when executing a Non Precision Approach until such time as the pilot has assured himself a safe landing may be made. The MDH should not be less than the published OCH for the category of the aircraft or the lowest acceptable MDH from the following table, whichever is the higher.

Lowest acceptable MDHs:

ILS/no glide-path	250 feet
ILS Back Beam	250 feet
PAR/no glide-path	250 feet
VOR	300 feet
VOR & DME	300 feet
SRA 0.5 nm	250 feet
SRA 1.0 nm	300 feet
SRA 2.0 nms	350 feet
NDB	300 feet
VDF	300 feet

When an OCH is published there is normally no need to apply a Position Error Correction, as the OCH already includes an altimeter correction allowance of fifty feet. This does not apply if the PEC is greater than fifty feet when the difference should then be added.

Minimum Descent Heights are related to threshold elevation for straight-in approaches and to aerodrome elevation for indirect approaches.

Runway Visual Ranges (RVRs)

The required minimum RVR for each instrument approach procedure is shown next to the Decision Height or Minimum Descent Height on the Aerad Operating Minima Pages. For aerodromes and runways where RVR is not measured and reported to pilots, operators should specify the minimum reported visibility below which an approach to land is not commenced or continued.

Selection of Alternate Aerodromes

Take-off at departure aerodromes should not normally be permitted unless a suitable return alternate is available within the time or distance specified below:

4 Turbine   120 mins or 500 nms
4 Piston   90 mins or 400 nms
3 Turbine   90 mins or 400 nms
3 Piston   60 mins
2 Turbine   60 mins
2 Piston   30 mins (typical training aircraft)

The APPROACH BAN!

An aircraft may only descend below 1,000 feet above the aerodrome elevation (during an approach to land) when the RVR reported for the intended runway or direction of landing is equal to or better than the minimum RVR specified for that runway or direction of landing when approached using the stated aid or method.

An aircraft should not continue an approach to land at any aerodrome by flying below the relevant specified Decision Height or descending below the relevant specified MDH, unless from that height the specified visual reference for landing is established and is maintained.

For Precision Approaches the specified visual reference should contain at least six consecutive lights which may be approach or runway lights or a combination of both.

For non-precision approaches, the specified visual reference should include the desired point of touch-down on the runway of intended landing or if lights are available at least seven consecutive lights as described above.

Finally for a visual circuit of the aerodrome after a visual approach or when manoeuvring after an instrument approach, a pilot should have continuous sight of ground features which will enable him to position the aircraft safely in relation to the aerodrome and subsequently remain within the notified visual manoeuvring area.

If visual reference is lost while circling to land from an instrument approach, the missed approach specified for that particular procedure must be followed. It is expected that the pilot will make an initial climbing turn towards the landing runway and overhead the aerodrome where he will establish the aircraft climbing on the missed approach track.

Chapter 12

The Asymmetric (Sub-section C) and When the Engine Fails!

During the go-around from the ILS the examiner will cover the throttles with his flight board. The asymmetric section begins! The pilot should, by this time, have cleaned the aircraft up, the gear and the flaps retracted and climb power will have been selected.

So, what is the examiner looking for? The aircraft should continue to be correctly controlled. This is the candidate's first priority. The heading should be maintained and the aircraft should continue to maintain a climb profile, albeit somewhat reduced. The necessary actions and the checks will then follow.

All aircraft are, of course, different. Checks for one aircraft may be completely different for another. The drills and checks that are covered here are those of a typical, twin piston-engined training aircraft such as the Grumman Cougar or Piper Seminole.

Typical Drills and Procedures

As the examiner retards the throttle, reduce your climbing attitude from the normal *seven degrees* pitch up to *four degrees* pitch up. This will delay the speed loss following the engine failure thus assisting the directional control, due to enhanced rudder effectiveness. The aircraft should still continue to climb and to maintain a climb for longer. There is no rush to achieve *blue line speed* (best rate of climb single engine). This speed will guarantee the best rate of climb only when the failed engine has been feathered, not before.

As the throttle is being pulled back by the examiner (he may do this quickly or slowly) apply rudder pressure to keep the balance ball centred and to maintain your planned climb out heading. This heading should be bugged.

Working on the *dead leg-dead engine principle* call out clearly which engine has failed: 'The right engine has failed!' Avoid long unnecessary monologues such as: 'My left leg is dead, therefore my right engine has failed'.

Just one simple statement is all that is required. The other famous line is : 'Right!! The left engine has failed!'

So be careful. Just a simple statement is needed: 'The left engine has failed'.

Assuming the failed engine has been correctly identified, the complete throttle quadrant will be revealed to the candidate for him to carry out the appropriate drills and checks.

Full Power	Mixtures fully forward.
	Propellers fully forward.
	Throttle(s) fully forward.
Gear & Flaps	Check both are fully retracted.
Feather Failed	
Engine	Left throttle close (check no swing, no change in engine note).
	Left propeller feather.
	Left mixture idle cut-off.
	Check for fire — left engine. No fire then:

Relax and Trim

Trim firstly in pitch to maintain attitude
for blue line speed; then trim in rudder to
reduce rudder forces whilst maintaining the
aircraft in balance and on heading.

Once the touch-drill feathering procedure has been completed it will be necessary to return the pitch attitude to seven degrees to maintain blue line speed. Only set the rudder trim once the elevator trim has been correctly and completely set.

During the asymmetric, it remains the candidate's responsibility to navigate according to instructions to liaise with Air Traffic Control. All turns asymmetric should remain 'Rate One'. Remember that any turns whilst asymmetric may seriously degrade the aircraft's climb performance. If ATC instructs the aircraft to climb to a higher than normal altitude the examiner may well return the throttles to a normal non-asymmetric setting to assist with the climb, only to reset asymmetric once the climb is complete, or shortly after.

Having completed the initial emergency actions, the securing checks should be followed as soon as is practicable. A typical check-list may proceed as follows:

The left engine has failed; secure the left engine.

Left fuel pump off.
Left fuel off.
Left cowl flap closed.
Left mags off in turn (Avoid touching the wrong mags).
Left alternator off.
The left engine is secure.
The right engine is live; protect the right engine.
Right fuel pump on.
Right fuel on (Note cross-feed is available).
Right cowl flap open.
Right mags on.
Right alternator on (load shedding available).
Right engine temperatures and pressures monitor (including suction).

The candidate will then simulate a call to Air Traffic to advise the nature of the problem and request priority permission to return either visually or by way of an instrument approach.

General Points

It is generally preferred practice in the United Kingdom, not to use the technique of applying five degrees of bank towards the live engine to reduce rudder forces.

Typically the aircraft used for the flight test will be in performance category 'E' which means a climb following an engine failure is not guaranteed at all weights. Candidates are therefore strongly advised that a minimum safe fuel loading is allowed, in order to confirm that the aircraft will climb following the simulated failure.

Chapter 13

The Asymmetric NDB Approach

Unlike the ILS, the NDB approach is a non-precision approach offering guidance in azimuth only. Knowledge of distance from threshold by way of a DME, NDB passage, or timing allows the pilot to decide where to descend. Descent is made eventually to a Minimum Descent Height to a missed approach point at which, if insufficient visual reference element exists, the pilot will commence a go-around.

One of the most difficult aspects of this approach is that it is asymmetric. Any change in power setting on the live engine will, unless checked with the appropriate rudder, have an effect on the heading. A golden rule results. Any change in power should be anticipated early and carried out gradually and progressively. If the power is changed too suddenly, the pilot may not be sufficiently prompt with the rudders to prevent the swing from the required heading. Move the levers slowly!

Most flight schools advise that the gear and flaps should not be selected until the aircraft is about to descend on final approach. This is because the majority of light twins at altitude have insufficient power to maintain height with the additional drag of gear and flaps.

It is important for the pilot to anticipate which rudder will be required to maintain heading. An increase in power to the right-hand engine will require an increase in right rudder pressure to maintain balance and heading. A reduction in power will require rudder pressure to be applied to the opposite rudder. A reduction in power on the left-hand engine will need an increase in rudder pressure on the right-hand rudder and vice versa. Pre-think rudder requirement before a power alteration is made.

Let's look at a typical profile:

The Cranfield Let Down plate calls for the aircraft, having reached the 'CIT' NDB to track away from the beacon on a track of 022° and to continue on this track for two minutes and thirty seconds. This timing should be adjusted for wind. For a ten knot tail-wind, the pilot should subtract twenty-five seconds from the outbound timing. This equates to one second per knot per minute of the leg.

Along this leg the pre-landing checks, with the exception of the gear and flaps, should be completed. The aircraft is then turned right to intercept the final approach track. This should be seen as a priority as, unless the aircraft is within five degrees of the designated track of 217°, it may not safely descend. Having established inbound, the pilot will report 'base turn complete'. Air Traffic will then normally offer descent clearance: 'G YD descent in the NDB procedure, report the beacon inbound'.

Descent is then commenced at a rate that equates as much as possible to a three degree descent path with a rate of descent that equates to five times the ground-speed. The aim should be to fly the vertical profile as closely as can be achieved to the picture of the vertical cross section of the approach. Passage through the beacon should occur at the beacon height of 1,220 feet (1,580 feet QNH). If that height is reached early, it should be maintained until beacon passage. Ideally both height and beacon passage should occur at the same time.

As the aircraft passes through the beacon, a very careful choice of heading should be made. Experience has shown that either a single drift heading should be flown or the track heading. This will depend upon the wind direction and the aircraft's position in relation to the track as the aircraft passes the beacon.

If the aircraft is passing to the north of track with a northerly wind, track heading should be maintained. If however the aircraft is passing to the south of track with a northerly wind, a single drift heading should be chosen.

Assuming the aircraft achieves a good beacon break and the needle swings promply around, turn immediately onto a single drift heading. Never steer or maintain an attack heading at the beacon passage. Always reduce to single drift or track. Never, never maintain an attack heading.

Being single-engined, certain different principles in speed and rate of descent should be applied when compared to the ILS. Think in terms of controlling the speed when asymmetric with attitude and the rate of descent with power. You will recall that this is the opposite technique to the one used to fly the ILS. The aircraft responds less quickly to the power change from a single engine and therefore anticipation in terms of height should be approximately one and a half times that for a two-engined approach. For example: Levelling off from a descent, whereas anticipation of 100 feet may be sufficient with two engines, 200 feet may be more appropriate with just one. This will of course depend upon weight and aircraft loading.

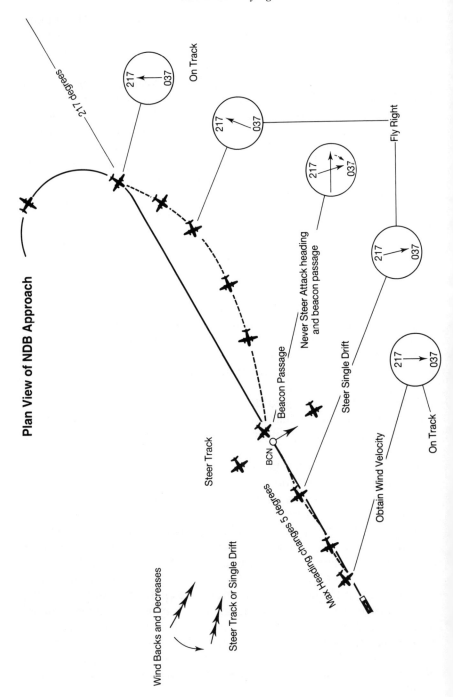

Plan View of NDB Approach

217 degrees

217 | 037 — On Track

217 | 037 — Fly Right

217 | 037 — Never Steer Attack heading and beacon passage

217 | 037 — Steer Single Drift

217 | 037 — On Track

Beacon Passage

BCN

Steer Track

Obtain Wind Velocity

Max Heading changes 5 degrees

Wind Backs and Decreases

Steer Track or Single Drift

The Asymmetric NDB Approach

The NBD Vertical Approach Profile

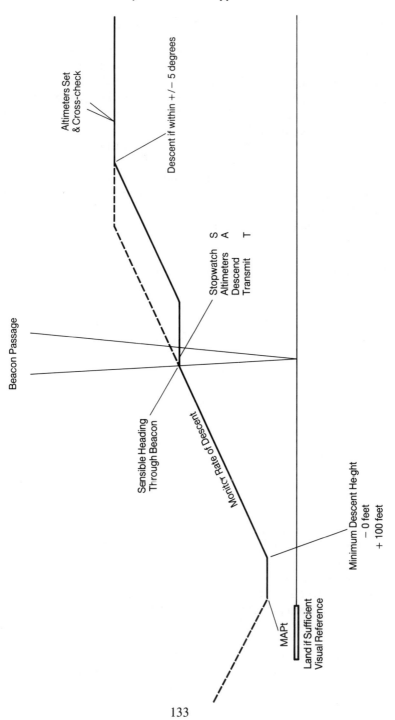

Altimeters Set & Cross-check

Descent if within +/– 5 degrees

Beacon Passage

Stopwatch — S
Altimeters — A
Descend
Transmit — T

Sensible Heading Through Beacon

Monitor Rate of Descent

Minimum Descent Height
– 0 feet
+ 100 feet

MAPt

Land if Sufficient Visual Reference

133

The Combined Instrument Rating Flight Test

Students who graduate from an Approved Ab-Initio Course are required to sit the Combined Instrument Rating Flight Test. The test differs only slightly from the normal IRT in that the candidate is required to visually carry out the appropriate actions at Minimum Descent Height himself and to complete a Fire Drill on climb out and an asymmetric circuit and landing. Let's go through it.

The candidate will have levelled the aircraft at Minimum Descent Height and answered the question: 'How much longer do we have to run to the threshold?' The examiner then removes the screens and the candidate is then expected to make a decision as to whether to land the aircraft or go-around.

This decision is based upon the following:

Is the runway clear?

Is the approach in all respects satisfactory?

Has landing clearance been given?

Typically from an NDB approach the aircraft may not be in line with the runway. It may be that by the time the runway has been sighted it is too far to one side of the aircraft for a safe manoeuvring to be made. A go-around must then be initiated.

If a landing is the option chosen, the candidate is expected to continue on the single engine to the flare, when both throttles should be closed together. Beware the swing! Do not select land flap as the aircraft descends below MDH until below the visual committal height and assured that a safe landing can be made. There may not be sufficient power in the conditions prevailing to overcome that increased drag from the one remaining engine.

If it is decided that a go-around is the best option, increase power to the live engine countering any further swing with rudder, reduce to blue line speed and clean the aircraft promptly and safely. If the gear and flaps are driven electrically, run them independently in order to prevent overload and possible failure of the one remaining generator.

If the runway is clear, maintain the runway centre-line as the aircraft is climbed to circuit height. If not, move to the right-hand side of the runway and keep any landing or departing aircraft in sight. Conform to local procedures and instructions should these differ from the aforesaid.

If the decision was to land, after landing, the examiner will return the trim settings to take-off and reset the flaps and expect the candidate to carry out a further take-off. During the climb-out the examiner will call out 'Engine fire right/left engine!!' Normal engine fire after take-off drills should be carried out. These typically might be as follows:

Full Power   Mixtures
               Propellers
               Throttles
Gear Up
Flaps Up
Confirming Fire Right Engine
     Feather   Right Throttle Close
                 Right Prop Feather (Touch drill on test)
                 Right Mixture ICO (Touch drill on test)

Has the fire gone out?

"It has."

Relax and trim.

Set cowl flaps.

The aircraft is then expected to be manually flown around the circuit to a second asymmetric landing. During the circuit the 'dead' engine should be secured 'touch drills only', gear and flaps delayed until abeam the touch-down point on down-wind and great care exercised not to go below blue line speed at any stage. Take particular care to continue monitoring the live engine and to exercise a thoroughly good look out now that you are flying visually. If VASI or PAPI are available on final approach make full use of them.

Chapter 14

Decision Heights, Minimum Descent Heights and What to Do

Decision Height

The Decision Height is the name given to the height on a Precision Approach at which a decision is made as to whether to continue the approach to a landing or to commence a 'go-around'. Decision Height is not a height that you may not therefore go below. Indeed if the procedure is followed correctly a short descent below DH should be anticipated.

Upon reaching Decision Height the pilot or co-pilot is expected to look up and decide whether there is sufficient visual reference for the approach to be continued. If not, a go-around or missed approach should be initiated. Climb power should be selected together with climb attitude. Once the decision to go-around has been made all subsequent actions should be such as to encourage an early rate of climb at the correct climbing speed and to clean the aircraft as soon as practicable.

Decision Heights are normally calculated by taking the highest of the following: System Minima plus fifty feet or OCH plus fifty feet. The fifty feet represents Position Error Correction or mismeasurements of the static pressure. Some operators will have different additions dependent upon the sophistication of the equipment.

Minimum Descent Height

This is the height that is used on a Non-Precision Approach procedure. Unlike the DH, the MDH may not be descended below until a decision has been made to continue the approach to a landing. The Non-Precision Approach is less accurate and its attendant MDH will naturally be higher than an ILS on the same runway.

MDH is normally maintained until what is known as the Missed Approach Point, although some operators actually initiate go-around at

MDH should they decide the landing can not be made safely. This can be defined as a timing from a facility, a beacon passage or perhaps the crossing of a radial or even a DME distance. In the event that the runway is not seen before the Missed Approach Point, go-around should be carried out at the MAP and again the pilot should seek to gain as much distance between him and the ground as soon as possible . . . maximum rate of climb.

Rates of Descent

For the Non-Precision Approach more and more operators are insisting that pilots compute a Rate of Descent that equates as closely as possible to the three degree approach path. This is typically five times the aircraft's ground-speed.

Circling Minima

In the event that either the Precision Approach or more likely the Non-Precision Approach are being used to locate the airfield and a landing is intended on a different runway a *Circle to Land Procedure* is carried out. The DH or MDH is now the Circling Minima and although your DH or MDH may be below circling minima, if your intention is to land on a different runway to the one you are using the instrument approach for, you *should not descend* below circling minima until established on final approach.

Offset Approaches

More common in Europe, the offset approach is designed to bring the aircraft to a satisfactory landing position although the approach may not be in line with that runway. Before the approach the pilot should pre-think in which part of the aircraft's windscreen the runway should appear.

Missed Approach Procedure whilst Circling

If during a 'circle to land' sight is lost of the runway, the pilot should carry out the missed approach procedure specified for the original runway approached. This will normally involve an initial climbing turn, towards the landing runway and overhead the aerodrome where the aircraft can resume the earlier final and missed approach track and procedure.

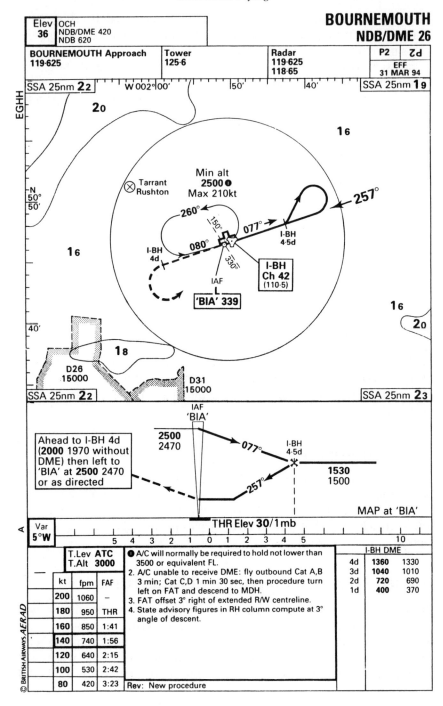

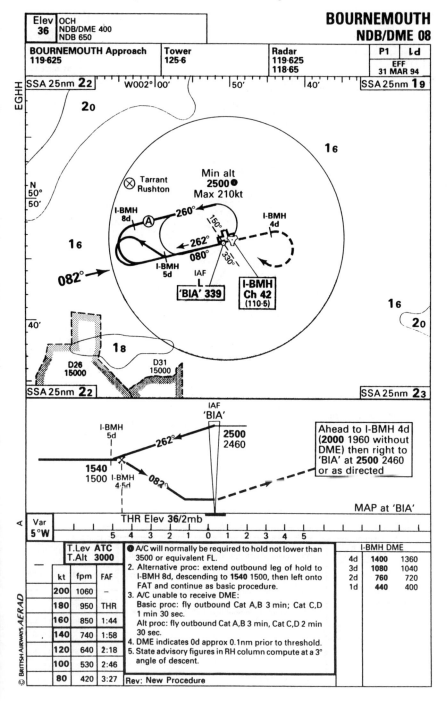

Elev 36	OCH NDB/DME 400 NDB 650			**BOURNEMOUTH** **NDB/DME 08**	
BOURNEMOUTH Approach 119·625	Tower 125·6		Radar 119·625 118·65	**P1**	**Ld**
				EFF 31 MAR 94	

EGHH — SSA 25nm **22** — W002° 00′ — 50′ — 40′ — SSA 25nm **19**

2 o

1 6

N 50° 50′

⊗ Tarrant Rushton

Min alt **2500●** Max 210kt

I-BMH 8d Ⓐ — 260°

I-BMH 4d

150°

1 6

← 262° — 330°

080°

082° →

I-BMH 5d

IAF L 'BIA' 339

I-BMH Ch 42 (110·5)

1 6

2 0

40′

1 8

D26 15000

D31 15000

SSA 25nm **22** — SSA 25nm **23**

IAF 'BIA'

I-BMH 5d — 262° — **2500** 2460

1540 1500 — I-BMH 4·5d — 082°

Ahead to I-BMH 4d **(2000** 1960 without DME) then right to 'BIA' at **2500** 2460 or as directed

MAP at 'BIA'

				THR Elev 36/2mb															
Var 5°W				5	4	3	2	1	0	1	2	3	4	5					

	T.Lev ATC T.Alt 3000		● A/C will normally be required to hold not lower than 3500 or equivalent FL. 2. Alternative proc: extend outbound leg of hold to I-BMH 8d, descending to **1540** 1500, then left onto FAT and continue as basic procedure. 3. A/C unable to receive DME: Basic proc: fly outbound Cat A,B 3 min; Cat C,D 1 min 30 sec. Alt proc: fly outbound Cat A,B 3 min, Cat C,D 2 min 30 sec. 4. DME indicates 0d approx 0.1nm prior to threshold. 5. State advisory figures in RH column compute at a 3° angle of descent.	I-BMH DME	
—				4d	**1400**	1360

	kt	fpm	FAF	
	200	1060	–	
	180	950	THR	
	160	850	1:44	
·	140	740	1:58	
	120	640	2:18	
	100	530	2:46	
	80	420	3:27	

I-BMH DME		
4d	**1400**	1360
3d	**1080**	1040
2d	**760**	720
1d	**440**	400

Rev: New Procedure

© BRITISH AIRWAYS *AERAD*

139

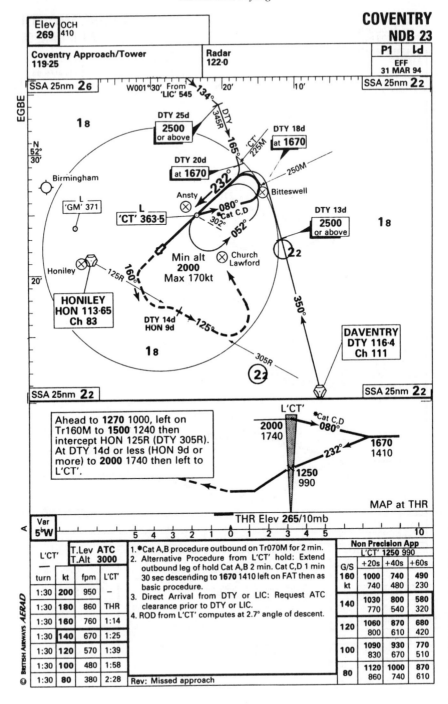

Elev 269	OCH 410				COVENTRY NDB 23

Coventry Approach/Tower 119·25	Radar 122·0	P1	Ld

EFF 31 MAR 94

SSA 25nm **26** — W001°30' From 'LIC' 545 — 134° — 20' — 10' — SSA 25nm **22**

EGBE

1 8

DTY 25d **2500 or above**

DTY 18d at **1670**

DTY 20d at **1670**

250M

232°

Birmingham

L 'GM' 371

L 'CT' 363·5

Ansty

Bitteswell

080° Cat C,D

302°   052°

DTY 13d **2500 or above**

1 8

Min alt **2000** Max 170kt

Church Lawford

22

Honiley

125R

160°

HONILEY HON 113·65 Ch 83

DTY 14d HON 9d

125°

1 8

350°

305R

22

DAVENTRY DTY 116·4 Ch 111

SSA 25nm **22** — SSA 25nm **22**

Ahead to **1270** 1000, left on Tr160M to **1500** 1240 then intercept HON 125R (DTY 305R). At DTY 14d or less (HON 9d or more) to **2000** 1740 then left to L'CT'.

L'CT'

*Cat C,D 080°

2000 1740

232°

1670 1410

1250 990

MAP at THR

THR Elev **265**/10mb

Var 5°W		5	4	3	2	1	0	1	2	3	4	5		10

L'CT'	T.Lev ATC T.Alt 3000			1. *Cat A,B procedure outbound on Tr070M for 2 min.		Non Precision App		

Non Precision App

L'CT'		T.Lev ATC		1. *Cat A,B procedure outbound on Tr070M for 2 min.	L'CT' 1250 990		
—		T.Alt 3000		2. Alternative Procedure from L'CT' hold: Extend outbound leg of hold Cat A,B 2 min. Cat C,D 1 min	G/S	+20s	+40s	+60s

turn	kt	fpm	L'CT'	...			
1:30	200	950	—	30 sec descending to **1670** 1410 left on FAT then as basic procedure.	160 kt	1000 740	740 480	490 230
1:30	180	860	THR	3. Direct Arrival from DTY or LIC: Request ATC clearance prior to DTY or LIC.	140	1030 770	800 540	580 320
1:30	160	760	1:14	4. ROD from L'CT' computes at 2.7° angle of descent.	120	1060 800	870 610	680 420
1:30	140	670	1:25		100	1090 830	930 670	770 510
1:30	120	570	1:39		80	1120 860	1000 740	870 610
1:30	100	480	1:58					
1:30	80	380	2:28	Rev: Missed approach				

© BRITISH AIRWAYS AERAD

Chapter 15

The VOR Hold/Let Down

Just as an aircraft may be asked to hold at an NDB facility, an aircraft may also be required to hold on or over a VOR or perhaps at the intersection of two VOR radials or perhaps on a VOR radial at a specific DME distance from a VOR. If an aircraft is equipped with an RMI that can be slaved to a VOR then there is little difficulty and equally little difference to holding on an NDB. Whilst the overhead of a VOR is slightly less well defined, there is normally no dip error. The RMI needle will not over-read in the turn, unlike the ADF needle.

However, if your aircraft is conventionally equipped, with the standard beam bar display for the VOR, should you be required to hold, I would like to suggest a few helpful hints that you may wish to put into practice.

The VOR Hold

Your aircraft will always be equipped with two VOR CDI displays tuned to two separate VOR receivers. Always have your number one VOR tuned to the holding station and have the OBS set to the inbound axis of the hold. On the number two VOR, which is also tuned to the holding station, you can firstly set this to the abeam QDR. For instance, if the hold is set for 270° inbound axis (right hand), have Number One VOR to 270° and Number 2 VOR set to 360°.

The stop-watch will be started initially on beacon passage. On the VOR (without RMI needle) this is taken to be when the TO/FROM flag changes to 'from'. In practice this will be slightly beyond the accurate overhead position but it will at least be in a consistent position for a given altitude.

The watch will be restarted in the abeam position. This can be seen in two ways. Firstly the TO/FROM flag will again return to TO as the aircraft passes through the abeam, as seen on the Number One VOR and secondly the Fly Right Indication on the Number Two VOR will become a FLY LEFT indication. As this swoops through the middle this is again an indication of passing the abeam.

Drift should be calculated in the normal way on the outbound leg of the hold, two or three times as the situation demands. Now, however we are without a 'gate angle' presentation. A suggestion is to now set the Number Two VOR to the 30° gate angle; in this case 060°. As you are, by now aware, the 30° gate angle is the approximate position that the aircraft should be in at the time to turn inbound.

Consequently, if this radial comes in too early it is a sign that the aircraft is too close to the inbound axis and should therefore steer out to avoid an overshoot. If the radial fails to come in at all at the end of the outbound timing, this may be a sign that the aircraft is too far from the inbound axis and that an undershoot may be the result.

Just prior to the inbound turn, I would recommend that the Number Two VOR is set to the inbound axis displaced by ten degrees, in this case 260°.

If the Number Two VOR is not active, by the time the aircraft passes a heading at a 60° angle to the inbound axis, stop on an intercept heading of approximately 40°, depending upon the wind. Wait for the Number Two VOR to become active and as the beam bar passes through the centre, the Number One VOR will become alive. This is an ideal warning as to the aircraft's proximity to the inbound axis.

The aircraft is now tracking towards the VOR. Typically there will only be a minute's worth of tracking time available. The indications will be becoming more and more sensitive to any heading change. Try to establish a sensible, single drift heading as early as possible and make all subsequent heading changes as small as you can to avoid shooting from one side of the track to the other.

VOR/DME Holding

You may be asked to hold on a VOR radial at a specific DME distance from that VOR/DME installation. This again is flown as a normal hold. The first turn is initiated at the published DME distance. The outbound heading should again be a multiple of the single drift required to maintain the inbound axis. Abeam position timing may also be at a DME distance or even a cross-cut. If it cannot be easily determined, simply start the timing as the wings are rolled level onto the outbound heading.

On some occasions the outbound leg's timing/distance may be determined by a DME range from the VOR or even a limiting radial that the aircraft is not permitted to extend beyond. If the two are combined, the aircraft may follow the limiting radial until the DME distance is reached, at which point the inbound turn is initiated.

A TYPICAL VOR APPROACH

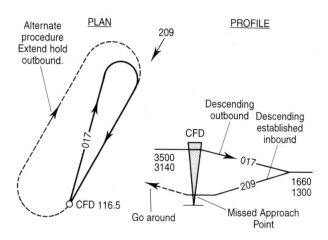

USE OF TWO VOR's IN THE HOLD: (GATE's)

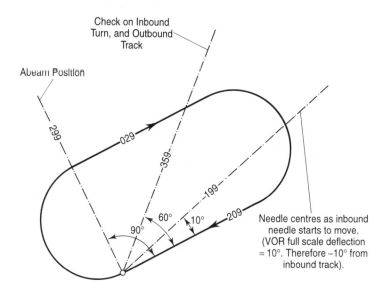

143

Use of No.2 VOR for 'GATE POSITIONS'

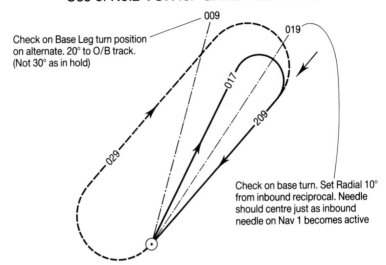

Check on Base Leg turn position on alternate. 20° to O/B track. (Not 30° as in hold)

Check on base turn. Set Radial 10° from inbound reciprocal. Needle should centre just as inbound needle on Nav 1 becomes active

The VOR Let Down

As with all let downs the VOR approach should not be attempted unless and until the plate has been completely understood, safety altitides, local obstructions and runway directions have been taken into account. It is quite common for the final approach track to not be completely in line with the runway QDM. This is known as an offset approach.

The VOR Let Down is a Non-Precision Approach. There is no electronic glide-path guidance. Descent may be simply based on timing, or more commonly these days on DME ranges. For example, at range four miles you should be passing 1,250 feet. At range three miles, you should be passing 950 feet. The pilot simply adjusts the rate of descent to meet these heights in accordance with the DME distance.

Being a Non-Precision Approach the VOR let down proceeds to a Minimum Descent Height that is maintained on reaching unless sufficient visual reference to the runway can be made for a continued descent to a safe landing can be made. The quoted Obstacle Clearance Height can be used for the MDH assuming the pilot is instrument rated. No increment need be added.

Descent on a VOR approach is not permitted unless the aircraft is within five degrees of track. This is represented by a maximum of one half-scale deflection on the VOR. Again the average heading for the approach should be pre-calculated and also the 'Time to Threshold' based upon the aircraft's average ground-speed. This, of course, serves as a back-up in the event, the DME if fitted, fails.

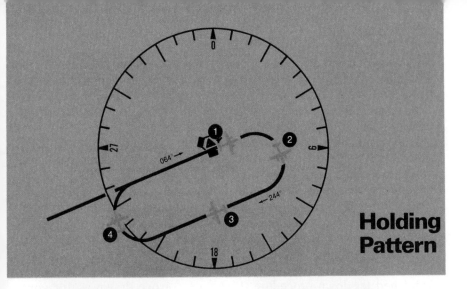

Holding Pattern

1. Approaching the STL VORTAC, the controller asks you to hold Southwest of the VORTAC on the 244° radial, right turns. You are now over the station with a 064° course selected (the TO/FROM Indicator has swung to "FROM"). (Set your Heading Bug to the reciprocal...or outbound heading...244° for easy reference and begin your right-turn holding pattern.)

2. Halfway through the outbound turn, the KI 525A display shows the Deviation Bar behind the symbolic aircraft. You know, therefore, that you must eventually fly back to the radial in order to be on course during the inbound leg of the holding pattern.

3. Outbound, you are using the Heading Bug as a reference for 244°. The 244° radial is off the right wing and parallel to your outbound course.

4. Halfway through your turn to the inbound 064° course, the KI 525A shows the symbolic aircraft approaching the Deviation Bar at a right angle. By keeping the top of the Deviation Bar on the Lubber Line, you can complete your turn and roll out precisely on course.

Missed approach procedure will be initiated at either the cessation of the timing, the expiry of the DME distance or on some approaches at the passage of the VOR. Once the decision to go-around has been made, minds should not be changed. Carry out the missed approach procedure unless directed otherwise by Air Traffic Control.

In the event that the let down track is not aligned with the landing runway, try to prepare yourself for the slightly unusual perspective that you may see on reaching the Minimum Descent Height. In the event that you see the runway too late, you may be forced to 'circle to land'. In this event, do not descend below your circling minima which becomes your minima for that approach. As you may appreciate, a VOR let down could simply be a cloud-break procedure designed to help you find the field, rather than a specific runway.

Finally a word of warning. Never ever construct your own, non-published let down procedure. If there's not one drawn up for your airfield, there's probably a very good reason why not! Don't go out to find the reason for yourself.

The Chichester VOR Approach (Runway 32)

This is the let down plate for the VOR approach at Goodwood (Chichester). What can be obtained from the plate. Top left will show us that the airfield elevation amsl is just 100 feet and that the OCH for a category A aircraft is 550 feet and for category B is 650 feet. The chart appears to have been last updated in January, 1991.

The frequency box shows an approach frequency of 122.45 and a tower frequency of 120.65. There are no radar frequencies shown. It can be assumed that only a procedural IFR service can be offered.

Sector safe altitudes to the North are both 2,100 ft, to the south-west 2,300 ft and to the south-east 2,000 ft. We can see that the ground to the North of the airfield rises very quickly.

The procedure is based on the Goodwood VOR, the GWC, frequency 114.75. There is a hold at this beacon which is right-handed about an axis of 160°. Pilots may take up this hold in the normal manner. Note the 70° degree line (see holds) has already been constructed for the pilot (050/230). The minimum holding altitude is 2,400 ft.

When cleared for the approach, pilots are to leave the GWC on a track of 160° descending to an altitude of 1,500 feet. This leg should last in still air two minutes and thirty seconds (bottom left-hand side). At which point the pilot should then turn left to intercept a track of 325° back to the VOR. Once on track and assuming within half-scale deflection (ie. five degrees) a descent, with clearance, may be made to Minimum Descent Height.

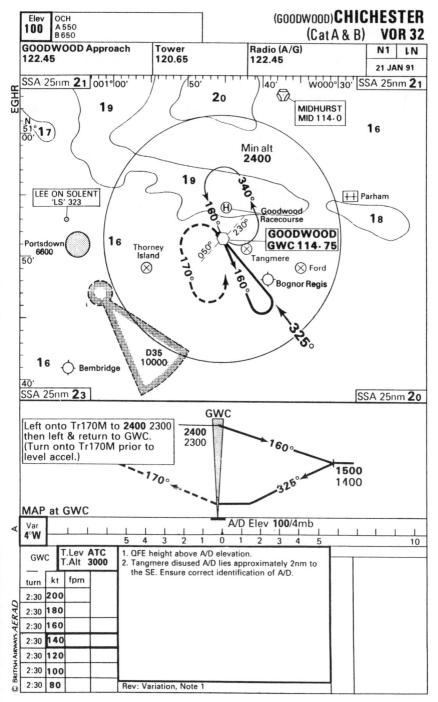

Elev **100**	OCH A 550 B 650			(GOODWOOD)**CHICHESTER** (Cat A & B) **VOR 32**		
GOODWOOD Approach **122.45**		Tower **120.65**		Radio (A/G) **122.45**	**N1**	**LN**
						21 JAN 91

Left onto Tr170M to **2400** 2300 then left & return to GWC. (Turn onto Tr170M prior to level accel.)

MAP at GWC

A/D Elev **100**/4mb

5 4 3 2 1 0 1 2 3 4 5 10

Var **4°W**

GWC	T.Lev **ATC** T.Alt **3000**	1. QFE height above A/D elevation. 2. Tangmere disused A/D lies approximately 2nm to the SE. Ensure correct identification of A/D.
turn	kt	fpm
2:30	200	
2:30	180	
2:30	160	
2:30	140	
2:30	120	
2:30	100	
2:30	80	

Rev: Variation, Note 1

© BRITISH AIRWAYS *AERAD*

147

This height should be maintained until sufficient of the runway can be determined in order to make a safe landing. In the event that contact is not made with the field or runway, a missed approach should commence no later than passage over the GWC. Note that an immediate left turn is called for, away from the high ground climbing to 2,400 feet on a track of 170°.

Maximum rate of climb speed should be maintained until on track 170°.

The editorial advises that Tangmere aerodrome is just two miles to the South-east and should not be confused with Goodwood. Transition Altitude for the aerodrome is 3,000 feet.

Points to note include the fact that *Danger Area* no D35 is occasionally active up to 10,000 ft to the South-west of the airfield.

Chapter 16

The Radar Approaches

Radar Vectors?

What did we do before radar?

The principal use of radar in the approach area is for the vectoring of aircraft onto an intercept heading for a final approach. This is most commonly the ILS. During the Instrument Rating Test radar vectors are permitted for one of the two approaches as long as the other approach is procedural.

When receiving vectors for an approach, expedite the turn once an instruction to change heading has been received. Do not delay. Typically the controller will inform you of your position in relation to the airfield and runway.

'Cabair zero three, your position is three miles to the south of the airfield on a downwind heading for runway twenty-two. You're number three in traffic, twelve track miles from touch-down'.

Distance to touch-down refers to the distance you will cover before touch-down and not straight line distance to the threshold. This gives you an indication of how much time you have left to complete your checks and drills. A controller may ask you 'what range of final do you require?' This refers to what distance from the threshold you wish to intercept final approach track. If you are in training a comfortable distance would be about eight nms. Any closer and things are going to happen quite quickly.

The controller is principally responsible for making due allowance for wind during the vectoring. He will have a good idea of the upper wind and your True Air Speed and will make sensible adjustments in heading to ensure correct tracking.

'Circuit adjustment, turn right ten degrees'.

The controller will also advise you to adjust height/altitude at the appropriate moments taking consideration of the sector safe altitudes in the area and the aircraft's position.

The aircraft will be directed onto a base leg and thence onto a final intercept heading. This heading is typically at an angle of fifty degrees to the final approach track.

'Turn left heading two seven zero degrees, closing the ILS localiser left to right (or from the left) report established'.

The words 'report established' are in effect a cancellation of the radar vectors. It is now up to the pilot to make the final adjustments in heading in order to capture the localiser. Once captured within half-scale deflection and on a heading that is sensible the pilot may then report: 'Cabair zero three localiser established'.

The controller will then confirm altimeter setting and offer 'Further Descent on the Glide-Path, report the Outer Marker (or report four miles)'.

Do remember that if the unit you are operating is not SSR equipped it is good airmanship to report arriving and vacating all levels/altitudes. This also applies if your aircraft is not equipped with a mode C transponder.

The Surveillance Radar Approach (the SRA)

In this approach the controller gives headings to steer in order to maintain an approach centre line and advisory heights/altitudes that the aircraft should be passing based on its range from the airfield.

The controller is equipped with a radar screen that is able to clearly see the aircraft and its displacement from the final approach track. The centre-line is painted onto the screen of the radar together with range marks at one and one half-mile intervals. The controller will have a list of the heights that the aircraft should be at for a given range. At four miles the aircraft should be passing 1,250 feet for instance. Probably the best way to understand this approach is to read a transcript

'Cabair zero three turn left heading 320 degrees, base leg.'

'Left 320 degrees, Cabair zero three.'

'Continue left heading 270 degrees, closing final approach track from the left at range seven miles.'

'270 degrees, Cabair zero three.'

'Left now heading 230 degrees, final approach.'

'230 degrees Cabair zero three.'

'Cabair zero three descent will begin at four miles to maintain a three degree glide-slope, do not acknowledge any further transmissions unless requested.'

'Left five degrees, heading 225 degrees slightly right of centre-line, stand-by to lose height.

Adjust power to commence descent. Range four miles from touch-down.

Range three miles. Height should be 950 feet, heading is good, on track.

Turn Right three degrees, heading 228 degrees drifting slightly left of centre.

At range two and one half miles height passing should be 800 feet, check your minimum descent height, confirm wheels down and locked. Acknowledge.'

This continues until ...

'Approaching a half nautical mile from touch-down, on track. I cannot assist you further, you are cleared to land from this approach, after landing contact tower on 123.2.'

It is up to the pilot, of course, to adjust rates of descent to meet the advisory passing heights.

The Precision Radar Approach. (PAR)

This is a similar concept to the SRA but this time the controller is able to *see* the aircraft's position not only in relation to the centre-line but also the glide-slope, with the use of two radar screens. The PAR is a precision approach and therefore a Decision Height is applicable and not a Minimum Descent Height. The controller will again give headings as he did for the SRA but instead of giving passing heights, he will quite literally advise the pilot his vertical displacement from the recommended glide-slope.

'You're going slightly high on the glide-slope, adjust rate of descent.'

BOURNEMOUTH
SURVEILLANCE RADAR APPROACH
K2
EFF
31 MAR 94

EGHH

R/W & OCH	FAC & GP	Term	MAPt	SRA Procedure	Missed Approach
		From TDZ			
08 420	080° 3°	2nm	1nm	Initial & intermediate approach as directed by radar. From FAF (5nm radar range) at 1590 (1550) or above, follow nominal GP advisory heights to MDH. Cross stepdown fix (3nm radar range) at 790 (750) or above.	Ahead to 2500 (2460) then as directed.
17 A/B 550 C/D 650	170° 3°	2nm	2nm	Initial & intermediate approach as directed by radar. From FAF (5nm radar range) at 1580 (1550) or above, follow nominal GP advisory heights to MDH.	Ahead to 2500 (2470) then as directed.
26 500	260° 3°	2nm	1nm	Initial & intermediate approach as directed by radar. From FAF (5nm radar range) at 1530 (1500) or above, follow nominal GP advisory heights to MDH. Cross stepdown fix (3.5nm radar range) at 930 (900) or above.	Ahead to 2500 (2470) then as directed.
35 A/B 550 C/D 650	350° 3°	2nm	2nm	Initial & intermediate approach as directed by radar. From FAF (5nm radar range) at 1580 (1550) or above, follow nominal GP advisory heights to MDH.	Ahead to 2500 (2470) then as directed.

A

© BRITISH AIRWAYS' *AERAD*

Rev: Missed approaches.

This is a very accurate and demanding approach for both the controller and the pilot requiring exacting flying skills from the pilot and a cool head for the controller who will have to take into account the changing wind effect during the descent.

Again all heading changes should be made promptly. Small heading changes require small bank angles but do remember to counter for adverse yaw with a touch of sympathetic rudder.

Chapter 17

Icing!

By the nature of instrument flying and the fact we only need to fly by reference to instruments when flying in IMC conditions, the likelihood of icing when flying by instruments must be considerably higher. However obvious this must sound, this simple statement still continues to elude a large number of pilots.

Many training aircraft are now equipped for flight into known icing conditions which are described as *Light, Moderate* or *Severe*. An aircraft cleared for flight into moderate icing may not enter severe icing but may of course fly in light icing conditions. The exact definition of these terms is not strictly necessary but relates to the rate of ice accumulation over a given period of time. Suffice to say that if an icing level is forecast, you should not fly in those conditions unless your aircraft is cleared so to do.

Systems

There are two main systems used for ice protection: *Boots* and *De-icing Fluid*. The former has the disadvantage that the pilot has to wait for ice to form and develop prior to use of the system. The boots are inflatable rubber strips located on the leading edges of the wings, tailplane and fin, which are pumped from air sourced from the engine driven suction or pressure pumps.

When inflated the boots cause the ice to crack and leave the aircraft in the slipstream. Premature use of the boots will cause the ice to simply expand but remain attached to the airframe. The pilot must therefore wait until a minimum level of icing is reached. Please note that this is primarily a de-icing system and not an anti-icing system.

The liquid de-icing system serves to prevent the formation of, as well as eradicate the ice should it form in the first place. De-icing fluid is pumped along the leading edges of all the flying surfaces and even the

Liquid De-icing Strip-Leading edge.

De-icing Nozzle for leading edge of propeller.

windscreen to keep the aircraft clear of ice. Normally two modes of ice protection are used which is dependent solely upon the amount of fluid delivered. This system is now common on many aircraft types and has less weight or maintenance penalties than the older fashioned 'rubber boot' system.

Propellers and windscreens can also be kept clear of ice using the fluid system. Other methods for these areas include heated windscreens and electrically heated propellers.

One disadvantage of the fluid system is that your flight in icing conditions can only last for as long as you have de-icing fluid in the tanks. The fluid can also be expensive and must not be flammable (most de-icing fluids are flammable).

Other parts of the de-icing system, and not to be neglected, include the pitot heat and also the aircraft heating system itself which may serve not only to keep your feet warm but also to keep the windscreen clear of ice.

All these systems will have their own 'self-checking' procedure which should of course be carried out prior to flight into known icing conditions. Since the Instrument Rating Test assumes these conditions, check that your aircraft's systems are fully serviceable and if necessary replenished.*

Icing is a killer. It adds weight to your aircraft affecting C of G positioning and overall weight. It changes the shape and lifting characteristics of your machine that even the bravest designer would not want to predict. Stalling speeds increase and aircraft handling can become a nightmare. Icing is not a condition to entertain lightly. If the outside air temperature is at or below zero and you are flying in IMC conditions, icing may be around the corner. The outside air temperature probe should be serviceable and checked. (Remember to check before flight that the OAT probe is measuring the correct ambient temperature.)

Prior to flight
If the aircraft has been parked in sub-zero conditions remember to check that all surfaces are clear of ice, frost or snow. Check all control hinge lines, undercarriage bays, drain holes, aerials, static vents and propellers. If intending to leave an aircraft outside in these conditions remember to park the propellers vertically in order to avoid ice accumulation in the spinners. If unable to clear the ice, consider moving the aircraft to a warm hangar. Don't hurry the process . . . Better to arrive late in this life than early in the next!!

* Please note: There is currently no single-engined aircraft on the CAA register that is permitted to fly into known icing conditions.

Engine Intake and Carburettor Icing

Carburettor icing is not confined to those days when the outside air temperature is low. If the relative humidity is fairly high, even in temperatures as high as plus thirty degrees centigrade, carburettor icing has been known to form. Use the carburettor heat control prior to power reduction and know your engine and the times when carb. heat should be permanently selected. Consider warming the engine during a prolonged descent.

Aircraft that are fuel injected and therefore do not have carburettors are often fitted with 'alternate air' sources which should be selected if icing is suspected.

If your aircraft is equipped with VP propellers controlled by constant speed units do not expect the RPM gauge to give you the first warning of icing. Instead look to the Manifold Pressure Gauge. Any drop in manifold pressure having been set at a constant altitude could be a warning of engine icing. *Beware as prisoners are not normally taken.*

So do take care to avoid those weather formations that encourage the formation of ice and in particular Cumulo Nimbus and Nimbo Stratus cloud formations and whenever in IMC conditions when the outside air temperature is below zero.*

What if you actually get icing that you are unable to clear? Immediately advise ATC of your problem and if necessary call a *PAN* or even a *MAYDAY*. This is a serious situation. If possible consider the options. Should you climb to clear the cloud layer or descend to where you know it to be warmer.

The risk of climbing is that another fifty miles along the track there may be more cloud above your new level. Unless an inversion is present, although new ice is unlikely to form, old ice is unlikely to clear. And, just how high do you have to climb in order to clear the cloud you are in?

Descending is the other option assuming you know that below you the temperature is above zero and that you will not come below your minimum safety altitude for that area.

Depending on level and other traffic, ATC may not be able to allow you to descend and it may therefore be necessary to leave Controlled Airspace and divert. Whatever you do, don't take too long to make your decision and don't delay to tell air traffic of your problems. Their assistance just may save your life.

Don't disregard the forecast and you are unlikely to be caught out!

* See information circular reprinted courtesy of the CAA.

Chapter 18

The Procedure Turn/Reversal Procedures

The procedure turn is the method most commonly used to reciprocate tracks.

The Normal 45° Procedure Turn

Let's firstly examine this in still air. Imagine an aircraft tracking 090° away from a facility. The pilot wishes to reverse this track and return on a QDM of 270° back to the facility. When ready, unless following a set procedure, turn *right* 45° from the heading/track you are presently steering. Steer heading 135°. The turn should take fifteen seconds.

Continue on the new heading for a further forty-five seconds and then turn left onto the reciprocal, heading 315°. Maintain this heading until the new track is re-intercepted. The total time from the start of the turn is one minute for category A and B aircraft. For category C, D and E aircraft this time is increased to one minute and fifteen seconds.

The direction of the first turn gives the name to the procedure. When the first turn is to the right, it will be called a *Right Hand Procedure Turn*. The time on the outbound leg may be adjusted in order to reduce distance travelled and therefore remain within the protected area.

If a wind is present, single or double drift may be applied to the initial leg. Double drift will help compensate for the effect of the wind during the turn back towards the reciprocal track. Timing on the straight leg may be adjusted as for the hold. Add or subtract one second for each knot of head or tail-wind.

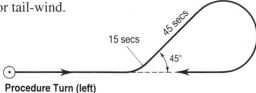

Procedure Turn (left)

158

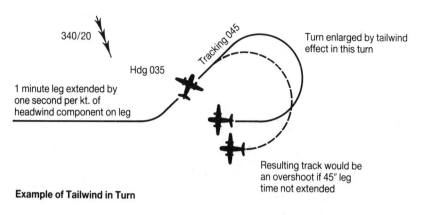

Example of Tailwind in Turn

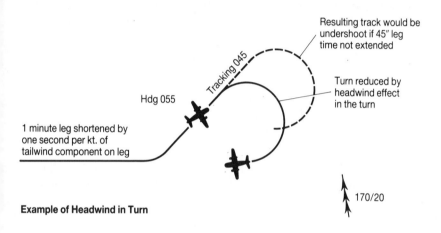

Example of Headwind in Turn

The 80° Procedure Turn

This is a far less common procedure. It consists of a specified track and timing from a facility or fix followed by an 80° turn away from the outbound track followed by an immediate 260° turn in the opposite direction to intercept the reciprocal track.

Base Turn

This differs from the procedure turns in that the first leg of the turn originates from the facility. This consists of a specified track and timing from the facility followed by a turn to intercept the inbound track. The track or timing may be adjusted for the different categories of aircraft.

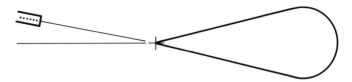

Race-track Procedure

This should not be confused with the hold. The race-track procedure consists of an initial turn from an inbound track through 180° from overhead the facility or fix onto an outbound track for a timing of one, two or three minutes. This is then followed by a 180° turn in the *same* direction to return to the inbound track. The 'timing' outbound may be substituted by a limiting radial or a DME distance. The join to the race-track procedure is similar to that for a holding procedure with some subtle differences:

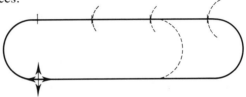

Offset Entry from sector two direction will limit the time on the 30° offset track to one minute and thirty seconds after which the pilot turns onto a heading to fly parallel to the outbound track for the remainder of the time. Should the published time on the outbound leg be only one minute then the time spent on the 30° offset track should be one minute also.

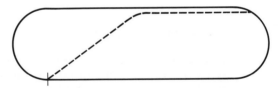

Parallel Entry may not return directly to the facility without first intercepting the inbound axis.

Flight Procedures for Race-track and Reversal Procedures

Bank Angles are based on rate one turns or twenty-five degrees of bank – whichever is the lesser.

Speeds may be specified within the procedure rather than aircraft categories and should be adhered to in order to remain within the protected area.

Entry. Reversal procedures should be entered from a track within 30° of the outbound track of the procedure. For base turns, if the +/-30° entry sector does not include the reciprocal of the inbound track, the entry sector is expanded to include it.

Timing outbound is always taken from abeam the facility or achieving the outbound heading, whichever comes later. This applies to a procedure based on a facility. If the procedure is based on a fix, timing is commenced upon achieving the outbound heading.

Chapter 19

Needle Tracking

Tracking a needle presentation has historically been the bane of many a pilot's life. What could be simpler than tracking towards a needle you might think and in 'still air' this is probably true. The problem comes when a wind is introduced and it's a rare day when the wind isn't blowing from somewhere.

The RBI (Relative Bearing Indicator)

First of all a few simple rules. Assuming the aid is tuned correctly and the aid is being used within its promulgated range and at the correct time of day, the ADF needle or RMI needle if tuned to a VOR will *point to the station*. As long as the pilot is able to maintain a constant heading, after having 'zeroed' the needle, any subsequent needle movement will indicate that a wind is present. If the needle should move to the left, the wind is from the left of the aircraft and if the needle should move to the right, the wind is from the right.

Let's imagine the aircraft is located due west of the station on a heading of 090° and the ADF needle is pointing directly ahead. The pilot is assuming zero wind conditions. Several minutes go by, and despite maintaining the heading of 090° very accurately, the needle has moved five degrees to the right. The aircraft has drifted to the North of track. The wind must therefore be from the South.

In order to regain track, the pilot must alter course to the right but by *how much*? A simple and effective rule of thumb is to *double the track error*. If the ADF needle is pointing five degrees to the right, turn right by ten degrees. Relative to the track of 090°, the pilot, steering 100 degrees, is steering ten degrees more than the required track. This we call + 10. When the ADF needle reads 350 degrees relative, the aircraft is back on track. 350 relative, we call -10. Just before the indication of -10 is seen the pilot should then turn onto a drift-corrected heading in order to remain on track despite the wind.

The greater the delay between correcting for track error and noting the error, the greater the displacement of the aircraft from track will be. As such, consideration could be made for increasing the attack above the standard *Double Track Error*. A suggested maximum attack of thirty degrees can be used when attacking into wind and ten degrees when attacking down-wind.

The pilot decides to steer 095° to take account of the southerly wind. He is now steering +5 looking for -5. The -5 position on the ADF dial is now the datum. Any movement away from this datum now signals that either the drift has been wrongly assessed or the wind has changed.

Movement of the needle to the right again, indicates the drift has been underestimated and needle movement in the opposite direction warns that the drift has been overestimated.

When winds are particularly strong, pilots may prefer to attack into wind by more than just double the track error. Figures of thirty degrees attack are not untypical. Remember, though, that if attacking the track with the wind behind you, it may be advisable to keep the attack to a minimum or even steer the track heading and allow the wind to blow you back onto track. This method should not be relied on if establishing a track before beacon passage is important.

In *still air conditions*, assuming no drift is being allowed and the pilot is steering the track heading, eg 090°, after beacon passage the needle should be indicating 180 degrees relative. It should be directly behind the aircraft. If the needle is to the right of this position it is a *fly right* indication and if it is to the left of this position it is a *fly left* indication.

If drift is being applied as in the case previously described, again ask yourself the following questions:

What am I steering?

What am I looking for?

Where is the needle?

eg I'm steering 095° (+5) and I'm looking for 175° relative (-5). If the needle is to the right of this position . . . fly right. If it is to the left of this position . . . fly left in order to regain track.

The RMI

Most training aircraft are today fitted with the RMI. This is simply a needle superimposed upon a moving DI which is normally slaved to the master direction indicator. As such the RMI gives a permanent indication of QDM to the facility. The same basic tracking principles apply.

After having zeroed the needle, the pilot can read off the QDM to the station. Let's suppose the QDM is 360 degrees. If the needle moves to the right (indicating wind from the right) the pilot must turn to the right to regain track. The simple rule is that he must turn sufficiently to place the needle to the left of the lubber line. In this way the needle can then 'drop down the dial' towards the required QDM of 360 degrees. It is important to remember that the needle only *drops down* the dial. If you find yourself waiting for the needle to climb up the dial, you'll have a long wait. Once the track has been regained, the normal method of track maintenance should be used.

Tracking Away could not be simpler than with an RMI. Just ask yourself what the needle should be pointing to. If the track 'to' is 360 degrees, the needle should be simply indicating the reciprocal track after beacon passage, namely 180 degrees. If the needle is to the right of this position, *fly right* and if it is to the left of this position *fly left* to regain track.

When using the RMI therefore ask these two questions:

What is the reciprocal of track required?

Is the needle left or right of this position?

The secret with all needle tracking is to keep the amount of drift applied to an absolute minimum. Too much drift will result in the aircraft passing from one side of the track to another in an annoying see-saw. Keep the drift to a minimum! A useful formula is as follows: Maximum Drift is equal to the *Wind-speed* multiplied by sixty and divided by the *True Airspeed*. For most training aircraft flying at and around 120 kts this means that the maximum drift is rarely much more than half the reported wind speed in degrees.

eg Wind speed thirty kts Max Drift fifteen degrees
(120 kts)

Dip Error

This is the error that causes the ADF needle to read incorrectly during turning. In a turn to the right with the station on the right the needle will give a relative bearing greater than is really the case. It will over-read. In a turn to the left, with the station on the left, the needle will give a relative bearing less than is really the case. Again it will over-read. The amount of over-read is a function of the bank angle and also the installation. The better the fit, the less will be the over-read. Familiarity with your aircraft will reduce the problems of dip error.

The error is always greatest when the beacon is either ahead of or behind the aircraft. The error increases with bank angle and with altitude and with proximity to the beacon. It follows that allowance should be made for this error when turning to establish on a QDM or a QDR and that the most accurate and therefore reliable indications are received only when the wings are level.

Chapter 20

Flying DME Arcs

The ability to fly a DME arc is becoming a necessary part of the instrument pilot's skills in the UK and Europe. They have been in more widespread use in the USA for some time, but one of the first UK instrument approach procedures to incorporate a DME arc is the VOR/DME procedure for Biggin Hill (page 167). Note that the arc is of seven nautical mile radius (the minimum possible) and extends for a relatively short distance, whereas the VOR/DME approach for Runway 08 at Catania (page 168) has arcs of sixteen nautical miles radius extending for much greater distances. Page 169 shows the Jeppesen presentation of the DME arc arrival procedure for Strasbourg.

Probably because a DME arc is not yet on the test menu for the Instrument Rating or most IMC Ratings there is a shortage of written material on the subject. This chapter gives some guidance on the three exercises of intercepting a DME arc from a radial, maintaining an arc, and intercepting a radial or localiser from an arc. The methods given here are probably not the only ones; readers might like to develop their own techniques on the basis of the guidance given.

It is always necessary to have a DME indicator in the aircraft, but techniques are given for using the Radio Magnetic Indicator/Relative Bearing Indicator (RMI/RBI), the Course Deviation Indicator (CDI), and the Horizontal Situation Indicator (HSI). It is interesting to note at this point that the FAA, who have considerable experience on this subject, make two points about flying DME arcs. Firstly, they recognise that the pilot, particularly in single crew operations, is too busy during an instrument approach to use formulae for the computation of lead angles and distances. (Some schools and authors of manuals who tend to treat the whole IR as an exercise in advanced mental trigonometry might do well to bear this expert opinion in mind.) Secondly, they recommend that unless the pilot is highly proficient in the use of the aircraft equipment

166

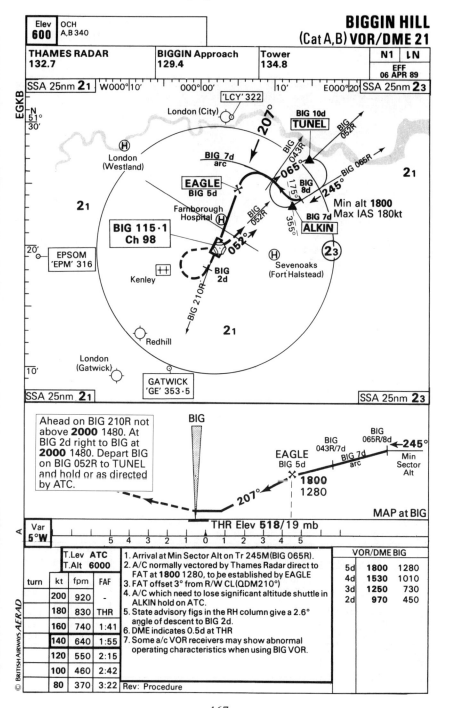

BIGGIN HILL
(Cat A,B) VOR/DME 21

Elev	OCH
600	A,B 340

THAMES RADAR 132.7	BIGGIN Approach 129.4	Tower 134.8	N1	LN
			EFF 06 APR 89	

SSA 25nm **21** · W000°10'   000°00'   10'   E000°20 SSA 25nm **23**

EGKB

London (City)
'LCY' 322

207°
BIG 10d
TUNEL
BIG 052R

N 51° 30'

⊕ London (Westland)

BIG 7d arc

BIG 043R
065°
175°
BIG 065R

BIG 8d
245°
Min alt **1800**
Max IAS 180kt

21

EAGLE
BIG 5d

Farnborough Hospital ⊕

BIG 052R
355°
BIG 7d
ALKIN

21

BIG 115·1
Ch 98

052°

⊕ Sevenoaks (Fort Halstead)
(23)

20'
EPSOM 'EPM' 316

Kenley
BIG 2d

BIG 210R

21

⊕ Redhill

London (Gatwick)
10'

GATWICK 'GE' 353·5

SSA 25nm **21** | SSA 25nm **23**

Ahead on BIG 210R not above **2000** 1480. At BIG 2d right to BIG at **2000** 1480. Depart BIG on BIG 052R to TUNEL and hold or as directed by ATC.

BIG

BIG 065R/8d ◄ **245°**
EAGLE BIG 5d · BIG 043R/7d · BIG 7d arc · Min Sector Alt

207° ✕ **1800** 1280

MAP at BIG

Var **5°W** | 5 4 3 2 1 0 1 2 3 4 5 |

THR Elev **518**/19 mb

	T.Lev ATC	1. Arrival at Min Sector Alt on Tr 245M(BIG 065R).	VOR/DME BIG		
	T.Alt **6000**	2. A/C normally vectored by Thames Radar direct to FAT at **1800** 1280, to be established by EAGLE	5d	1800	1280
turn	kt fpm FAF	3. FAT offset 3° from R/W CL(QDM210°)	4d	1530	1010
	200 920 -	4. A/C which need to lose significant altitude shuttle in ALKIN hold on ATC.	3d	1250	730
	180 830 THR	5. State advisory figs in the RH column give a 2.6° angle of descent to BIG 2d.	2d	970	450
	160 740 1:41	6. DME indicates 0.5d at THR			
	140 640 1:55	7. Some a/c VOR receivers may show abnormal operating characteristics when using BIG VOR.			
	120 550 2:15				
	100 460 2:42				
	80 370 3:22	Rev: Procedure			

© BRITISH AIRWAYS *AERAD*

167

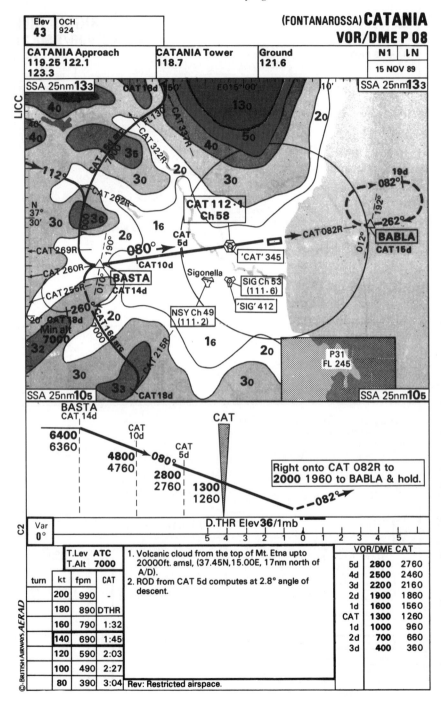

(FONTANAROSSA) **CATANIA**
VOR/DME P 08

Elev	OCH
43	924

CATANIA Approach	CATANIA Tower	Ground	N1	LN
119.25 122.1 123.3	118.7	121.6	**15 NOV 89**	

Right onto CAT 082R to
2000 1960 to BABLA & hold.

		BASTA CAT 14d				
		6400 6360				
			4800 4760	080°		
				2800 2760	**1300** 1260	
						---082°

D.THR Elev **36**/1mb

Var		5	4	3	2	1	0	1	2	3	4	5
0°												

	T.Lev **ATC** T.Alt **7000**	1. Volcanic cloud from the top of Mt. Etna upto 20000ft. amsl, (37.45N,15.00E, 17nm north of A/D).	VOR/DME CAT		
turn	kt	fpm	CAT	2. ROD from CAT 5d computes at 2.8° angle of descent.	5d	**2800**	2760

turn	kt	fpm	CAT			
	200	990	-	5d	**2800**	2760
	180	890	DTHR	4d	**2500**	2460
	160	790	1:32	3d	**2200**	2160
	140	690	1:45	2d	**1900**	1860
	120	590	2:03	1d	**1600**	1560
	100	490	2:27	CAT	**1300**	1260
	80	390	3:04	1d	**1000**	960
				2d	**700**	660
				3d	**400**	360

Rev: Restricted airspace.

© BRITISH AIRWAYS *AERAD*

C2

168

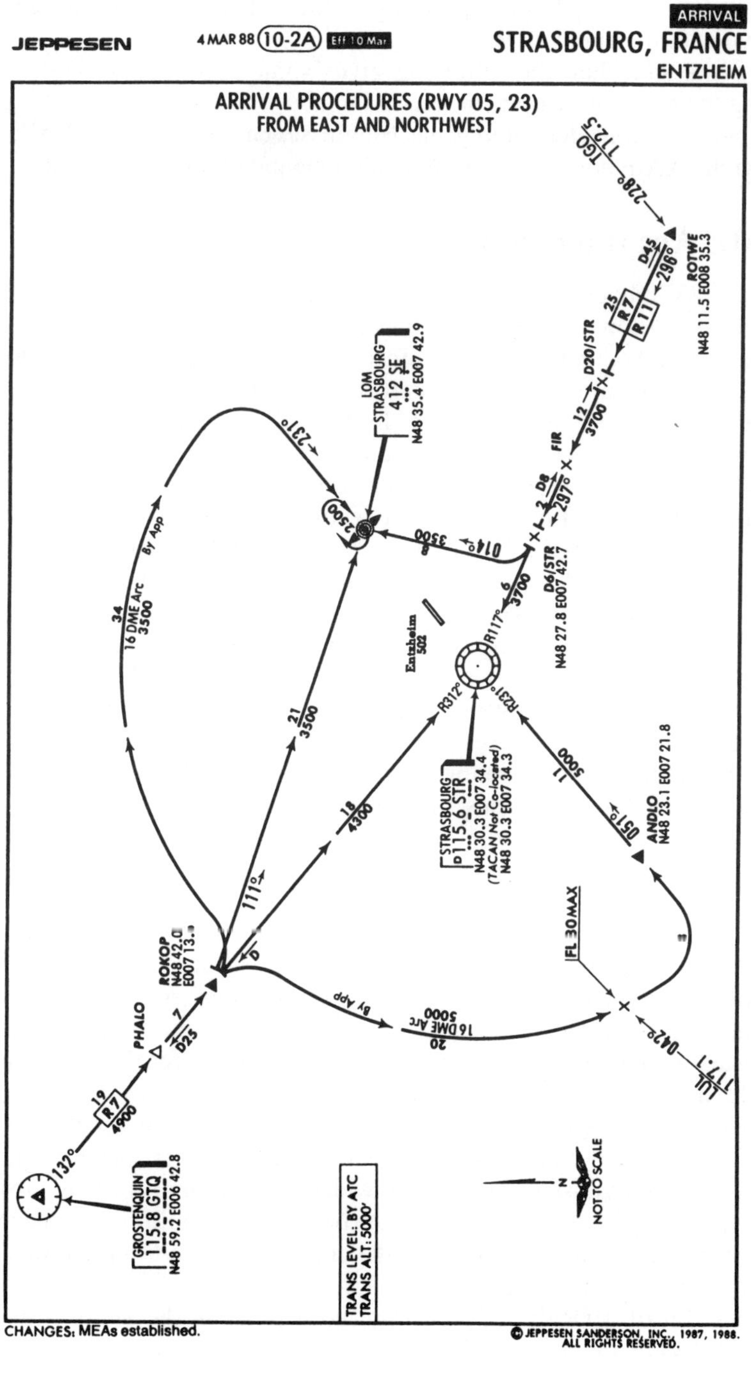
ARRIVAL
JEPPESEN
4 MAR 88 (10-2A) Eff 10 Mar
STRASBOURG, FRANCE
ENTZHEIM
ARRIVAL PROCEDURES (RWY 05, 23)
FROM EAST AND NORTHWEST
TGO 112.5
228°
ROTWE
N48 11.5 E008 35.3
D45
296°
R7
R11
25
D20/STR
12
3700
FIR
D8
2
297°
D6/STR
N48 27.8 E007 42.7
6
3700
R117°
014°
3500
LOM
STRASBOURG
412 SE
N48 35.4 E007 42.9
2500
231°
34
16 DME Arc
3500
By App
21
3500
Entzheim
502
R312°
R231°
STRASBOURG
D 115.6 STR
N48 30.3 E007 34.4
(TACAN Not Co-located)
N48 30.3 E007 34.3
18
4300
111°
11
5000
051°
ANDLO
N48 23.1 E007 21.8
FL 30 MAX
ROKOP
PHALO
7
D25
20
16 DME Arc
5000
By App
042°
LUL 117.1
132°
19
R7
4900
GROSTENQUIN
115.8 GTQ
N48 59.2 E006 42.8
TRANS LEVEL: BY ATC
TRANS ALT: 5000'
NOT TO SCALE
CHANGES: MEAs established.
© JEPPESEN SANDERSON, INC., 1987, 1988.
ALL RIGHTS RESERVED.

and in flying the specific approach procedure, DME arcs should only be flown with the aid of an RMI.

Having said that, the following gives some guidance on DME arcs using the types of instrument referred to above. Referring again to figure 66, we will consider joining the Biggin seven nautical mile DME arc from the Alkin hold — that is, tracking inbound on the 065° radial.

DME Arc Interception

Track 245° inbound on the 065° radial to intercept the seven nautical mile DME arc. Allow 0.5 nm lead distance at ninety knots to give you a lead point where you commence the ninety degree turn at Rate One on to the arc. Therefore in our example start the turn on to 335° when the DME distance is 7.5 nm. Note the lead distance of one nm given on the plate showing commencement of the turn at eight nautical miles; this distance might not be suitable for slow aircraft. If we were tracking 065° outbound on the 065° radial at ninety knots we would start the turn on to 335° at 6.5 nm. At 120 knots use a lead of +/- 0.7 nm. The DME distance should be closely monitored during the intercepting turn. Roll out of the turn early if the arc is being undershot; continue the turn past the nominal ninety degrees if the arc is being overshot. This assumes that the intercept is being made at ninety degrees; if the intercepting turn is less than ninety degrees then the lead distance needs to be reduced. An intercepting turn of more than ninety degrees needs an increased lead distance. Note that the procedure for intercepting an arc is the same whether RMI, HSI or CDI is used. Allowance must of course be made for drift.

Maintaining the DME Arc — General

As in all instrument approach procedures, the pilot must have a continuous mental picture of his position. This means knowing his DME distance relative to the desired arc, the current radial and the wind effect. Wind effect is particularly critical because heading and therefore drift are constantly changing. Wind can move the aircraft nearer the arc (helpful) or further away from it (not helpful). Larger arcs are easier to fly, whereas higher ground-speeds make life more difficult because of the higher rate of deviation and correction. The task is made easier by keeping slightly inside the curve, in which case the arc is turning towards the aircraft and re-interception can be made by holding the heading constant. If the aircraft is outside the curve the arc is turning away, and greater corrections are required.

The aim of a DME arc procedure is to position the aircraft on to a specific VOR radial or an ILS localiser. Throughout the arc procedure it is essential to monitor the aircraft's proximity to, and closure rate with, the target radial or localiser because the aircraft should not overshoot this target. Similarly, intermediate radials or other cross-cut fixes might be specified in the procedure where the aircraft is to alter altitude, and these must remain in mind. The Catania procedure has examples of this.

Maintaining the DME Arc — RMI/BRI

This method is equally applicable to the RMI and RBI, as it only uses the relative position of the bearing pointer. An ADF only RMI/RBI can of course only be used where the VOR/DME has a co-located NDB; ADF dip error is an added difficulty. It can also be used by the poor man's RMI, the RBI with manually rotated compass card, but I do not like this instrument because there is always the danger of forgetting to turn the card after the aircraft changes heading, especially when the turn has been an inadvertent one.

In zero wind the pilot should theoretically be able to fly an exact arc by maintaining a relative bearing of 090 or 270 degrees, but in practice and when there is wind, a series of short straight lines is flown. Obstacle clearance is provided for quite some distance either side of the arc, therefore small deviations from the arc are permissible. Obstacle clearance is in fact 300 metres (1,000 feet) for 2.5 nm either side of the arc, with further clearance areas for another 2.5 nm either side, tapering from 300 metres to zero. The procedure for maintaining the arc is as follows:

1. Having made the initial ninety degree turn on to the arc and with the aircraft at the required DME distance, establish the RMI/RBI bearing pointer on the 090 or 270 degree wing tip reference on the dial. Maintain heading and allow the pointer to move five or ten degrees behind the wing tip, the DME range will increase slightly.

2. Turn the aircraft towards the DME facility to place the bearing pointer five to ten degrees ahead of the wing tip. The DME distance will begin to decrease.

3. Maintain this heading until the pointer is again five to ten degrees behind the wing tip.

4. Continue this procedure to maintain the approximate arc.

5. If drift is blowing the aircraft away from the facility, establish the reference ahead of the wing tip. If drift is blowing the aircraft towards the facility, establish the reference behind the wing tip. If there is any wind, remember that the drift will not be constant.

6. This procedure should bracket the required arc. If a correction needs to be made to the aircraft's DME range, alter heading so as to change the relative bearing ten to twenty degrees for each half mile deviation from the desired arc, the amount of correction depending on the rate of deviation. For example, if the aircraft is half a mile outside the arc and the bearing pointer is on the chosen reference (in other words the aircraft is bracketing an arc half a mile too wide), turn the aircraft ten to twenty degrees towards the facility to return to the arc and reassess your drift correction.

Maintaining the DME Arc — CDI

Orientation is more difficult because the pilot does not have a direct azimuth reference. Referring again to figure 66, and for still air conditions:

1. The rollout on to the 335 degree heading should place the aircraft on the required 7 nm arc.

2. Immediately set the OBS to 055 degrees (ten degrees past the 065 degree interception radial in the direction of flight around the arc). The CDI should read left of centre with deviation decreasing, and the DME distance should be increasing, to show that the aircraft has not yet crossed but is approaching the 055 degree radial and is going outside the arc. Turn left by a suitable amount to achieve crossing the 055 degree radial simultaneously with intercepting the required 7 nm arc (what the Americans term 'making the bread come out even with the peanut butter').

3. Set the OBS ahead twenty degrees to 035 degrees. Alter heading 100 degrees from the radial the aircraft is currently on 055 degree to a heading of 315 degrees.

4. Maintain this heading until the 035 degree radial is crossed or the arc is intercepted. At this point, use the OBS to centre the deviation indicator if necessary and then set the OBS ahead another twenty degrees. Alter heading 100 degrees from the current radial.

This technique will maintain a track slightly inside the required arc. Allow for drift as necessary, one method being to adjust the 100 degree figure in a similar way to 6 above.

Maintaining the DME Arc — HSI

Again with reference to figure 66, we pick up the story where the aircraft has just turned on to a heading of 335 degrees from the interception radial.

1. As the aircraft circles anti-clockwise, the radials crossed will decrease and the 065 degree interception radial will be left behind. Turn the OBS anti-clockwise until the deviation indicator (beam bar) on the CDI moves just to full-scale deflection ahead. It seems better to use 'five dots' or its equivalent rather than go to the mechanical stop. Alter heading to fly towards the beam bar at a right-angle to it, that is, the beam bar lies horizontal at the top of the HSI.

2. The beam bar will then move down the HSI; when it reaches the centre, rotate the OBS to place the beam bar again just a full-scale deflection ahead and alter heading to place it horizontal at the top of the HSI.

3. Periodically check the DME distance to monitor drift. If the distance is significantly greater than the required 7 nm, a turn of ten degrees is a good initial correction. If the distance is significantly less than 7 nm, maintaining heading should result in intercepting the arc. When the arc is intercepted, turn the OBS to give full-scale deflection and alter heading to place the beam bar horizontal at the top of the HSI again, but this time make an immediate further adjustment to the heading to allow for anticipated drift.

Intercepting a VOR Radial or ILS Localiser from a DME Arc

The amount of lead required will depend on the arc radius and the aircraft g/s. Lead radials, shown on instrument approach plates, such as the 043 degree radial in figure 66, might not be appropriate for slow aircraft. As general guidance for speeds of 150 knots or less, the required lead will be less than five degrees. There is no practical difference between intercepting a radial or a localiser from an arc and intercepting if from a straight track. The same considerations about rate of closure etc., apply. However, bear in mind that the intercept angle will probably be ninety degrees.

As with all new procedures and techniques, you should not attempt to fly DME arcs 'for real' until you have been trained by an appropriately qualified instructor. A flight simulator or procedure trainer would be a good way to practise, and perhaps to develop your own techniques. May all your arcs be de triomphe!

(courtesy of *Pilot Magazine*) and of Peter Cox.

Chapter 21

The Debrief

The test is not over until you have said 'Good-bye' to the examiner. If you have not passed or have achieved only a 'partial pass' you may have to meet him again and examiners like elephants have long memories.

Use the debrief to your best advantage and listen carefully to all the points that the examiner raises. Use pencil and paper to take notes of the criticisms. It is always very difficult to recall after a test what is discussed. Your mind is not at its most receptive. However, the examiner, will have a lot of experience that you should draw on. After all, you've paid a small fortune for his time and you should make sure you are getting good value.

If you do not understand the debrief or perhaps are not in agreement with a decision that has been made, feel free to discuss it. Examiners have been known not to make their minds up as to the result until some way into the debrief. Use this knowledge to your advantage. If an examiner is querying a certain technique, give lucid reasons or explanations as to your choice.

In the event of a partial pass, the examiner will give you a slip of paper which outlines your retest requirements. Do make sure you understand this. Any section or sub-section that is to be retested will have to be flown. Normally the departure will always be retested even though it has been passed on the first attempt. It is not unheard of for a person who has passed a section on the first attempt fail it on his second attempt. *So be careful.*

The slip of paper that you are given must be handed to your examiner on your next attempt, so don't lose it.

If you are unhappy with the conduct of the test you can appeal to higher authority. Note the appeal is against the conduct and not the result. So, if you feel the examiner was not doing his job properly or put you off in some way, you can and should appeal to the chief examiner

175

who will lend a sympathetic ear to your case. Appeals are few and far between and some are lost and some are won. The CAA maintains a very impartial line in the hope of the fairest of assessments. So, if you feel you have a case — appeal. You have seven days after the test to make it. After that you have no redress.

Speaking as an instructor it is always of value to hear the truthful and accurate reasons for an unsuccessful result. Always tell your instructor the truth, even if it causes you some embarrassment to admit your mistake. It will help him improve his instructing and thus benefit the next student. As someone once said to me, 'show me someone who has never made a mistake and I'll show you someone who has never done anything'.

Your taxi after the flight is <u>not</u> the time to relax.

Chapter 22

General Points of Interest

Air Traffic Control

Air Traffic Control is there to help the pilot and to assist and expedite the flow of traffic. Within controlled airspace they offer a *Radar Control Service* in which they provide a safe separation from other traffic conforming to certain minima.

Outside of controlled airspace a radar unit may offer a *Radar Information Service* or *Radar Advisory Service*. Radar information offers information to the pilots of aircraft in his vicinity that could pose a collision risk.

It is up to the pilot to make a decision as to whether or not to take avoiding action. Radar advisory service offers the same information but the controller will require the pilot to turn onto instructed headings in order to maintain minimum separations.

During Radar Information service, the pilot is wholly responsible for maintaining separation from other aircraft, whether or not the controller has passed traffic information. During receipt of a radar information service the pilot is required to advise the controller of any change in level or heading.

Both radar advisory or radar information service may be requested during any weather condition. However, if a radar advisory service is requested, pilots should not request a service where compliance would require flight into IMC, unless they are legally able to fly in such conditions.

Rates of Descent or Climb

If accepting a radar advisory or control service and instructed to climb or descend, pilots should comply to a minimum rate of climb or descent of 500 feet per minute.

Transition Altitude

This is defined as the altitude at and below which vertical separation is described in terms of altitude (rather than height or flight level). Not all transition altitudes are the same as the following list explains:

Aberdeen CTR/CTA	5,000 ft
Belfast CTR/CTA	4,000 ft
Birmingham CTR/CTA	4,000 ft
Edinburgh CTR	6,000 ft
Glasgow CTR	6,000 ft
Leeds Bradford CTR/A	4,000 ft
London TMA	6,000 ft
Manchester TMA	4,000 ft
Scottish CTR/TMA	4,000 ft
Teesside CTR/CTA	5,000 ft

For Aberdeen, Leeds Bradford and Teesside, outside the notified hours of operation the Transition Altitude is 3,000 feet.

Flight Plan Filing

A flight plan may be filed for any flight. A flight plan must be filed:

1. For all flights within Class A airspace.
2. For all flights in Controlled Airspace in IMC or at night (except for Special VFR flights).
3. For all flights in Controlled Airspace in VMC if the flight is to be conducted in accordance with IFR.
4. For all flights within Class B, C and D control zones/areas irrespective of flight rules.
5. For all flights within the Scottish and London Upper Flight Information Regions.
6. For any flight from an aerodrome of departure within the UK being a flight whose destination is more than 40 kms from the departure aerodrome and the aircraft's maximum all-up weight exceeds 5700 kgs.
7. For any flight to or from the UK which will cross the UK FIR Boundary.
8. For a flight where it is intended to make use of the Air Traffic Advisory Service.

It is advisable that a flight plan is filed if a flight involves flying over the sea, more than ten miles from the UK coast, or flying over sparsely populated areas where Search and Rescue Operations would be difficult.

Normally flight plans should be filed on the ground with the ATS unit at the aerodrome of departure at least thirty minutes before clearance to start-up or taxi is requested. For those flights intending to operate in or through controlled airspace, the time should be ideally one hour. Airborne flight plans may also be filed with at least ten minutes warning of entry into controlled airspace.

Transponders

Carriage of serviceable SSR transponders is mandatory for IFR flight within controlled airspace. It is also required for VFR flight within the whole of UK airspace at and above Flight Level 100. The Scottish TMA between 6,000 ft and FL 100 requires mode A transponders to be carried. The Internationally recognised codes are as follows:

7700   Emergency
7600   Radio Failure
7500   Unlawful Interference (Hijack)
2000   When entering UK airspace from an adjacent region where the operation of transponders was not required.
7007   Code for aircraft engaged on airborne observation flights.

Mode C should normally be selected unless requested otherwise.

The Conspicuity Code: 7000

This code is normally to be used when flying VFR in uncontrolled airspace. Whilst this is a recommendation below FL100 it is mandatory at and above FL 100. The exceptions to the above rule include those times when the aircraft is receiving a service from an ATS unit which requires a different setting or when circumstances require the use of one of the special purpose codes. If an aircraft intends to remain within an aerodrome traffic pattern below 3,000 feet agl the transponder should be selected to stand-by.

Instrument Flight Rules

Subject to Rule 5 (The Low Flying Rule) requirements, an aircraft when flying IFR may not fly less than 1,000 ft above the highest obstacle within five nms unless on a route notified for the purpose of this rule, for take-off and landing and when flying at 3,000 ft amsl or below if clear of cloud and in sight of the surface.

When flying above 3,000 ft amsl but below FL 245, pilots should adhere to the quadrantal rules (previously described) unless they are complying to instructions from an ATC unit. Above FL 245 the semi-circular rules apply (previously described).

For any flight within controlled airspace under IFR, a pilot must file a flight plan and obtain an ATC clearance based upon it. The flight must obey this clearance and with the notified holding and approach procedures at the destination.

An aircraft flying outside Controlled Airspace but under IFR may change to VFR if VMC may be maintained.

Unless the flight plan is cancelled the pilot is required to advise ATC when the aircraft lands within, or leaves Controlled Airspace.

Position Reports must be made in accordance with ATC instructions with Position, Time, Level and Estimate for the next position.

Chapter 23

The AERADS and How to Interpret Them

Users of AERAD documentation should be aware that Instrument Approach charts currently appear in the Flight Guide in two different specifications.

The older, single-colour charts are being progressively replaced by two-colour charts showing high ground and obstacles in excess of 500 feet above A/D elevation encompassed within green layer tints referred to as Minimum Safe Altitude Contour envelopes (MSA).

Section Layout of New Specification IACs

The layout of the new specification charts is grouped into five main sections viz: TITLE, COMMUNICATION FREQUENCIES, PLAN, PROFILE and INFORMATION AREA.

1. The TITLE panel incorporates obstacle clearance limit (OCL) or obstacle clearance height (OCH) information. Where OCH information is extensive it may also be found in the information area.

2. The COMMUNICATION FREQUENCY PANEL contains Approach, Director, Tower, Ground and ATIS frequencies (the call-sign being quoted only once), alphanumeric chart reference and date.

3. THE PLAN

   3.1 MSA Contour envelopes.
   Terrain is shown by way of contour envelope layers tinted in up to five shades of green and adjusted where necessary to include all known obstructions. The shade of green used (Emerald) has

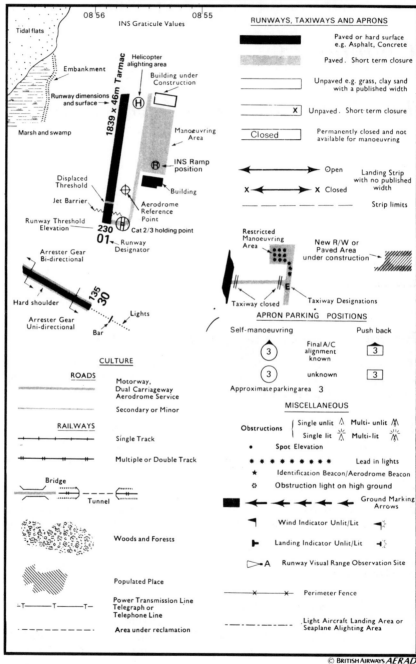

RUNWAYS, TAXIWAYS AND APRONS

Paved or hard surface e.g. Asphalt, Concrete

Paved. Short term closure

Unpaved e.g. grass, clay sand with a published width

Unpaved. Short term closure

Closed — Permanently closed and not available for manoeuvring

Open / Closed — Landing Strip with no published width

Strip limits

New R/W or Paved Area under construction

APRON PARKING POSITIONS

Self-manoeuvring / Push back

Final A/C alignment known

unknown

Approximate parking area 3

MISCELLANEOUS

Obstructions: Single unlit / Multi-unlit / Single lit / Multi-lit

Spot Elevation

Lead in lights

Identification Beacon/Aerodrome Beacon

Obstruction light on high ground

Ground Marking Arrows

Wind Indicator Unlit/Lit

Landing Indicator Unlit/Lit

Runway Visual Range Observation Site

Perimeter Fence

Light Aircraft Landing Area or Seaplane Alighting Area

CULTURE

ROADS

Motorway, Dual Carriageway Aerodrome Service

Secondary or Minor

RAILWAYS

Single Track

Multiple or Double Track

Bridge

Tunnel

Woods and Forests

Populated Place

Power Transmission Line / Telegraph or Telephone Line

Area under reclamation

© BRITISH AIRWAYS *AERAD*

NEW SPECIFICATION
APPROACH CHART LEGEND

02 FEB 87   **5**

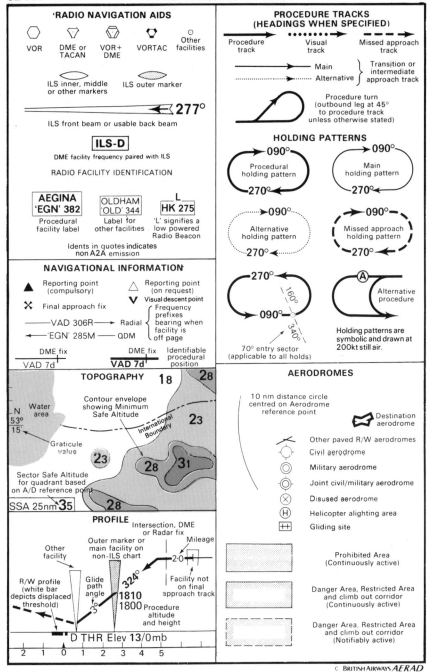

RADIO NAVIGATION AIDS

VOR · DME or TACAN · VOR+DME · VORTAC · Other facilities

ILS inner, middle or other markers · ILS outer marker

≪277°

ILS front beam or usable back beam

ILS-D

DME facility frequency paired with ILS

RADIO FACILITY IDENTIFICATION

AEGINA 'EGN' 382 — Procedural facility label

OLDHAM 'OLD' 344 — Label for other facilities

L HK 275 — 'L' signifies a low powered Radio Beacon

Idents in quotes indicates non A2A emission

NAVIGATIONAL INFORMATION

▲ Reporting point (compulsory)
△ Reporting point (on request)
✕ Final approach fix
▽ Visual descent point

VAD 306R — Radial
'EGN' 285M — QDM

Frequency prefixes bearing when facility is off page

DME fix — VAD 7d
DME fix — VAD 7d (Identifiable procedural position)

TOPOGRAPHY

Contour envelope showing Minimum Safe Altitude

N 53° 15' — Water area

Graticule value

International Boundary

Sector Safe Altitude for quadrant based on A/D reference point

SSA 25nm **35**

PROFILE

Intersection, DME or Radar fix

Outer marker or main facility on non-ILS chart — Mileage

Other facility

R/W profile (white bar depicts displaced threshold)

Glide path angle **1810**

324° Facility not on final approach track

1800 Procedure altitude and height

D THR Elev **13/0mb**

2 1 0 1 2 3 4 5

PROCEDURE TRACKS (HEADINGS WHEN SPECIFIED)

Procedure track · Visual track · Missed approach track

Main — Transition or intermediate approach track
Alternative

Procedure turn (outbound leg at 45° to procedure track unless otherwise stated)

HOLDING PATTERNS

→090° Procedural holding pattern 270°←
→090° Main holding pattern 270°←
→090° Alternative holding pattern 270°←
→090° Missed approach holding pattern 270°←

270° / 160° / 090° — 340°
70° entry sector (applicable to all holds)

(A) Alternative procedure

Holding patterns are symbolic and drawn at 200kt still air.

AERODROMES

10 nm distance circle centred on Aerodrome reference point

Destination aerodrome
Other paved R/W aerodromes
Civil aerodrome
Military aerodrome
Joint civil/military aerodrome
Disused aerodrome
(H) Helicopter alighting area
Gliding site

Prohibited Area (Continuously active)

Danger Area, Restricted Area and climb out corridor (Continuously active)

Danger Area, Restricted Area and climb out corridor (Notifiably active)

© BRITISH AIRWAYS *AERAD*

been selected to give the best appearance, especially under flight deck lighting at night.

To ensure that the area immediately surrounding the aerodrome remains white contours are selected to commence at the first suitable contour nearest to 500 feet above A/D elevation. This allows an aircraft, flying at the MSA applicable to the white area, to fly anywhere within that white area with a clearance of at least 1,000 feet above obstacles and terrain while remaining at a circuit height of 1,500 feet above A/D elevation. Isolated obstacles within this white area are shown by a green circle of radius three millimetres (approximately one nautical mile). The two, or exceptionally three, digits overprinted in black represent minimum vertical clearances in thousands and hundreds of feet above terrain and obstructions according to the following table:-

Elevation of Obstacle	Vertical Clearance
Up to and including 5,000 ft	1,000 ft
Above 5,000 ft up to and including 10,000 ft	1,500 ft *
Above 10,000 ft	2,000 ft

* AERAD charts are being changed to conform with CAA requirements for a minimum clearance of 2000 ft for terrain or obstacles above 5,000 ft (CAP 360, Chap 2/15 April 1990).

3.2 Sector Safe Altitudes (SSA).

Sector Safe Altitudes are computed and displayed in the same fashion as MSA, the twenty-five nautical mile quadrants being based on the A/D reference point. In computing these altitudes an additional five nm around each sector is taken into account. Each SSA shown is the higher of the calculated figure or the State published figure and in no case will be less than 1,600 feet (16).

3.3 Scale

Charts are drawn to a standard scale of 1:½ m (approx. seven nms to one inch). Exceptionally a smaller scale may be used.

3.4 Procedure

The procedure is drawn at a speed of 180 kt; holding patterns at a speed of 200 kt. Various line weights and styles are employed according to the emphasis placed upon them. DME distances are signified by a short bar annotated with the ident, distance and suffix 'd'. Holding pattern entry sectors are shown by a pecked line at 70° to the axis of the hold.

4. The PROFILE

Procedure altitudes and heights are 'rounded off' to the nearest ten feet in each case and are the minimum to be observed.
The profile distance scale is zeroed at the ILS reference point or touch-down point with the magnetic variation box sited to its left.
The touch-down zone (TDZ) or threshold elevation (THR) in feet is shown with its millibar (mb), Hectopascal (hPa) or inches mercury (Hg) equivalent.

5. INFORMATION AREA

The information area is divided into three main components consisting of:

LEFT — Facility to turn and facility to threshold timing with a rate of descent table in feet per minute and an inset displaying Transition Level and Transition Altitude.

CENTRE — A warnings box containing all important notes grouped together for easy reference.

RIGHT — A DME descent slope table for non-precision approaches featuring up to twelve advisory DME altitudes and heights. Alternatively altitude and height may be expressed at twenty, forty and sixty seconds past the marker for the relevant non-precision approach (LLZ, VOR or NDB).

Sectional Layout of Old Specification IACs

Symbols displayed are in common with those found on the approach chart with the addition of the following:-

SID/STAR
designator

A/W
designator

Speed limit
point

Noise
measurement
site
(where applicable)

End of
noise
abatement
(where applicable)

<<<<<<<<<<   Radar Vector

TITLE

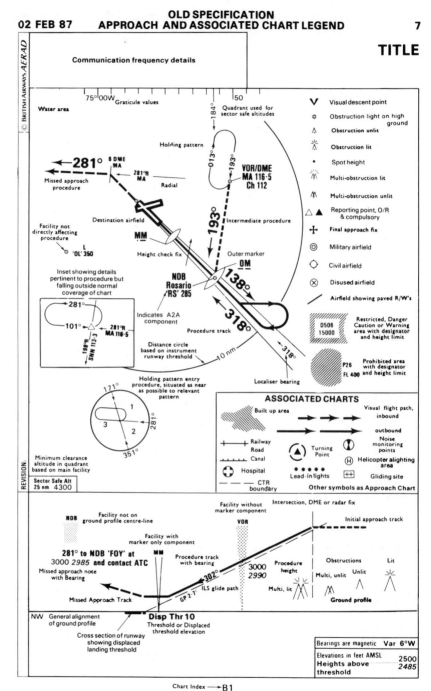

© BRITISH AIRWAYS *AERAD*

Communication frequency details

75°00W Graticule values

Water area

Quadrant used for sector safe altitudes

Holding pattern

←281° 6 DME MA

281°R MA

Missed approach procedure

Radial

VOR/DME MA 116·5 Ch 112

Facility not directly affecting procedure

Destination airfield

Intermediate procedure

L 'OL' 350

MM

Height check fix

Outer marker OM

Inset showing details pertinent to procedure but falling outside normal coverage of chart

NDB Rosario 'RS' 285

281°

101°

281°R MA 116·5

Indicates A2A component

Procedure track

198°R SNN 113·3

Distance circle based on instrument runway threshold

10 nm

Holding pattern entry procedure, situated as near as possible to relevant pattern

Localiser bearing

Minimum clearance altitude in quadrant based on main facility

Sector Safe Alt 25 nm 4300

V	Visual descent point
✿	Obstruction light on high ground
∆	Obstruction unlit
☆	Obstruction lit
•	Spot height
⋔	Multi-obstruction lit
Ϻ	Multi-obstruction unlit
△ ▲	Reporting point, O/R & compulsory
✛	Final approach fix
◎	Military airfield
○	Civil airfield
⊗	Disused airfield
/	Airfield showing paved R/W's

| D506 15000 | Restricted, Danger Caution or Warning area with designator and height limit |
| P26 FL 400 | Prohibited area with designator and height limit |

ASSOCIATED CHARTS

Built up area

Visual flight path, inbound

outbound

Railway

Road

Canal

Turning Point

Noise monitoring points

Hospital

Lead-in lights

Ⓗ Helicopter alighting area

⧺ Gliding site

CTR boundary

Other symbols as Approach Chart

NDB Facility not on ground profile centre-line

Facility without marker component

Facility with marker only component

281° to NDB 'FOY' at 3000 *2985* and contact ATC

MM Procedure track with bearing

302°

GP 2·7° ILS glide path

VOR Intersection, DME or radar fix

Initial approach track

3000 *2990* Procedure height

3000 *2990*

Obstructions

Multi, unlit

Lit

Unlit

Multi, lit

Ground profile

Missed approach note with Bearing

Missed Approach Track

NW General alignment of ground profile

Cross section of runway showing displaced landing threshold

Disp Thr 10
Threshold or Displaced threshold elevation

Bearings are magnetic	**Var 6°W**
Elevations in feet AMSL	2500
Heights above threshold	2485

The old specification charts in existence differ in the following ways:

1. They are drawn to a speed of 150 kt.

2. Obstructions and spot-heights on plan and profile appear where they penetrate the slope.

3. Sector Safe altitudes are based on the main aid for the procedure with the quadrantal lines drawn true but labelled with magnetic bearings.

4. Spot-heights and obstructions are labelled with both QNH and QFE values determined from the following datum points.

   (a) The Lowest threshold at the A/D on charts where the legend is at the top of the page.
   (b) Threshold elevation of the RW in use for that procedure on charts where the legend box is positioned lower right corner of the page.

   The exceptions to the above are break cloud procedures, where the datum is the aerodrome elevation, and parallel approaches where the datum is the lower landing threshold of the two runways.

Aerodrome/Landing Charts

With these charts the differences are minor, the new specification charts featuring improvements such as:

An INS ramp position at the head of the chart symbolised by an R within a circle and cross-referenced onto the associated ramp chart using the same symbol. When no convenient ramp position is available the A/D reference point is substituted.

Runway dimensions published in metres with the conversion to feet quoted in a box on the plan.

A redesigned, abbreviated, lighting table with runways paired up, true bearings and landing distances incorporated and the average slope between R/W ends expressed as a percentage.

A warnings box lower right of chart as featured on the IACs.

Standard Instrument Departure and Arrival Charts

SID and arrival charts are presented in diagrammatic form with, in the case of SIDs the routes grouped by SID clearance on each page. Arrival routes terminate at the main entry or holding point. On both charts transitions are shown as thin lines.

In pre-flight briefing the SID text should be read in conjunction with the diagram. Magnetic tracks towards a VOR are indicated as e.g. Tr358M (BKY 178R). Crossing altitudes or flight levels are quoted both in the test and on the diagram thereby making it impossible to fly the SID using the diagram without further reference to the text.

A pecked line showing an approximate twenty-five nm radius for the A/D, together with a quartered circle indicating the Sector Safe Altitudes for the quadrants, is provided. Beneath this a MSA figure based on 10 nm either side of the SID track is published. This applies to the full length of the SID from the runway end to the exit point.

Approximate distances from the inbound entry points to touch-down and from take-off to the point at which straight tracks commence are quoted.

Danger, restricted or prohibited areas are shown only where they overlap, or are adjacent to, a route shown on the chart.

Visual Approach and Visual Routes Charts

These three-colour charts are of variable scale and take the form of a topographical location chart showing principal rivers, roads, railways, built-up area etc together with contours spot-heights and obstructions in relation to any visual procedures at the aerodrome.

Routes together with visual reporting points, controlled airspace etc are shown when published by the State and a text description where it applies.

Other features of the chart are in accordance with the new Specification Approach and Aerodrome chart legends.

Radio Navigation Charts/Route Facility Charts

Radio Navigation charts are being supplemented or replaced by the Route Facility chart. This is an en route chart drawn to a larger scale and printed in either two or four colours with revised features and symbology to improve clarity.

DME Altitude/Height Table

(New specification charts only). The DME altitude/height table in the information area of the approach charts is provided to assist pilots to judge straight-in and visual approaches and is *ADVISORY ONLY.*

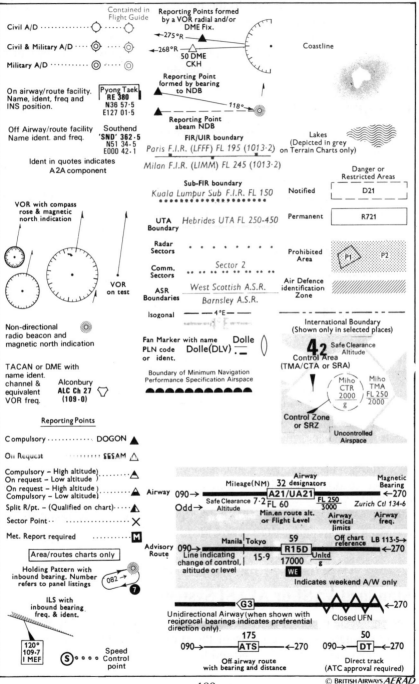

© British Airways *AERAD*

Where a horizontal line is incorporated in the table the heights shown below the line relate directly to the procedure, whereas those above the line are calculated to indicate the approach slope on an extension of the procedure up to approximately ten nautical miles from the A/D.

These advisory DME altitudes/heights are not valid when the aircraft is displaced from the extension to the procedure.

Hectopascals (hPa)

Some states are changing from millibars to hectopascals as the unit of measurement for altimeter setting.

Hectopascals are numerically equivalent to millibars and as such no conversion is necessary.

New specification AERAD approach charts will show either mb or hPa adjacent to the threshold elevation in the profile.

Visual Descent Point

On some procedures a Visual Descent Point (VDP) is published.

This is a defined point on the final approach path of a non-precision, straight-in approach from which normal descent from the MDA (minimum descent altitude) to the runway touch-down point may be commenced providing that the approach lights or other markings identifiable with the approach end of that runway are clearly visible to the pilot.

The MDA concerned should be that published by the State which may not necessarily coincide with the ADM published in company operations manuals.

The VDP will normally be identifiable by DME or VOR and Locator procedures and by seventy-five MHz marker beacons on NDB procedures. They are not a mandatory part of the procedure but one intended to provide additional guidance when used in conjunction with the VASI.

Pilots of aircraft not able to use the VDP for any reason should fly the approach as though no VDP is provided.

Visual Approach Slope Indicator
Standard VASI or AVASI System

The full system comprises twelve units which are arranged to form two lighted wingbars on each side of the runway and which project white light above the glide-slope and red below. They are generally located at

150 metres and 300 metres up the runway with the innermost lights positioned not less than fifteen metres outside the runway edge.

An abbreviated VASI system (AVASI) is one where a reduced number of light units are used for each wing are either on one, or both, sides of the runway.

During an approach the aircraft should remain within the white sector of the nearer bars and the red sector of the further bars in order to touch-down at the correct point. If both bars are red the aircraft is too low, if white, the aircraft is too high. If well below the glide-path the red bars will tend to merge into one bold signal on each side of the runway, and care must be taken not to continue an approach in the pink sector of the nearer bars.

Pilots are advised of the following operational considerations when using VASIs.

1. At maximum range on the approach slope the white bars of the system may become visible before the red bars and under certain conditions may appear yellowish.

2. In poor visibility both pairs of red bars may not be seen until reaching the runway threshold and the system can then be used only to indicate a possible undershoot.

3. The azimuth coverage of the system varies between 10° either side of the centre-line in daylight and 15° either side at night. Indications may be visible in areas where obstruction clearance protection is not guaranteed and they should not be used for approach slope guidance until the aircraft is aligned with the runway.

4 On precision approach runways the VASI normally brackets the ILS or GCA glide-path but in certain cases it is not possible to achieve mutual alignment. The divergence of the VASI red/white channel is normally contained within 1½ dots fly-up to the 1½ dots fly-down sector of the ILS where full-scale deflection is equivalent to five dots. Where the ILS and GCA glide-path deviation to maximum tolerance and other factors have a cumulative effect, a red/red or white/white VASI signal may coincide with an 'on glide-path' signal from the ILS or GCA and it should be borne in mind that where a VASI signal other than red/white is observed during the final stages of an approach, adjustment to the flight path should be made.

5. Captains of long-bodied aircraft are warned that they should not rely on this system for approach slope guidance since this would cause the

aircraft to touch down too soon. At some airfields the standard system has been modified by the addition of two more sets of wingbars (one either side) known as the three-bar VASI. This enables long-bodied aircraft to carry out a safe approach using VASI. A full description of this system is contained in the following pages.

Visual Approach Slope Indicator
Three-Bar VASI System

The addition of a third (upper) bar to the standard VASI results in the three-bar VASI system. This system ensures sufficient wheel clearance over the threshold for very large aircraft where there can be a significant difference in height (i.e. in excess of approx fifteen feet) between the pilot's eye and the landing gear.

Long-bodied aircraft should use the second and third (upper) bars and ignore the first (lower) bar. Flying on the low side of the second and third bars would cause the touchdown point to be 570 feet, or less, while flying on the high side would cause the touchdown point to be at 1,450 feet or more. This would give a wheel height across the threshold of thirty feet on the low side and eighty-eight feet on the high side.

Other aircraft types should use the first and second bars and ignore the third (upper) bar.

Correct selection of the pair of bars appropriate to the aircraft type is essential. Flying the wrong pair could result in an unacceptably long, or short, touch-down.

Note: In the lighting table on AERAD aerodrome/landing charts the abbreviation LB is used to signify a three-bar VASI.

Visual Approach Slope Indicator
('T' Type VASI System)

The system consists of one group of lights on each side of the runway arranged in the form of a 'T'. Glide-slope indication is obtained by the relative appearance of the 'T's.

On the correct glide-slope (normally 3°), only the crossbars of the 'T' will appear. Should the full 'T's appear with the legs towards the approaching aircraft, the aircraft is below the correct glide-slope, whilst the appearance of the legs in the opposite direction indicates an approach above the glide-slope.

The azimuth spread through which the system is visible in the approach phase varies between day and night. Normally the azimuth cover for daylight operation is 10° either side of the extended runway centre-line whilst at night the cover is not less than 15° either side of the centre-line. As the system is visible in areas where obstruction clearance protection is not guaranteed, it must not be used for approach slope guidance until the aircraft is aligned with the runway. Because of the large azimuth cover the system does provide information to aircraft on base leg but this information should not be solely relied on for descent purposes.

During light ground-fog conditions all the white lights of the system (crossbar, fly up and fly down) may be visible at the same time. This phenomenon is the result of lights from the 'T' VASI units being reflected from water droplets adjacent to the units. Under these conditions the pilot will see, in addition to the direct light from the 'T' VASi, reflected lights from the fly up and fly down lights. The reflected light has a fuzzy appearance and is less distinct than the direct lights. It will be apparent to the pilot that this signal is abnormal and the approach should be made on the direct light. If there is any doubt the 'T' VASI should not be used.

Visual Approach Slope Indicator
Non Standard VASI (French)

The French authorities have equipped certain aerodromes in their territories with a VASI system which does not conform to the ICAO standard specification.

This system comprises two groups of three lights in the form of a triangle positioned on each side of the approach end of the runway. A runway may only have one group and in this case it will be positioned to the left of the runway.

All lights have white characteristics and glide-slope guidance is obtained by the relative brilliance of the apex lights and the base lights of the triangle or triangles.

On the correct glide-slope all lights will have equal brilliance. If the apex light is brighter the aircraft is above the glide-path and if the base lights are brighter it is below the glide-path.

Precision Approach Path Indicator (PAPI)

The Precision Approach Path Indicator (PAPI) is a development of the VASI and uses the same principle giving red and white visual signals indicating the required approach angle. The essential differences are the number and arrangement of the light units and their interpretation.

With PAPI the pink transition sector is virtually eliminated, giving a sharp transition characteristic.

In a full PAPI array eight units are mounted in wing bars, four units either side of the runway adjacent to the touch-down point. The outermost units are set ½° lower than the required approach angle with progressive increments of setting angle for each unit inboard, the innermost unit being ½° higher than the approach angle. If greater threshold crossing heights are required for aircraft with large eye-to-wheel-heights, the wing bar is positioned above 120 metres further upwind and the on slope channel opened out to ½°. More commonly PAPI is installed as a four-unit array located on the left-hand side of the runway.

Low Intensity Two-Colour Approach Slope System (LITAS)

LITAS is a simplified version of the standard VASI system. It consists of one unit upwind and one unit downwind, usually on the left-hand side of the runway and is a low intensity system designed to be used at night but it can also be useful in poor light conditions during the day.

Pulse Light Approach Slope Indicator (PLASI)

This installation is aligned to a 3° glide-slope and is located on the left-hand side of the runway fifteen metres outside the R/W edge and 150 metres upwind from the threshold.

The system emits pulsing white and red lights to indicate when the aircraft is too high or too low. A steady white light indicates when the aircraft is on the glide-path and a steady red light signifies the aircraft is just below the glide-path.

Chopper Approach Path Indicator (CHAPI)

The installation consists of two boxes placed side by side three metres apart emitting white, green and red signals.

If set for a 7° approach; green will be observed from both boxes at between 6½° and 7½°. With any tendency to fly low the right-hand box will change to red while the left-hand box will remain green. If the aircraft remains low both boxes will indicate red.

Should the approach be high the boxes will show white and green respectively, changing to white if the approach remains high.

Safe Clearance Altitudes

Altitudes shown thus 42 (4,200 ft amsl), indicate safe clearance above highest known terrain and notified obstructions within degrees of latitude and longitude, in accordance with the table below. The symbol ± indicates an estimated value in areas where relief date is incomplete.

Where the above method of portrayal is not used, the Safe Clearance Altitudes are shown along airways thus, 7.5 (7,500 ft amsl) and indicate safe clearance above highest known terrain and notified obstructions within a thirty nm range of a prescribed track and include a semi-circular area of thirty nm radius at either end of the track, in accordance with the table below.

The altitudes have been established from the best available maps but warning is given that contours and spot-heights shown on these maps can be inaccurate.

Elevation of Obstacle	Vertical Clearance
Up to and including 5,000 ft	1,000 ft
Above 5,000 ft up to and including 10,000 ft	1,500 ft *
Above 10,000 ft	2,000 ft

* AERAD charts are being changed to conform with CAA requirements for a minimum clearance of 2,000 feet for terrain or obstacles above 5,000 ft (CAP 360, Chap 2/15 April 1990).

General

1.1 Not only are there different AERAD chart specifications but there are also two different criteria used for the construction of Instrument Approach Procedures. The new criteria, introduced recently by ICAO, produce charts which look very much the same as before, however, some important changes have been made which must be fully understood and which are described in subsequent paragraphs.
Since nearly every Instrument Approach Procedure has to be re-surveyed or re-drawn, it is taking time for State Aviation Authorities to amend their procedures to conform to the new criteria. During this changeover period, charts drawn to both the old and the new criteria will co-exist. It is essential, therefore, that pilots should be able to identify which criteria apply to the procedure in use.

1.2 All procedures drawn to the new criteria use OCA/H as the basic obstacle clearance element for calculating minima.

All procedures drawn to the old criteria will continue to use OCL (Obstacle Clearance Limit).

1.3 To identify the criteria in use, look for the letters OCH (or OCL) as shown below:

On new specification MSA contour Charts:

Elev	OCH
202	Cat 1 A140,B151,C164,D182. Cat 2 A48,B59;C72,D84. LLZ 550.

Changes Introduced by the New ICAO Criteria

Aircraft Categories

ICAO have grouped aircraft into the following categories according to their threshold speeds.

Aircraft Category	Vat	Range of speeds for initial approach	Range of final approach speeds	Max Speeds for Visual Manoeuvring (Circling)	Max Speeds for Missed Approach	
					Inter-mediate	Final
A	91	90/150 (110*)	70/100	100	100	110
B	91/120	120/180 (140*)	85/130	135	130	150
C	121/140	160/240	115/160	180	160	240
D	141/165	185/250	130/185	205	185	265
E	166/210	185/250	155/230	240	230	275

Vat – Speed at threshold based on 1.3 times stall speed in the landing configuration at maximum certificated landing weight.

* – Maximum speed for reversal and race-track procedures.

These speeds have been used to calculate the airspace and obstacle clearance required for each procedure. Normally, procedures are designed to provide protected clearance for all aircraft categories up to and including C and D. However, where airspace requirements are critical, procedures may be restricted to either a lower speed category, or a specified maximum IAS.

It is essential that pilots comply with the procedures and speed limits applicable to their aircraft's category.

Typical aircraft categories are as follows :

Category	Aircraft Type
A	All Helicopters
B	HS 748
C	1-11, B737, B757
D	L1011, B747, Concorde

Note 1. AERAD will not publish any procedures for Cat E aircraft.

Note 2. Where States publish variations of the same basic procedure for different aircraft categories, AERAD will draw the procedure for the faster category (usually C and D) on the plan and annotate it accordingly. The procedural differences for the slower categories will be noted in the Warnings Box.

Procedure Turns

Direct Entry to Procedure Turn
Unless specified otherwide the procedure shall be entered from a track within 30° either side of the outbound track of the procedure turn.

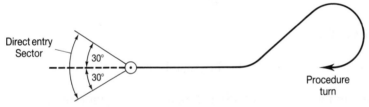

Procedure Turn 45°/180°
Timing shall commence from start of turn

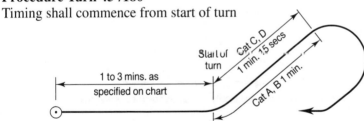

Procedure Turn 80°/260°

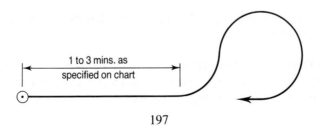

197

AERAD charts will always show the State published procedure. Pilots may substitute either type of procedure turn for the other, unless specifically excluded by a note in the Warnings Box.

Base Turns

Direct Entry to Base Turn
Base turns shall be entered from a track within 30° either side of the outbound track. (Where this direct entry sector does not include the reciprocal of the inbound track, the sector is expanded to include it).

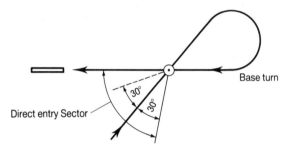

The Base Turn

Timing and track from the facility shall be as specified on the chart.

A base turn may **not** be substituted for a procedure turn (or vice versa).

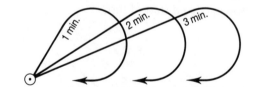

Timing and track from the facility shall be as specified on the chart

Race-Track Procedures

A race-track procedure is a new type of intermediate procedure. It is not a holding pattern.

Entry to Race-track Procedures
Race-track procedures shall be entered in the same way as holding patterns, but with the following differences:

(a) Offset entry from sector 2.

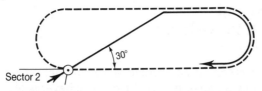

The time on the 30° offset track shall be no more than 1 min. 30 sec, after which, the pilot shall turn to a heading to parallel the outbound track for the remainder of the outbound time. If the outbound time is only 1 min, the time on the 30° offset track shall be 1 minute also.

(b) Parallel entry from Sector 1.

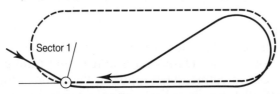

When proceeding to the final segment of the approach procedure, aircraft shall intercept the inbound track and not return direct to the facility.

(c) All manoeuvring shall be done in so far as possible on the manoeuvring side of the inbound track.

The Race-Track

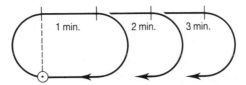

(a) When a race-track is based on a facility, the outbound timing shall start from abeam a facility, or on attaining the outbound heading, whichever comes later.

(b) When a race-track is based on a fix, the outbound timing shall start from attaining the outbound heading.

(c) The turn back on to the inbound track shall be started within the specified time, or on reaching any DME distance, or the radial/bearing specifying a limiting distance, whichever comes first.

All Entry Procedures, Procedure Turns, Base Turns and Race-Track Procedures

Bank Angle
Procedures are based on an average achieved bank angle of 25°, or the bank angle giving a rate of turn of 3°/sec, whichever is less.

Descent
Aircraft shall cross the fix or facility and fly outbound on the specified track descending as necessary to the specified altitude. If a further descent is specified after the inbound turn, this descent shall not be started until established within 5° of the inbound track.

Wind Effect
The pilot shall make due allowance in both heading and timing for the effects of known wind. Outbound headings and timings should be adjusted to achieve correct interception of the inbound track. When a limiting DME distance or radial/bearing is specified, it shall not be exceeded when flying on the outbound track.

Final Approach Segment

Precision Approach
The final approach segment begins at the Final Approach Point (FAP) — the point on the centre-line of the localiser at which the intermediate approach altitude intersects the glide-path.

Descent on the glide-path shall not be initiated until the aircraft is established within a half-scale deflection of the localiser.

A fix or facility, usually the outer marker, is provided to permit verification of the glide-path/altimeter relationship. Descent below the fix crossing altitude should not be made before crossing the fix.

Non-Precision Approach
The final approach segment begins at the Final Approach Fix (FAF) and ends at the Missed Approach Point (MAP). The FAF should be crossed at or above the specified altitude before descent is initiated. When no FAF is shown, descent should not be initiated until the aircraft is established inbound within 5° of the final approach track.

Step down fixes should, if depicted, be crossed at or above their associated minimum crossing altitudes.

Descent Slope Guidance

Where a suitable DME exists, descent slope guidance will be provided in the form of a table of altitudes/heights against DME distances. This information is not mandatory but is provided to assist pilots on straight-in and non-precision approaches.

Obstacle Clearance Altitude/Height (OCA/H

OCA/H is the lowest altitude (OCA), or alternatively, the lowest height (OCH) above the relevant runway threshold (or aerodrome elevation), used in establishing compliance with the appropriate obstacle clearance criteria.

All OCA/Hs include a suitable height margin dependent on aircraft category.

All charts drawn to the new criteria will show the relevant OCHs at the top of the chart. In the absence of AERAD AOM pages, minima may be calculated from these figures by using the information contained in the appropriate Operations Manual. Pilots should take particular care to ensure that they select the correct OCH for their aircraft category and the procedure in use.

Missed Approach Point (MAP)

This is the point in an instrument approach procedure at or before which the prescribed missed approach must be initiated in order to ensure that the minimum obstacle clearance is not infringed. A missed approach must be carried out if the missed approach point is reached before visual reference is acquired.

If a turn is specified in the missed approach procedure, the turn shall not be initiated until the a/c has passed the MAP and is established in climb.

Pilots should be aware that the MAP is not necessarily a point in space from which a safe landing can be made.

Precision Approach

The missed approach point is defined by the intersection of the glide-path with the relevant Decision Altitude/Height (DA/H) and therefore is not shown on the chart.

No Glide-path Approach (LLZ)

The MAP is normally located at the middle marker in which case it is not shown on the chart. The (LLZ) map is only shown when it is defined by other means.

All other Non-Precision Approaches

The MAP is defined by either a fix, a facility or by timing and is shown on both the plan and the profile. When it is defined by a fix or a facility, timing shall not be used to determine the MAP since the radio fix tolerance is considerably smaller than the timing tolerance.

The timing table shows times from the FAF to the threshold of the landing runway except when the MAP is defined by timing. In this case only, the times shown are those from the FAF to the MAP.

Missed Approach

For the purposes of providing sufficient obstacle clearance, the missed approach is assumed to be initiated not lower than the DA/H in precision approaches, or at the MAP and not lower than MDA/H in a non-precision approach. A short initial phase is allowed for establishing the climb, thereafter the aircraft is assumed to climb at a gradient of not less than 2.5%. It must be emphasised that not all aircraft can achieve this gradient with an engine out, at maximum certificated gross weight.

This 2.5% gradient is assumed to extend up to a point at which the aircraft can fly level for 6 nms to accelerate and clean up. Normally this horizontal segment is a minumum of 820 feet, above the aerodrome elevation, however, when obstacle clearance requires it, the height of the horizontal segment is raised and the procedure annotated accordingly.

Pilots must ensure that they do not accelerate and clean up their aircraft below 820 feet above aerodrome elevation or the specified minimum altitude as shown above.

Note: Company Ops Manuals may specify a higher acceleration altitude.

Appendix A

Definitions

Aerodrome Elevation
The elevation of the highest point of the landing area.

Base Turn
A turn executed by the aircraft during the initial approach between the end of the outbound track and the beginning of the intermediate or final approach track.

Circling Approach
An extension of an instrument approach procedure which provides for visual circling of the aerodrome prior to landing.

Decision Altitude/Height
A specified altitude/height in the precision approach at which a missed approach must be initiated if the required visual reference to continue the approach has not been established.

Flight Level (FL)
A surface of constant atmospheric pressure which is related to a specific pressure datum, 1013 mbs.

Altimeters when set to QNH will indicate Altitude
Altimeters when set to QFE will indicate Height.
Altimeters when set to 1013 (QNE) will indicate Flight Level.

Minimum Descent Altitude/Height
A specified altitude/height in a non-precision approach below which descent may not be made without visual reference.

Minimum Sector Altitude
The lowest altitude which may be used under emergency conditions which will provide a minimum clearance of 1,000 ft above all objects located in an area contained within a sector of a circle twenty-five nms radius centred on a radio aid to navigation.

Missed Approach Point
That point in an instrument approach procedure at or before which the prescribed missed approach procedure must be initiated in order to ensure that the minimum obstacle clearance is not infringed.

Procedure Turn
A manoeuvre in which a turn is made away from a designated track followed by a turn in the opposite direction to permit the aircraft to intercept and proceed along the reciprocal of the designated track.

Transition Altitude
The altitude at or below which the vertical position of an aircraft is controlled by reference to altitudes.

Transition Level
The lowest flight level available for use above the transition altitude.

Transition Layer
The airspace between the transition level and transition altitude.

Appendix B

Abbreviations

ATC	Air Traffic Control
ATS	Air Traffic Service
C/L	Centre-line
DA/H	Decision Altitude/Height
DME	Distance Measuring Equipment
FAF	Final Approach Fix
FAP	Final Approach Point
GP	Glide-path
IAF	Initial Approach Fix
IAS	Indicated Air-speed
IF	Intermediate Approach Fix
ILS	Instrument Landing System
ISA	International Standard Atmosphere
LLZ	Localiser
MAPt	Missed Approach Point
MDA/H	Minimum Descent Altitude/Height
MM	Middle Marker
MSA	Minimum Sector Altitude
MSL	Mean Sea-level
NDB	Non Directional Beacon
OM	Outer Marker
PAR	Precision Approach Radar
RAS	Radar Advisory Service

Appendix C

The CAP 54

CHAPTER 14   THE INSTRUMENT RATING (AEROPLANES)

14.1   THE INSTRUMENT RATING PRIVILEGES

14.1.1   The privileges of the Instrument Rating (Aeroplanes) are specified in Schedule 8 to the Air Navigation Order. In general terms, the holder of a professional pilot's licence (aeroplanes) is required to hold a valid Instrument Rating:

14.1.1.1   on any flight as pilot-in-command (PIC) or co-pilot in controlled airspace notified for the purpose of Schedule 8 of the Air Navigation Order (ANO): or

14.1.1.1.1   in conditions such that the pilot cannot comply with the specified weather provisions; or

14.1.1.1.2   in circumstances which require compliance with Instrument Flight Rules.

14.1.1.2   as PIC on a scheduled journey;

14.1.1.3   as PIC of an aeroplane exceeding 2300 kg maximum total weight authorised flying for the purposes of public transport, except a flight beginning and ending at the same aerodrome and not extending beyond 25 nautical miles from that aerodrome;

14.1.1.4   as PIC at night when passengers are carried or flying instruction is given, unless the licence holder has certain specified recent night flying experience.

14.1.2   A BCPL(A) or CPL(A) may be issued without it having to contain an Instrument Rating but its privileges will not include flights under the circumstances detailed above.

14.1.3   An ATPL(A) will not be issued unless the applicant has qualified for inclusion in the licence of an Instrument Rating. Should the rating at any time become invalid, the privileges of the licence will be restricted accordingly.

14.1.4   The flight test for the Instrument Rating (Aeroplanes) is normally conducted in a multi-engine aeroplane, other than a centreline thrust aeroplane, as if it were being flown by a single flight crew member. This is regarded as the most demanding case and the privileges conferred by a rating gained as the result of such a test may be exercised in single-engine or multi-engine and single-crew or multi-crew aeroplanes.

14.1.5   An applicant for a flight test for the Instrument Rating (Aeroplanes) to be conducted in a multi-engine aeroplane, other than a centre-line thrust aeroplane, must hold a current type or group rating on multi-engine aeroplanes, or have passed the 1179 flight test (or Group B rating flight test) in the previous 6 months. The applicant must provide documentary evidence of such a qualification to the Flight Examiner prior to undertaking the first attempt in a series.

14.1.6   At the applicant's request, however, the test may be conducted in:

14.1.6.1   a single-engine aeroplane. The rating will be endorsed accordingly and its privileges may be exercised only in single-engine aeroplanes;

14.1.6.2 a multi-crew aeroplane. The rating will be endorsed accordingly and its privileges may be exercised only in aeroplanes certificated for two pilots. Grant of such a restricted rating is normally confined to service pilots who have qualified in the UK military forces and who hold a current Procedural Instrument Rating, or to holders of a current SCPL(A) or ATPL(A) and Instrument Rating issued by another ICAO Contracting State. The test will normally be conducted only in aeroplanes requiring two pilots when flying for the purpose of public transport in compliance with the Instrument Flight Rules.

14.1.7 Should an applicant wish to take the Instrument Rating flight test in a centreline thrust multi-engine aeroplane he should consult the CAA (FCL 4) on what approved training, if any, and flight test requirements have to be met, and on what restrictions may be placed on the rating privileges.

14.2 APPROVED TRAINING

14.2.1 Unless qualifying for exemption as detailed in paragraph 14.2.4, persons wishing to obtain an Instrument Rating (Aeroplanes) will, before they may take the Instrument Rating flight test, be required to complete an approved course of training. This will comprise:

14.2.1.1 for an unrestricted rating, not less than 45 hours dual instruction in instrument flying. This must include not less than 25 hours dual instruction in instrument flying in single-engine or multi-engine aeroplanes, of which not less than 15 hours must be in multi-engine aeroplanes. The remaining experience, up to a maximum of 20 hours, may be gained in an approved flight simulator or an approved procedure trainer;

14.2.1.2 for a rating with privileges restricted to single-engine aeroplanes, not less than 40 hours dual instruction in instrument flying. This must include not less than 20 hours in single-engined aeroplanes. The remaining experience, up to a maximum of 20 hours, may be gained in an approved flight simulator or an approved procedure trainer;

14.2.1.3 for the holder of a rating restricted to single-engine aeroplanes wishing to obtain an unrestricted rating, not less than five hours dual instruction in instrument flying in multi-engine aeroplanes.

14.2.2 The experience gained on an approved course of training may be counted toward satisfying the experience requirements for the rating as specified in paragraph 14.3.

14.2.3 A list of flying training organisations (FTOs) which conduct approved courses of training for the Instrument Rating (Aeroplanes) may be obtained from the CAA (FCL 3) at the address given in Appendix A.

14.2.4 **Exemption from approved training**

Exemption from having to undergo an approved course of training will normally be given to the following :

14.2.4.1 *Holders of a UK Instrument Rating (Helicopters)*

Pilots who hold, or have held within the three years preceding the date of receipt in the CAA of the application for the Instrument Rating (Aeroplanes), a valid UK Instrument Rating (Helicopters).

The CAP 54

14.2.4.2   *UK military pilots*

Qualified service pilots in the UK military forces who meet the experience requirements specified in paragraph 14.3.2.

14.2.4.3   *Other experienced pilots*

Pilots meeting the detailed experience requirements as specified in paragraphs 4.5.6 to 4.5.8.5.

14.2.5   **Reduction of Approved Training**

14.2.5.1   *Holders of a valid UK IMC rating*

The minimum training requirements as laid down in paragraph 14.2 may be reduced for pilots holding a UK PPL which includes a valid IMC Rating. The reduced requirements are tabulated at Appendix M.

14.3   **FLYING EXPERIENCE REQUIREMENTS**

14.3.1   The normal method of recording flight time and the way in which it will be credited toward meeting the flying experience requirements is given in Appendix C.

14.3.2   The minimum flying experience required for grant of an Instrument Rating (Aeroplanes) to a pilot who does not already hold an Instrument Rating (Helicopters) is 200 hours as pilot of aeroplanes, which must include:

14.3.2.1   not less than 100 hours as PIC, of which not less than 35 hours must be cross-country flying;

14.3.2.2   not less than 40 hours as pilot by sole reference to instruments, of which up to 20 hours may be in an approved flight simulator, approved procedure trainer or helicopter.

14.3.3   Where a pilot holds, or has held within the three years preceding the date of receipt in the CAA of the application for the Instrument Rating (Aeroplanes), a valid Instrument Rating (Helicopters), the minimum experience required in aeroplanes is:

14.3.3.1   50 hours as PIC, of which not less than 20 hours must be cross-country flying;

14.3.3.2   20 hours as pilot by sole reference to instruments. Up to 10 hours of this may be in an approved aeroplane simulator.

14.3.4   Flight time in microlight aeroplanes, as defined in the footnote to Appendix C, may not be counted toward satisfying any of the requirements specified in paragraphs 14.3.2 or 14.3.3. Flight time in self-launching motor gliders may not be counted toward satisfying the minimum PIC or pilot by sole reference to instruments requirements and may only be counted toward satisfying the total experience requirements specified in paragraph 14.3.2 when the aircraft is under power.

Instrument Flying

14.4 GROUND EXAMINATION REQUIREMENTS

Persons who have passed the ground examinations for grant of a professional pilot's licence, or who have been exempted from having to take them, will not normally be required to take any ground examinations for grant of an Instrument Rating.

14.5 THE INSTRUMENT RATING FLIGHT TEST

14.5.1 All applicants for the grant of an Instrument Rating (Aeroplanes) will be required to pass an Instrument Rating Flight test conducted by a CAA Flight Examiner. The test for an unrestricted rating will be conducted in a multi-engine aeroplane (other than a centreline thrust aeroplane; see paragraph 14.1.6) having a UK Certificate of Airworthiness which permits it to be flown by a single flight crew member. The syllabus for the test comprises;

Section 1 : Departure procedures

Section 2 : Airways procedures

Section 3 : ILS instrument approach procedure

Section 4 : NDB or VOR instrument approach procedure

NOTE: At the conclusion of Section 3, the applicant will be asked to carry out a missed approach from decision height in the course of which and at a safe height an engine failure will be simulated. Section 4 will then be conducted on asymmetric power and will terminate at minimum descent height after the applicant has levelled the aircraft and has given the Flight Examiner an estimate of the time or distance to run to the aerodrome boundary, runway threshold or the facility, as appropriate.

Sub-section A : Preliminary and external checks

Sub-section B : Holding procedures

Sub-section C : Engine failure procedures

14.5.2 The full syllabus for the test, the conditions and assumptions upon which it will be conducted and the level of acceptable performance are given in Appendix M.

14.5.3 The test syllabus for a rating restricted to multi-crew aeroplanes is the same as that for an unrestricted rating, but there may be minor variations in the conduct of the test. These will be explained by the Flight Examiner before the test begins.

14.5.4 The test syllabus for a rating restricted to single-engine aeroplanes is the same as that given in paragraph 14.5.1, less Sub-section C and with no simulation of engine failure as referred to in the Note.

14.5.5 In the test for an unrestricted or single-engine rating, the applicant will be required to fly the aeroplane from the PIC position and to carry out the test as if he were the sole flight crew member. The Flight Examiner will, however, be the designated PIC.

14.5.6   In the test for a multi-crew rating, the applicant may take the test as handling pilot in either the PIC or in the co-pilot position and will be expected to call upon the other flight crew members to assist him in the conduct of the flight in accordance with the normal crew drills for that type of aeroplane. Where the Flight Examiner occupies the PIC or co-pilot position, he will be designated as PIC of the aeroplane. Where he does not occupy either of these positions, the pilot occupying either one who is not undergoing the test will be designated as PIC and must be a person authorised by the operator of the aeroplane to act as a training or check captain on the type.

14.5.7   The applicant, together with the remainder of the flight crew in the case of a test on a multi-crew aeroplane, will be briefed by the Flight Examiner before the test. The applicant will be responsible for ensuring that he has all equipment and documentation necessary for the planning and execution of the flight.

14.5.8   The route for the test flight will be chosen by the Flight Examiner. It may start and finish at the same aerodrome or may end at another aerodrome. The applicant may not decline to fly the nominated route solely because he is not familiar with it. He should be prepared to be examined along any route terminating at a suitably equipped aerodrome within 150 nm of departure.

14.5.9   **The combined GFT/IR test**

For students who have completed an unabridged course of training for grant of a CPL(A) and Instrument Rating (see paragraph 4.4.3), the Instrument Rating flight test is combined with the General Flight Test. The combined GFT/IR test is conducted to a syllabus and under arrangements agreed by the CAA with the FTOs which conduct such combined courses. The student will be given all the information he needs concerning the test by the FTO which carries out his training. Details are not included in this publication.

14.6   INSTRUMENT RATING FLIGHT TEST: PASS CONDITIONS

14.6.1   Before an applicant may take the Instrument Rating flight test he must obtain a form FCL 170A, signed by a person authorised to sign such forms, certifying that he has satisfactorily completed any training which may have been required of him and that, in the judgement of the person signing the form, he is fully ready to take the test. This requirement will apply whether or not the applicant has had to undergo an approved course of training. The 170A is valid for a period of 6 months from the date of signature and the first attempt to pass the test must be taken within this period of validity. If a partial pass is obtained during this period, then the 170A may be extended to allow the candidate to complete satisfactorily all the outstanding items within a period of six months from the date of first obtaining a partial pass. If the candidate fails to pass the test during this extended validity period, the 170A is cancelled.

14.6.2   All four sections and three sub-sections (two sub-sections in the case of a test in a single-engine aeroplane) of the test must be taken at the first attempt.

14.6.3   An applicant is required to demonstrate that he can satisfactorily complete in one flight any three sections of the four sections. He will be required to take the failed section again in the next attempt at the test, together with such other items in the test as may have been failed.

14.6.4   In the course of a re-test, Section 1 (Departure Procedures) will be re-tested regardless of any previous satisfactory completion of this section. Also, if in course of re-test the applicant is required for operational reasons to take up a hold, he will be re-assessed on Sub-section B, whether or not there is a test requirement to take the sub-section again.

14.6.5   Where, under the provisions of paragraphs 14.6.3 and 14.6.4, the applicant has to take only part of the test again, he must satisfactorily complete all the outstanding items within a period of six months from the date of first obtaining a partial pass, or the whole of the test must be taken again.

14.6.6   Failure to achieve a valid pass in all sections and required sub-sections of the test in three attempts, including attempts at outstanding items following a partial pass, will exhaust the first series of attempts the applicant is permitted to make and require him, before he may make the first attempt in the second series, to:

14.6.6.1   complete in the six months preceding the date of receipt in the CAA of the application for the first test in the second series such further training as the CAA may prescribe;

14.6.6.2   obtain a form FCL 170A, signed by a person authorised to sign such forms certifying that the prescribed training has been satisfactorily completed and that the applicant is fully ready to take the test.

14.6.7   The first attempt in the second series will cover the whole test and the series will be subject to the same pass conditions as the first series. If, within three attempts at the test in the second series, including attempts at outstanding items following a partial pass, the applicant has still not obtained a valid pass in all sections and required sub-sections of the test, he will, before he may start the third series of attempts, be required to:

14.6.7.1   show that he has not less than 500 hours experience as pilot-in-command of aeroplanes;

14.6.7.2   complete in the six months preceding the date of receipt in the CAA of the application for the first test in the third series, an approved course of training as specified in paragraph 14.2.1.1 or 14.2.1.2 as appropriate;

14.6.7.3   obtain a form FCL 170A, signed by a person authorised to sign such forms, certifying that he has satisfactorily completed the required training and is fully ready to take the test.

14.6.8   The first two attempts at the test in the third series will be conducted subject to the same pass conditions as in the earlier series. If a third attempt is necessary, however, even though it may be within six months of the applicant having gained a partial pass, the whole of the test will have to be taken again.

14.6.9   If, at the conclusion of the third attempt in the third series, the applicant has still not obtained a valid pass in all sections and required sub-sections of the test, he will be considered unsuitable to hold an Instrument Rating and will not normally be permitted to make any further attempts at the Instrument Rating test. The CAA will, however, without prejudice to his rights under the Civil Aviation Authority Regulations (see paragraph 1.7), be prepared, at his written request, to review the circumstances and results of all the tests he has taken to determine whether any further attempt may be permitted. Any such further attempt, if allowed, would be subject to such conditions as the CAA may decide to impose.

14.6.10   **Termination of a test by the applicant**

Once a test has started, should the applicant choose not to continue with it for reasons not considered adequate by the Flight Examiner, he will be regarded as having failed those items not attempted. Failure of the test on these grounds will be counted against the number of attempts the applicant is permitted to make.

14.6.11   **Termination of a test by the Examiner**

The Examiner may stop the test at any stage if he considers that the candidate's standard of flying warrants a complete re-test.

14.7   FLIGHT TEST ARRANGEMENTS

14.7.1   There are Instrument Rating flight test centres at Bournemouth/Hurn, Perth/Scone, Cambridge, Cranfield and Leeds/Bradford aerodromes. Examiners are also available at Oxford/Kidlington and Prestwick aerodromes.

14.7.2   Where an applicant for an Instrument Rating has undergone an approved course of training, arrangements for the flight test, including the provision of a suitable aircraft, will normally be made by the FTO which conducted the training. It will also normally provide the applicant with a form FCL 170A certifying that, in its judgement, he is fully ready to take the test. This must be produced to the CAA Flight Examiner conducting the test.

14.7.3   Applicants who have been exempted from having to undergo an approved course of training will be required to make their own arrangements for the test with the CAA (See Appendix A), stating the preferred location. They must also make their own arrangements to provide an aircraft for the test. Such aircraft must be maintained and equipped to CAA requirements and be approved by the Authority for the conduct of the test, including the method of ensuring that it can be flown by sole reference to instruments. Visors will not be acceptable for this purpose. Full details concerning the test aircraft requirements are contained in CAA Document No. 7 obtainable from the test booking office referred to above.

14.7.4   Applicants who have been exempted from having to undergo an approved course of training will also be required to produce to the Flight Examiner who is to conduct the test a form FCL 170A as prescribed in paragraph 14.6.1.

14.7.5   Payment of the statutory charge for the test must be made to CAA (FCL) in advance.

Instrument Flying

14.8 THE INSTRUMENT RATING CERTIFICATE OF TEST

14.8.1 The privileges of an Instrument Rating may not be exercised unless the licence contains a valid Certificate of Test (C of T) in respect of the functions to which the rating relates. The period of validity of a C of T in relation to an Instrument Rating is 13 months from the date of effect of the certificate.

14.8.2 On grant of an Instrument Rating the C of T will be completed by the CAA with a date of effect as from the date on which the Instrument Rating flight test was successfully completed.

14.8.3 Before the certificate can be completed again the licence holder must pass a further test conducted by a CAA Flight Examiner, or by an authorised Instrument Rating Examiner (IRE), in an aeroplane or in an approved flight simulator. Access to such simulators can normally only be obtained through the operator who holds the simulator approval. Most operators have on their own staff, or have an arrangement with, an IRE able to conduct test on their pilots. Alternatively, the CAA (FCL4) will provide names of IREs with whom it should be possible to arrange a test. Payment for the test will be a matter between the applicant and the IRE concerned.

14.8.4 Any suitable means of simulating instrument flight conditions in an aeroplane may be used, including the use of visors.

14.8.5 The test will comprise, Section 1, Departure procedures, Section 2, Airways procedures, and a modified Section 3, ILS instrument approach procedure, consisting of an approach to land, go-around and missed approach procedure, Sub-section A, Preliminary and external checks, and Sub-section B, Holding procedures. Simulated failure of an engine and flight on asymmetric power will not be tested in Section 3.

14.8.6 A failure of more than one section of Sections 1, 2 and 3 will require the whole of the test to be taken again. If only one of these sections is failed the examiner, at his discretion, may ask the applicant to repeat the failed procedure during the course of the test. Should a further flight test be necessary, only the failed section need be taken again except that where a retest of Section 3 is required it will start from the holding pattern and the candidate will be re-assessed on Sub-section B as well as Section 3: If, in the course of any other retest, the applicant is required for operational reasons to take up a hold, he will be re-assessed on Sub-section B: In a retest of Sub-section B, Section 1 will also be retested. If in the course of a retest a section or sub-section which has previously been passed is performed unsatisfactorily a retest in that section or sub-section may be required at the discretion of the examiner.

14.8.7 The whole of the test must be satisfactorily completed within 30 days from the initial attempt, or all passes gained will become invalid and the whole of the test must be taken again in one attempt, the pass conditions applying as before.

14.8.8 On successful completion of the test, the C of T will be signed by the examiner who conducted it, with a date of effect as from the date on which the test was successfully completed.

214

The CAP 54

14.8.9   **Expiry of C of T by a period of more than five years**

If a period of more than five years has elapsed since the period of validity of the C of T expired, the licence holder will be required, before the C of T can be revalidated, to pass a full Instrument Rating flight test conducted by a CAA Flight Examiner as for the grant of the rating; see paragraph 14.5. On the test being passed, the C of T will be completed by the CAA effective from the date on which the test was concluded. Where a licence holder has remained in instrument flying practice, on a foreign licence and Instrument Rating or HM Forces Procedural Instrument Rating for example, this requirement may be waived. Advice should be sought from the CAA (FCL4).

14.9   TEST FOR REMOVAL OF THE MULTI-CREW OR SINGLE-ENGINE AEROPLANE RESTRICTION

14.9.1   The holder of an Instrument Rating valid only for multi-crew aeroplanes or only for single-engine aeroplanes may have the restriction removed by passing a flight test conducted by a CAA Flight Examiner in an aeroplane of the type specified in paragraph 14.5.1, with the applicant acting as sole flight crew member. The arrangements to be observed for the test are as described in paragraph 14.7. Visors will not be acceptable as a means of ensuring flight by sole reference to instruments.

14.9.2   For removal of the multi-crew restriction the test will be conducted to the same syllabus and subject to the same pass conditions as that for an unrestricted rating; see paragraphs 14.5.1 and 14.6. On the applicant passing the test, the CAA will remove the restriction on the rating and complete the C of T effective as from the date on which the test was completed.

14.9.3   Before the test can be taken for removal of the single-engine aeroplane restriction, the applicant will, unless he is exempt under the terms of paragraph 14.2.4, be required to complete an approved course of training as specified in paragraph 14.2.1.3.

14.9.4   The test for removal of the single-engine restriction will be that described in paragraph 14.5.1, less Section 2 and Sub-section B, except that if a holding procedure is operationally necessary the applicant will be assessed on it.

14.9.5   Successful completion of the test will allow removal by the CAA of the single-engine restriction from the rating, but will not allow the C of T to be revalidated. For this to be done, the applicant will also be required to pass Section 2, Airways procedures, and Sub-section B, Holding procedures. Applicants wishing to have these items included in the test should request it at the time of making the arrangement for the test.

Professional pilots' licences

14.9.6   A failure of more than one of Sections 1, 2 if taken, 3 and 4 will require the whole test to be taken again. If only one of these sections is failed the examiner, at his discretion, may ask the applicant to repeat the failed procedure during the course of the test. Should a further flight test be necessary only the failed section need be taken again, except that where a retest of Section 3 is required the retest will start from the holding pattern and the candidate will be re-assessed on Sub-section B as well as on Section 3. If, in the course of any other retest, the applicant is required for operational reasons to take up a hold he will also be re-assessed on Sub-section B. In a retest of Sub-section B, Section 1 will also be retested. If in the course of a retest a section or sub-section which has previously been passed is performed unsatisfactorily a retest in that section or sub-section may be required at the discretion of the examiner.

14.9.7   The whole of the test must be satisfactorily completed within 30 days from the initial attempt, or all previous passes will become invalid and the whole of the test must be taken again in one attempt, the pass conditions applying as before.

Appendix D

Some interesting reading from the Air Pilot

Aerodrome Operating Minima - Non-Public Transport Flights By Aircraft

1   Introduction

1.1   This section of the AIP specifies the requirement for non-public transport aircraft to observe Aerodrome Operating Minima (AOM) and gives the information needed for a pilot to calculate his minima for a particular approach. It is concerned with take-off and landing in weather conditions corresponding to Category 1 operations, or better. For Category 2 and 3 operations advice should be obtained from the Civil Aviation Authority, Flight Operations Policy Department, Gatwick.

1.1.1   The holder of a Private Pilots Licence who does not hold a valid instrument rating or IMC rating is prohibited from flying an Instrument Approach in cloud.

1.2   Under the provisions of the Air Navigation Order 1989 (as amended), the operator of a non-public transport flight shall observe AOM when conducting an approach to a runway with an Instrument Approach Procedure (IAP). In the absence of an Operations Manual containing AOM the operator must comply with minima calculated in accordance with the directions contained in this section of the UK AIP. **Calculated minima are mandatory and shall not be lower than those published in Table 1 at paragraph 6.4.2.1 or Table 2 at paragraph 6.4.2.2.**

1.3   The take-off minima published in this section are advisory, but operators are strongly recommended to operate in accordance with this advise to obtain adequate levels of safety.

2   Glossary of Terms

2.1   These explanations of terms are offered as a practical guide. For formal definitions refer to Article 106 in the Air Navigation Order 1989, as amended.

2.2   Aerodrome Operating Minima (AOM)

2.2.1   The minimum conditions of cloud ceiling and Runway Visual Range for take-off, and of Decision Height/Minimum Descent Height, Runway Visual Range and visual reference for landing.

2.3   Aeronautical Information Publication (AIP)

2.4   Approach to Landing

2.4.1   'Approach to landing' means that portion of the flight of the aircraft, when approaching to land, in which it is descending below a height of 1000 ft above the relevant specified Decision Height or Minimum Decision Height.

2.5   Circling Approach

Some interesting reading from the Air Pilot

2.5.1   An extension of an AIP which provides for visual circling of the aerodrome to position for landing.

2.6   Cloud Ceiling

2.6.1   'Cloud Ceiling' in relation to an aerodrome means the vertical distance from the elevation of the aerodrome to the lowest part of any cloud visible from the aerodrome which is sufficient to obscure more than one-half of the sky so visible.

2.7   Decision Height (DH)

2.7.1   The height in a precision approach at which a missed approach must be initiated if the required visual reference to continue the approach has not been established.

2.8   Instrument Approaches

2.8.1   Instrument Approaches are divided into non-precision approaches:

      (a)   Non precision approach
      An Instrument Approach to landing which does not use electronic glidepath guidance;

      (b)   Precision Approach
      An Instrument Approach to landing using ILS, MLS or PAR for guidance in both azimuth and elevation.

      Categories of precision operations

      Category 1 operation
      A precision Instrument Approach and landing with a DH not lower than 60 m (200 ft) and a Runway Visual Range not less than 550 m.

      Category 2 operation
      A precision Instrument Approach and landing with a DH lower than 30 m (100 ft) and a Runway Visual Range not less than 300 m.

      Category 3 operation
      A precision Instrument Approach and landing with a DH, if any, lower than 30 m (100 ft) and an appropriate Runway Visual Range.

2.9   Instrument Approach Procedure (IAP)

2.9.1   A series or pre-determined manoeuvres by reference to flight instruments with specified protection from obstacles from the Initial Approach Fix or, where applicable, from the beginning of a defined arrival route, to a point from which a landing can be completed and thereafter if a landing is not completed, to a position at which holding or en-route obstacle clearance criteria apply.

2.10   Minimum Descent Height (MDH)

2.10.1   The height in a non-precision approach below which descent may not be made without the required visual reference.

2.11   Missed Approach Point (MAPt)

2.11.1   That point in a non-precision approach procedure at or before which the prescribed missed approach procedure must be initiated in order to ensure that the minimum obstacle clearance is not infringed.

2.12   Notified

2.12.1   Information set forth in a document published by an Authority and entitled Supplement (NOTAM) or AIP and for the time being in force.

2.13   Runway Visual Range (RVR)

2.13.1   The distance in the direction of take-off or landing over which the runway lights or surface markings can be seen, calculated by either human observation or instruments.

2.14   Visual Reference

2.14.1   A view of the section of the runway and/or the approach area and/or their visual aids, which the pilot must see in sufficient time to assess whether or not a safe landing can be made from the type of approach being conducted.

3   **Determination of Take-off Minima**

3.1   The take-off minima chosen by the pilot of a non-public transport aircraft should be calculated not only by considering the requirement for directional control in poor visibility but also against a background of the prospect of engine failure after take-off. Pilots taking-off in bad weather should therefore be confident of their ability to deal with an engine failure as well as to fly on instruments. Weather minima limitations in licence privileges may override some of the recommended minima.

Some interesting reading from the Air Pilot

3.2   Single Engine Aircraft

3.2.1   The minima selected for single engine aircraft should be adequate to ensure a high probability of a successful forced landing being made should a failure of the engine occur soon after take-off. The recommended minima for take-offs are 600 ft cloud ceiling and 1800 m RVR. These should apply irrespective of the licence qualifications of the pilot. It should be noted that the minimum cloud ceiling for public transport operations in single engine aircraft is 1000 ft aal.

3. 3   Multi-engined Aircraft

3.3.1   Multi-engined Aircraft under 5700 kg MTWA.

3.3.1.1   The selection of suitable take-off minima for multi-engined aircraft will depend on the aircrafts engine-out climb performance and handling characteristics, realistically assessed taking into account prevailing conditions of wind and temperature, obstacles that might affect the aircraft during its initial climb, together with the pilot's currency and experience on type.

3.3.1.2   For aircraft with no engine-out climb capability the recommended minima should equal that for single engine aircraft; 600 ft cloud ceiling and 1800 m RVR.

3.3.1.3   For aircraft with a positive engine-out climb capability of less than 150 ft per minute; recommended minima are 600 ft cloud ceiling and 1500 m RVR.

3.3.1.4   For aircraft that expect an engine-out rate of climb exceeding 150 ft per minute; recommended minima are 300 ft cloud ceiling and 800 m RVR.

3.3.1.5   It is stressed that these recommended minima are the absolute minimum that the non-public transport pilot should accept for take-off. Consideration should be given to increasing minima to take account of the obstacle environment and to assist with a landing on the departure runway in the event of an engine failure.

3.3.2   Multi-engined Aircraft over 5700 kg MTWA

3.3.2.1   Numerous multi-engined aircraft over 5700 kg MTWA, that are used for non-public transport operations, have performance characteristics which ensue a good climb profile following an engine failure on take-off. If the performance of the aircraft does not justify this confidence the recommended minima mentioned in paragraph 3.3.1 should be used. When the aircraft has a performance capability equivalent to performance groups A of B the minima recommended for take-off are governed by the visibility necessary to maintain directional control of the aircraft on the runway during a normal take-off or in the event of an engine failure for stopping safely or continuing the take-off after decision speed. Having taken account of the performance aspects of the take-off, effective control of the aircraft depends on the visual aids available at the take-off runway. The recommended take-off minima associated with particular visual aids are specified in the following table for aircraft displaying these good performance characteristics.

3.3.2.2   Recommended Minima

Available Visual Aids for Take-off	Recommended Take-off Minima RVR (m)
High Intensity (HI) Runway centre-line lighting	150
HI Runway edge lighting and Runway centre-line marking	200
HI Runway edge lighting (day and night). Low intensity (LI) Runway edge lighting (night only). No Runway markings	300
No lighting or L1 Runway edge lighting, with Runway centre-line marking (day only)	350
No lighting or marking	500

4   Determination of Landing Minima

4.1   General

4.1.1   The operator of any non-public transport aircraft must calculate appropriate minima for landing before carrying out an Instrument Approach Procedure. The minima will consist of:

> (a)   A Decision Height or Minimum Descent Height (DH/MDH);
> (b)   a Runway Visual Range (RVR);
> (c)   the Visual Reference required.

4.1.2   The minima for a particular IAP at a UK licensed aerodrome are published in the UK AIP at RAC 4-3-9.

4.1.3   When the actual weather conditions at the aerodrome of intended landing includes an RVR which is less than that calculated for the AOM, a legal approach ban is specified in Article 32A of the Air Navigation Order, 1989 (as amended).

Note: To calculate an RVR from a meteorological visibility refer to the table at paragraph 6.3.

Some interesting reading from the Air Pilot

4.1.4   The Approach Ban has two parts:

(a)   Firstly, an aircraft when making a descent at an aerodrome to a runway in respect of which there is a notified IAP shall not descend below 1000 ft above the height of the aerodrome if the relevant RVR for that runway is at the time less than the calculated minimum for landing;

(b)   Secondly, an aircraft when making a descent to a runway in respect of which there is a notified IAP shall not:
(i)   continue an approach to landing at such a runway by flying below the relevant calculated DH; or
(ii)   descend below the relevant calculated MDH;
unless in either case from such height the specified visual reference for landing is established and is maintained.

4.2   Factors affecting Decision Heights and Minimum Descent Heights

Note: The information in this section gives guidance to calculate DH/MDH when the appropriate minima is not published in the AIP, eg military and unlicensed aerodromes, or an operations manual. Pilots are recommended to read this section as it contains valuable background information.

4.2.1   Decision Heights (DH) and Minimum Descent Heights (MDH) are the lowest heights to which particular Instrument Approaches may safely be continued without the specified visual reference. DH is related to precision approaches and MDH is related to non-precision approaches. The determination of both DH and MDH is governed by three factors.

4.2.2   Obstacle Clearance Height (OCH)

4.2.2.1   The DH/MDH for an approach is determined in part by considering obstacles which could affect the approach of a particular aircraft. In broad terms, the more accurate the aid supporting the approach to be flown and the slower the approach speed of the aircraft the smaller the area in which obstacles need be considered. The height which is calculated to clear all obstacles by a defined margin within a particular area is called Obstacles Clearance Height (OCH).

4.2.2.2   The OCH is the lowest height above the elevation of the relevant runway threshold or above the aerodrome elevation used in establishing compliance with the appropriate obstacle clearance criteria.   The OCH is calculated, in part, in relation to an Aircraft Category which is defined as follows:

Aircraft Category	Nominal Vat (kt)
A	Less than 91
B	91 - 120
C	121 - 140
D	141 - 165

The nominal Vat is the indicated stalling speed in the approach configuration at maximum certified landing mass multiplied by 1.3 and is taken to be a fixed value for categorization purposes.   Helicopters are categorized as Aircraft Category A and are subject to the Approach Ban in Article 32A.

4.2.3   System Minimum

4.2.3.1   The lowest safe height to which an aircraft may descend using a particular system of guidance is called the System Minima. The specific minimum will vary according to the accuracy of the individual approach aid used.

4.2.3.2   The system Minimum for Category 1 precision approach aids are:

Aid	Minimum (ft)
ILS	200
MLS	200
PAR	200

Note: Off-set Localizers.   The DH should not be less than the height on the nominal glidepath at which the localizer intersects the runway extended centre-line.

Some interesting reading from the Air Pilot

4.2.3.3   The system minimum for non-precision approach aids are:

Aid	Minimum (ft)
ILS (no glidepath	250
SRA (terminating at 0.5 nm)	250
SRA (terminating at 1 nm)	300
SRA (terminating at 2 nm)	350
VOR	300
NDB	300
VDF (QDM or QGH)	300
NDB/DME	300
VOR/DME	300

4.2.4   Altimeter Error

4.2.4.1   When calculating DH, account must be taken of the errors of indicated altitude which occur when the aircraft is in the approach configuration. Details of the Presure Error Correction (PEC) should be available from the aircraft manual of hand book. In the absence of this information a PEC of plus 50 ft has been found to be suitable for a wide range of light aircraft and should be used. This addition of 50 ft need only be applied to DH; MDH included sufficient margin to allow for altimeter errors.

4.2.4.2   The use of a radio altimeter is only applicable to approved Cat III operations. For an aircraft flying a Cat 1 IAP, DH/MDH is indicated on the pressure altimeter. At Cat 1 DH > MDH any readings from a radio altimeter may be unreliable because of the large area of terrain providing return signals to the instrument.

4.3   Determination of DH/MDH

4.3.1   Instrument Rating Holders in Current Practice

4.3.1.1   If the minima for the IAP to be flown are not published at RAC 4-3-9 et seq, the procedure for determining the DH?MDH for a pilot with a valid instrument rating and who is in current practice is as follows:

(a)   Determine the OCH for the aircraft's Category from the approach plate or from the appropriate AIP;
(b)   determine system minimum;
(c)   take the higher of (a) and (b);
(d)   If a precision approach, add PEC; if the correction is not reliably known, add 50 ft. When calculating MDH for non-precision approach, altimeter correction need not be considered.

4.3.1.2   For UK, the minimum DH/MDH for Category A aircraft using the above criteria, including a standard 50 ft altimeter correction for DHs, is given at RAC 4-3-9 et seq.

4.3.2   IMC Rating Holder in current Practice

4.3.2.1.   Pilots with a valid IMC rating are recommended to add 200 ft to the instrument rated pilots' DH/MDH, but with absolute minima of 500 ft for a precision approach and 600 ft for a non-precision approach. The UK IMC rating may not be valid outside UK territorial airspace, therefore IMC rated pilots should check the validity of their rating for the State in which they intend to fly. If the rating is not valid pilots must comply with the basic licence privileges, subject to the regulations of that State.

4.3.3   Pilots Not in Current Practice

4.3.3.1   If a pilot has not flown Instrument Approaches within the previous few weeks he should try to avoid having to make an Instrument Approach in bad weather. If he has to make an Approach, even if he is fully confident of his abilities, he is advised to add 100 ft to his calculated DH/MDH. Further increments should be added depending on when the pilot was last in full practice, his or her familiarity with the aircraft, the procedure and the aerodrome environment.

Note: A pilot who has conducted an actual Instrument Approach during the previous 28 days can be considered as being in current practice.

4.4   DH/MDH Multi-Engined Aircraft - Engine-out Approach

Some interesting reading from the Air Pilot

4.4.1   Having to fly an engine-out Instrument Approach in poor weather conditions presents a pilot with a situation which is best avoided. If faced with this prospect a diversion to an aerodrome with VMC should be seriously considered so that the asymmetric landing can be accomplished without the complication of having to fly an Instrument Approach in IMC.

4.4.2   If an Instrument Approach is unavoidable, account of the engine-out condition must be made in the calculation of an appropriate DH/MDH. A single engine go-around from the normally selected DH/MDH may well be beyond the capability of some aircraft due to either the increase in the height lost in the transition from descent to climb or the shallow climb out path. Consequently, in an engine-out approach, the lowest DH is effectively determined by the Missed Approach performance.

4.4.3   The lowest height from which a light multi-engined aircraft can make a successful go-around, whether IMC or VMC, is known as the Asymmetric Committal Height (ACH). Below this height the pilot must consider himself committed to land. Typically in aircraft below 5700 kg MTWA the accepted range of ACHs is 300 ft to 500 ft. The major element of ACH is the height needed for the transition from descending to climbing flight which is known as the Engine-Out Allowance (EOA). Advice of ACH/EOA may be contained in aircraft manuals or handbooks.

4.4.4   Determination of Engine-out DH/MDH

4.4.4.1   Having calculated the all engines operating DH/MDH element of the ACH, if known, should be added to this DH/MDH. If it is not known, and this is normally the case, pilots are advised to add 100 ft to the DH/MDH. If the particular aeroplane type is known of having a high ACH pilots are advised to add 200 ft. The determined DH/MDH must not be lower than the ACH.

4.4.5   In every case an **Urgency** or **Distress** message should be made. This will normally result in the aircraft being given a priority landing thus lessening the risk of having to make an engine-out Missed Approach.

5   **Visual Reference Element**

5.1   Having reached DH or MAPt, whichever is the earlier, a Missed Approach must be initiated unless the required visual reference for landing or circling is established and can be maintained. This visual reference must contain sufficient physical features to ensure that the aircraft's position relative to the desired flight path can be positively and immediately identified. It should include an element for lateral control, eg a cross-bar of the Calvert approach lighting system, or barrettes on the approach lighting system where there are no cross-bars available.

5.2   For a precision approach, the specified visual reference should contain at least six consecutive lights which may be approach lights or runway lights, or a combination of both.

5.3   For a non-precision approach, when approach lighting is not available, the visual reference should include the desired point of touchdown on the runway of intended landing. If approach lights are available it is not essential that the touchdown point should be in view at MDH, but the segment of lighting should contain at least 7 consecutive lights, which may be approach lights or runway lights, or a combination of both.

6   **Runway Visual Range (RVR)**

6.1   The DH/MDH is calculated with due regard to the type of approach, obstacles, and the pilots experience. On reaching DH/MDH the pilot must have a reasonable chance of being able to complete the approach to a landing by visual reference. The visibility required to achieve a landing will increase the higher the DH/MDH. An improved chance of landing will be obtained if high intensity lights are in use at the aerodrome.

6.2   Therefore, for each DH/MDH there is a corresponding RVR depending upon the type of approach and runway lights in use. If the weather at the aerodrome includes an RVR worse than this minimum there is not a reasonable prospect of achieving a landing and consequently the pilot shall not commence or continue the approach to landing.

6.3   At an aerodrome where measured RVRs are not available, the following table gives a conversion factor that may be applied to meteorological visibility to obtain an equivalent RVR

Lighting Elements Available	RVR = Reported Met Vis x	
	Day	Night
Hl Approach and Runway lighting	1.5	2.0
Any other type of lighting installation	1.0	1.5
No lighting	1.0	-

6,4   Determination of Runway Visual Range (RVR)

6.4.1   The RVR that determines whether or not an approach ban exists for any particular notified Instrument Approach Procedure is that published at RAC 4-3-9 et seq.

Some interesting reading from the Air Pilot

6.4.2   To determine the recommended RVR when the DH/MDH for a particular approach has been increased to take account of currency (see paragraph 4.3) or an asymmetric power condition (see paragraph 4.4) or when the minima is not published in the AIP, refer to the following tables which are applicable to all aircraft categories.

6.4.2.1   Precision Approach

Table 1

DH (ft)	Approach Lighting Length (m) and Type (Key below)			
	LA	LB	LC	LD
200 - 250	600*	700	800	900
251 - 300	650	800	900	1000
301 - 350	700	900	1000	1100
351 - 400	750	1000	1100	1200
401 - 450	800	1100	1200	1300
451 - 500	900	1200	1300	1400
501 - 550	1000	1300	1400	1500
551 - 600	1100	1400	1500	1500
601 - 650	1200	1500	1500	1500
651 - 700	1300	1500	1500	1500
Over 700	1500	1500	1500	1500

* Note: If Runway centre-line, touchdown zone and threshold lighting is in use, an
RVR   550 m is permitted when the DH is 200 ft.

LA   720 m or more High Intensity (HI). 5 cross-bars with coded CL or 1 cross-bar with centre-line barrettes.

LB   400 m to 719 m HI. At least 1 cross-bar with coded CL or centre-line barrettes.

LC   Up to 399 m HI. At least 1 cross-bar or centre-line barrettes.

LD   No approach lighting or any system not meeting the above specifications.

Instrument Flying

MDH (ft)	Approach Lighting Length (m) and Type (Key below)			
	LA	LB	LC	LD
250	650	800	900	1000
251 - 300	700	900	1000	1100
301 - 350	800	1000	1100	1200
351 - 400	900	1100	1200	1300
401 - 450	1000	1200	1300	1400
451 - 500	1100	1300	1400	1500
501 - 550	1200	1400	1500	1500
551 - 600	1300	1500	1500	1500
601 - 650	1400	1500	1500	1500
651 - 700	1500	1500	1500	1500
Over 700	1500	1500	1500	1500

LA 720 m or more High Intensity (HI). 5 cross-bars with coded CL or 1 cross-bar with centre-line barrettes.

LB 400 m to 719 m HI. At least 1 cross-bar with coded CL or centre-line barrettes.

LC Up to 399 m HI. At least 1 cross-bar or centre-line barrettes.

LD No approach lighting or any system not meeting the above specifications.

6.4.3 The process of determining AOM is complicated; pilots are therefore recommended to complete their calculations before commencing an IAP.

7 Visual Manoeuvring after an Instrument Approach - Aircraft

7.1 Visual Manoeuvring (Circling)(VM(C)) onto another runway following an IAP is to be conducted with the pilot maintaining continuous sight of ground features which will enable him to position the aircraft safely in relation to the aerodrome and subsequently remain within the visual manoeuvring area. The visual circuit height or the visual manoeuvring OCH is specified in the RAC 4-2 Section and should never be less than the values tabulated below.

Aircraft Category	Minimum Circling Height (ft)	Minimum In Flight Circling Visibility (km)
A	400	1.9
B	500	2.8
C	600	3.7
D	700	4.6

Some interesting reading from the Air Pilot

8   Determination of Minima Additional Cases

8.1   Military aerodromes in UK Territorial Airspace

Note: Military Aerodromes are not encompassed by Air Navigation Order Article 32A and AOM are not therefore mandatory. However, pilots are strongly advised to calculate minima and operate with regard to this minima.

8.1.1   For military aerodromes, a Procedure Minimum for each AIP is shown on the RAF Approach chart in a table of Aircraft Categories (CAT); the words 'Procedure Minimum' are not shown. The Procedure Minimum shown in bold print is a minimum altitude (Minimum with QNH set on the altimeter) with the minimum height (the equivalent of OHC) shown in light print beside to the right. The Procedure Minimum (Minimum Altitude) will also be passed by ATC who will request the pilots DA or MDA and intentions.

8.1.2   Precision Approaches, ILS and PAR, for which the absolute minimum is 200 ft above touchdown elevation, are normally based on a 3° glidepath. The glidepath angle, also shown on the chart, may be as low as 2.5°. The following increments should be made to the given Procedure Minimum to obtain the equivalent of OCH. There is no provision for the use of radio altimeters.

Nominal Glidepath Angle°	Aircraft Categories (ft)			
	A	B	C	D
2.5	NIL	10	20	30
2.6	10	20	30	40
2.7	10	20	30	40
2.8	20	30	40	50
2.9	20	30	40	50
3.0	30	50	50	60

8.1.3   For non-precision approaches the Procedure Minimum may be taken to the OCH.

8.1.4   DH and MDH should then be determined as previously described. The related RVR continues to be obtained from Table 1 or 2 at paragraph 6.4.

8.1.5   For VM(C), the OCH should be determined by adjusting the published RAF values, shown on the Approaches Charts, as follows:

Aircraft Category	Increment (ft)

231

Instrument Flying

8   Determination of Minima Additional Cases

8.1   Military aerodromes in UK Territorial Airspace

Note: Military Aerodromes are not encompassed by Air Navigation Order Article 32A and AOM are not therefore mandatory. However, pilots are strongly advised to calculate minima and operate with regard to this minima.

8.1.1   For military aerodromes, a Procedure Minimum for each AIP is shown on the RAF Approach chart in a table of Aircraft Categories (CAT); the words 'Procedure Minimum' are not shown. The Procedure Minimum shown in bold print is a minimum altitude (Minimum with QNH set on the altimeter) with the minimum height (the equivalent of OHC) shown in light print beside to the right. The Procedure Minimum (Minimum Altitude) will also be passed by ATC who will request the pilots DA or MDA and intentions.

8.1.2   Precision Approaches, ILS and PAR, for which the absolute minimum is 200 ft above touchdown elevation, are normally based on a 3° glidepath. The glidepath angle, also shown on the chart, may be as low as 2.5°. The following increments should be made to the given Procedure Minimum to obtain the equivalent of OCH. There is no provision for the use of radio altimeters.

Nominal Glidepath Angle°	Aircraft Categories (ft)			
	A	B	C	D
2.5	**NIL**	10	20	30
2.6	**10**	20	30	40
2.7	**10**	20	30	40
2.8	**20**	30	40	50
2.9	**20**	30	40	50
3.0	**30**	50	50	60

8.1.3   For non-precision approaches the Procedure Minimum may be taken to the OCH.

8.1.4   DH and MDH should then be determined as previously described. The related RVR continues to be obtained from Table 1 or 2 at paragraph 6.4.

Some interesting reading from the Air Pilot

8.1.5   For VM(C), the OCH should be determined by adjusting the published RAF values, shown on the Approaches Charts, as follows:

Aircraft Category	Increment (ft)
A and B	zero
C and D	+ 100

The minimum visibility should be determined as described in paragraph 7.1.

8.1.6   OCH information will not be used at British Military Aerodromes.

8.1.7   Instrument Approaches at British Military Aerodromes (except Royal Navy Aerodromes) are flown on aerodrome QNH until approaching the Final Approach Fix or Point, when QFE is set for the remainder of the approach. All flying in the visual circuit is on QFE. At Royal Navy Aerodromes instrument and visual approaches are flown on QFE. Aircraft who are unable to comply with the above procedures will be accommodated wherever possible.

8.2   Overseas Aerodromes

8.2.1   AOM at overseas aerodromes should not be lower than those published as State Minima or permitted by the privileges of the pilot's licence by the UK or overseas State.

8.3   Aerodromes Without Published Instrument Approach Procedures

8.3.1   Legislation prohibits Instrument Approaches being made to aerodromes for which there are no published IAPs. For landings at these aerodromes pilots should either:
(a)   Descend in VMC and visual contact with the ground, then fly to the destination;
(b)   fly an IAP at a nearby aerodrome and proceed as in (a); or
(c)   If neither (a) nor (b) is possible, first obtain an accurate fix and then descend not lower than 1000 ft above the highest obstacle within 5 nm of the aircraft. If visual contact (as at (a) above) has not been established at this height, the pilot should divert to a suitable alternate with a published Approach Procedure.

233

Instrument Flying

Aerodrome Operating Minima - Non-Public Transport Flights By Aircraft

Note 1: Minima for any Aerodrome Approach Procedures, and minima for Runway Approach Procedures at military or unlicensed aerodromes are recommended only.

Note 2: IMC rated pilots and pilots not in current practice should read paragraph 4.3 to establish recommended increments for their DH/MDH.

Note 3: The OCH has been calculated using Aircraft Category A (see paragraph 4.2.2). The Decision Heights, for precision approaches, published in column 5 include a standard 50 ft Altimeter Pressure Error Correction (PEC) (see paragraph 4.2.4.1).

Aerodrome and Approach Lighting Category	Runway	Approach Aid	OCH (ft)	Minima.	
				DH/MDH (ft)	RVR (m)
1	2	3	4 Note 3	5 Note 3	6
ABERDEEN/Dyce					
Runway 16 LA	16	ILS	160	250	600
	16	ILS (GP inoperative)	400	400	900
	16	NDB(L) AOS	650	650	1400
	16	RADAR (2 nm termination range)	780	780	1500
Runway 34 LA	34	RADAR (2 nm termination range)	750	750	1500
	34	ILS	163	250	600
	34	ILS (GP inoperative)	500	500	1100
	34	NDB(L) ATF	1000	1000	1500
Alderney					
Runway 08 LC	08	NDB(L) ALD	390	390	1200
Runway 26 LC	26	NDB(L) ALD	380	380	1200
BELFAST/Aldergrove					
Runway 07 LC	07	VOR/DME BEL	350	350	1100
	07	VDF	560	560	1500
	07	RADAR (2 nm termination range, 1 nm MAPt)	350	350	1100
Runway 17 LA	17	ILS	162	250	600
	17	ILS (GP inoperative)	270	270	700
	17	VOR/DME BEL	370	370	900
	17	VOR BEL	420	420	1000
	17	RADAR (2 nm termination range, 1 nm MAPt)	350	350	800
Runway 25 LA	25	ILS	136	250	600
	25	ILS (GP inoperative)	400	400	900
	25	VOR/DME BEL	400	400	900
	25	NDB(L) OY	530	530	1200
	25	RADAR (2 nm termination range)	650	650	1400
Runway 35 LC	35	VOR/DME BEL	450	450	1300
	35	RADAR (2 nm termination range, 1 nm MAPt)	430	430	1300
BELFAST/City					
Runway 04 LC	04	LLZ/DME HBD	480	480	1400
	04	NDB(L) HB	1000	1000	1500
	04	NDB(L) HB/DME HBD	620	620	1500
	04	RADAR (0.5 nm termination range)	470	470	1400
Runway 22 LA	22	ILS/DME	280	330	700
	22	ILS/DME (GP inoperative)	450	450	1000
	22	NDB(L) HB	980	980	1500
	22	NDB(L) HB/DME I BFH	750	750	1500
	22	RADAR (0.5 nm termination range)	440	440	1000
Benbecula					
Runway 06 LD	06	VOR BEN/DME BEZ	300	300	1100
	06	VOR BEN	350	350	1200
Runway 24 LD	24	VOR BEN/DME BEZ	300	300	1100
	24	VOR BEN	490	490	1500
Biggin Hill					
Runway 21 LB	21	ILS	280	330	900
	21	ILS (GP inoperative)	300	300	900
	21	VOR/DME BIG	350	350	1000

Some interesting reading from the Air Pilot

Aerodrome and Approach Lighting Category	Runway	Approach Aid	OCH (ft)	Minima	
				DH/MDH (ft)	RVR (m)
1	2	3	4 Note 3	5 Note 3	6
Birmingham					
Runway 06 LC	06	RADAR (2 nm termination range)	600	600	1500
Runway 15 LA	15	ILS	163	250	600
	15	ILS (GP inoperative)	410	410	1000
	15	NDB(L) GX	470	470	1100
	15	RADAR (2 nm termination range)	510	510	1200
Runway 24 LC	24	RADAR (2 nm termination range)	600	600	1500
Runway 33 LA	33	ILS	162	250	600
	33	ILS (GP inoperative)	420	420	1000
	33	NDB(L) GM	470	470	1100
	33	RADAR (2 nm termination range)	470	470	1100
Blackpool					
Runway 10 LC	10	NDB(L) BPL/DME I BPL	410	410	1300
	10	NDB(L) BPL	410	410	1300
	10	VDF	540	540	1500
	10	RADAR (0.5 nm termination range)	320	320	1100
	10	RADAR (2 nm termination range)	410	410	1300
Runway 13 LD	13	RADAR (2 nm termination range)	310	350	1200
Runway 28 LC	28	ILS/DME	135	250	800
	28	ILS/DME (GP inoperative)	350	350	1100
	28	NDB(L) BPL/DME I BPL	450	450	1300
	28	NDB(L) BPL	500	500	1400
	28	RADAR (0.5 nm termination range)	350	350	1100
	28	RADAR (2 nm termination range)	500	500	1400
Runway 31 LD	31	RADAR (2 nm termination range)	340	350	1200
Bournemouth					
Runway 08 LC	08	ILS	170	250	800
	08	ILS (GP inoperative)	340	340	1100
	08	NDB(L) BMH	400	400	1200
	08	RADAR (2 nm termination range)	420	420	1300
Runway 17 LC	17	RADAR (2 nm termination range)	550	550	1500
Runway 26 LA	26	ILS	180	250 –	600 –
	26	ILS (GP inoperative)	330	330	800
	26	NDB(L) HRN	420	420	1000
	26	RADAR (2 nm termination range)	500	500	1100
Runway 35 LC	35	RADAR (2 nm termination range)	550	550	1500
Bristol					
Runway 09 LB	09	NDB(L) BRI	340	340	1000
	09	VDF	370	370	1100
	09	RADAR (2 nm termination range)	270	350	1000
	09	ILS/DME	155	250	700
	09	ILS/DME (GP inoperative)	260	260	900
	09	NDB(L) BRI/DME	290	300	900
Runway 27 LB	27	ILS/DME	176	250	700
	27	ILS/DME (GP inoperative)	340	340	1000
	27	NDB(L) BRI/DME	340	340	1000
	27	NDB(L) BRI	570	570	1500
	27	VDF	570	570	1500
	27	RADAR (2 nm termination range)	340	350	1000
Brough					
	Aerodrome Approach 125° MAG	NDB(L) BV	910	910	1900

Instrument Flying

Aerodrome and Approach Lighting Category	Runway	Approach Aid	OCH (ft)	Minima	
				DH/MDH (ft)	RVR (m)
1	2	3	4 Note 3	5 Note 3	6
Cambridge					
Runway 05 LD	05	NDB(L) CAM/DME CAB	450	450	1400
	05	NDB(L) CAM	580	580	1500
	05	VDF	640	640	1500
	05	RADAR (0.5 nm termination range)	300	300	1100
Runway 23 LC	23	NDB(L) CAM/DME CAB	350	350	1100
	23	NDB(L) CAM	540	540	1500
	23	VDF	540	540	1500
	23	RADAR (0.5 nm termination range)	330	330	1100
Cardiff					
Runway 12 LA	12	ILS/DME	137	250	600
	12	ILS/DME (GP inoperative)	310	310	800
	12	NDB(L) CDF	420	420	1000
	12	RADAR (2 nm termination range)	480	480	1100
Runway 30 LA	30	ILS	155	250	600
	30	ILS/DME (GP inoperative)	310	310	800
	30	ILS (GP inoperative)	360	360	900
	30	NDB(L) CDF/DME	330	330	800
	30	NDB(L) CDF	380	380	900
	30	VDF	420	420	1000
	30	RADAR (2 nm termination range)	350	350	800
Carlisle					
Runway 07 LD	07	NDB(L) CL	450	450	1400
	07	VDF	510	510	1500
	07	NDB(L) CL/DME CO	330	330	1200
Runway 25 LD	25	NDB(L) CL/DME CO	300	300	1100
CHICHESTER/Goodwood					
Runway 32 Nil	32	VOR GWC	550	550	1500
	32	VDF	820	820	1500
	Aerodrome Approach 275° MAG	VDF 275°	900	900	2000
Coventry					
Runway 05 LC	05	RADAR (0.5 nm termination range)	350	350	1100
Runway 23 LC	23	ILS	280	330	1000
	23	ILS (GP inoperative)	370	370	1200
	23	NDB(L) CT	410	410	1300
	23	VDF	570	570	1500
	23	RADAR (0.5 nm termination range)	370	370	1200
Cranfield					
Runway 22 LC	22	ILS	136	250	900
	22	ILS (GP inoperative)	300	300	1000
	22	NDB(L) CIT	340	340	1100
	22	VDF	400	400	1200
	22	VOR	350	350	1100
Dundee					
Runway 10 LC	10	NDB(L) DND	600	600	1500
	10	LLZ	470	470	1400
	10	NDB(L) DND/DME DDE	550	550	1500
	10	LLZ/DME	350	350	1100

236

Some interesting reading from the Air Pilot

Aerodrome and Approach Lighting Category	Runway	Approach Aid	OCH (ft)	Minima	
				DH/MDH (ft)	RVR (m)
1	2	3	4 Note 3	5 Note 3	6
East Midlands					
Runway 09 LA	09	ILS	180	250	600
	09	ILS (GP inoperative)	350	350	800
	09	NDB(L) EMW	430	430	1000
	09	RADAR (2 nm termination range)	480	480	1100
Runway 27 LA	27	ILS	160	250	600
	27	ILS (GP inoperative)	350	350	800
	27	NDB(L) EME	350	350	800
	27	RADAR (2 nm termination range)	360	360	900
Edinburgh					
Runway 07 LA	07	ILS/DME	160	250	600
	07	ILS/DME (GP inoperative)	550	550	1200
	07	ILS (GP inoperative)	720	720	1500
	07	NDB(L) UW/DME	600	600	1300
	07	NDB(L) UW	720	720	1500
	07	RADAR Vectored Aerodrome Approach (4 nm termination range)	1250	1250	5000
Runway 13 LB	13	RADAR (2 nm termination range)	650	650	1400
Runway 25 LA	25	ILS/DME	160	250	600
	25	ILS/DME (GP inoperative)	460	460	1100
	25	ILS	160	250	600
	25	ILS (GP inoperative)	460	460	1100
	25	NDB(L) EDN/DME	550	550	1200
	25	NDB(L) EDN	550	550	1200
	25	RADAR (2 nm termination range)	600	600	1300
Runway 31 LB	31	RADAR Vectored Aerodrome Approach (4 nm termination range)	1600	1600	5000
Exeter					
Runway 08 LD	08	RADAR (1 nm termination range)	360	360	1300
	08	RADAR (2 nm termination range)	600	600	1500
Runway 26 LC	26	ILS	200	250	800
	26	ILS (GP inoperative)	780	780	1500
	26	ILS (GP inoperative) with radar fix at 2.5 nm	500	500	1400
	26	NDB(L) EX	780	780	1500
	26	RADAR (1 nm termination range)	480	480	1400
	26	RADAR (2 nm termination range)	720	720	1500
	Aerodrome Approach	VDF 004°	830	830	2000
Filton					
Runway 09 LC	09	ILS/DME	280	330	1000
	09	ILS/DME (GP inoperative)	340	340	1100
	09	NDB(L) OF/DME	450	450	1300
	09	NDB(L) OF	500	500	1400
	09	RADAR (2 nm termination range)	500	500	1500
	09	VDF 093°	600	600	1500
Runway 27 LA	27	ILS/DME	290	340	700
	27	ILS/DME (GP inoperative)	310	310	800
	27	NDB(L) OF/DME	500	500	1100
	27	RADAR (2 nm termination range)	600	600	1300
	27	VDF 277°	870	870	1500

Instrument Flying

Aerodrome and Approach Lighting Category	Runway	Approach Aid	OCH (ft)	Minima	
				DH/MDH (ft)	RVR (m)
1	2	3	4 Note 3	5 Note 3	6
Glasgow					
Runway 05 LA	05	ILS	160	250	600
	05	ILS (GP inoperative)	750	750	1500
	05	ILS (GP inoperative)/DME GOW	400	400	900
	05	VOR/DME GOW	400	400	900
	05	VOR GOW	900	900	1500
	05	NDB(L) AC	900	900	1500
	05	RADAR (2 nm termination range)	1040	1040	1500
Runway 10 LD	10	RADAR (2 nm termination range)	450	450	1400
Runway 23 LA	23	ILS	160	250	600
	23	ILS (GP inoperative)	650	650	1400
	23	ILS (GP inoperative)/DME GOW	440	440	1000
	23	VOR/DME GOW	440	440	1000
	23	NDB(L) GLG	680	680	1500
	23	RADAR (2 nm termination range)	650	650	1400
Runway 28 LD	28	RADAR (2 nm termination range)	650	650	1500
Gloucestershire					
	Aerodrome Approach	NDB(L) GST App Dir 115° MAG	750	750	2000
Runway 09 LD	09	NDB(L) GST/DME GOS	350	350	1200
	09	RADAR (0.5 nm termination range)	310	310	1200
Runway 22 LD	22	RADAR (2 nm termination range)	650	650	1500
Runway 27 LC	27	NDB(L) GST/DME GOS	420	420	1300
	27	RADAR (0.5 nm termination range)	330	330	1100
Guernsey					
Runway 09 LA	09	ILS	140	250	600
	09	ILS (GP Inoperative)	330	330	800
	09	ILS (GP inoperative)/DME GUR	280	280	700
	09	NDB(L) GRB/DME GUR	280	300	700
	09	NDB(L) GRB	330	330	800
	09	VOR/DME GUR	280	300	700
	09	VOR GUR	330	330	800
	09	VDF	330	330	800
	09	RADAR (2 nm termination range)	280	280	700
Runway 27 LA	27	ILS	142	250	600
	27	ILS (GP inoperative)	380	380	900
	27	ILS (GP inoperative)/DME GUR	330	330	800
	27	NDB(L) GRB/DME GUR	330	330	800
	27	NDB(L) GRB	380	380	900
	27	VOR/DME GUR	330	330	800
	27	VOR GUR	380	380	900
	27	VDF	410	410	900
	27	RADAR (2 nm termination range)	360	360	800
Hatfield					
Runway 06 LC	06	RADAR (0.5 nm termination range)	390	390	1200
	06	RADAR (2 nm termination range)	600	600	1500
Runway 24 LC	24	ILS	163	250	800
	24	ILS (GP inoperative)	490	490	1400
	24	ILS (GP inoperative)/DME BKY	340	340	1100
	24	RADAR (0.5 nm termination range)	340	340	1100
	24	RADAR (2 nm termination range)	600	600	1500
Hawarden					
Runway 14 LD	14	RADAR (0.5 nm termination range) (Day only)	340	340	1200
	14	RADAR (2 nm termination range)	600	600	1500
Runway 23 LD	23	RADAR (1 nm termination range)	350	350	1200
Runway 32 LD	32	NDB(L) HAW	530	530	1500
	Aerodrome Approach 340°MAG	VDF	500	500	2000
	32	RADAR (1 nm termination range) (Day only)	350	350	1200
	32	RADAR (2 nm termination range)	600	600	1500

Some interesting reading from the Air Pilot

Aerodrome and Approach Lighting Category	Runway	Approach Aid	OCH (ft)	Minima	
				DH/MDH (ft)	RVR (m)
1	2	3	4 Note 3	5 Note 3	6
Humberside					
Runway 03 LA	03	NDB(L) KIM/DME I HS	450	450	1000
	03	NDB(L) KIM	450	450	1000
	03	RADAR (2 nm termination range)	470	470	1100
Runway 21 LA	21	ILS/DME	150	250	600
	21	ILS/DME (GP inoperative)	370	370	900
	21	ILS (GP inoperative) without DME	440	440	1000
	21	NDB(L) HBR/DME I HS	390	390	900
	21	NDB(L) HBR	440	440	1000
	21	NDB(L) KIM/DME I HS	390	390	900
	21	NDB(L) KIM	640	640	1400
	21	RADAR (2 nm termination range)	420	420	1000
Inverness					
Runway 06 LD	06	VOR/DME INS	400	400	1300
	06	VOR INS	525	525	1500
Runway 24 LC	24	VOR/DME INS	350	350	1100
	24	VOR INS	400	400	1200
Islay					
Runway 13 LD	13	NDB(L) LAY	450	450	1400
	Aerodrome Approach 165°	NDB(L) LAY	700	700	2000
ISLE OF MAN/Ronaldsway					
Runway 03 LD	03	RADAR (2 nm termination range)	600	600	1500
Runway 08 LC	08	RADAR (2 nm termination range)	420	420	1300
	08	VOR/DME IOM	450	450	1300
	08	NDB RWY/DME I RY	420	420	1300
Runway 26 LC	26	ILS/DME	145	250	800
	26	ILS/DME (GP inoperative)	400	400	1200
	26	NDB RWY/DME I RY	550	550	1500
	26	NDB RWY	600	600	1500
	26	RADAR (2 nm termination range)	600	600	1500
Runway 35 LD	35	RADAR (2 nm termination range)	600	600	1500
Jersey					
Runway 09 LC	09	ILS	139	250	800
	09	ILS/DME (GP inoperative)	310	310	1100
	09	ILS (GP inoperative)	360	360	1200
	09	NDB(L) JW/DME I JJ	310	310	1100
	09	NDB(L) JW	360	360	1200
	09	RADAR (2 nm termination range)	360	360	1200
Runway 27 LA	27	ILS	156	250	600
	27	ILS/DME JSY (GP inoperative)	350	350	800
	27	ILS (GP inoperative)	480	480	1100
	27	NDB(L) JEY/DME JSY	400	400	900
	27	NDB(L) JEY	480	480	1100
	27	VOR/DME JSY	390	390	900
	27	VOR JSY	480	480	1100
	27	RADAR (2 nm termination range)	420	420	1000
Kirkwall					
Runway 09 LD	09	NDB(L) KW/DME KWL	520	520	1500
	09	VOR/DME KWL	520	520	1500
Runway 25 LD	25	NDB(L) KW/DME KWL	460	460	1500
	25	NDB(L) KW	510	510	1500
Runway 27 LD	27	VOR/DME KWL	440	440	1400
	27	VOR KWL/MKR	440	440	1400
	27	VOR KWL	550	550	1500
	27	NDB(L) KW/DME KWL	440	440	1400
	27	NDB(L) KW/MKR	440	440	1400
	27	NDB(L) KW	550	550	1500

Instrument Flying

Aerodrome and Approach Lighting Category	Runway	Approach Aid	OCH (ft)	Minima	
				DH/MDH (ft)	RVR (m)
1	2	3	4 Note 3	5 Note 3	6
Leavesden					
Runway 06 LD	06	RADAR (0.5 nm termination range)	450	450	1400
	06	RADAR (2 nm termination range)	600	600	1500
Runway 24 LD	24	RADAR (0.5 nm termination range)	450	450	1400
	24	RADAR (2 nm termination range)	600	600	1500
Leeds Bradford					
Runway 14 LA	14	ILS/DME	150	250	600
	14	ILS/DME (GP inoperative)	360	360	900
	14	ILS (GP inoperative)	970	970	1500
	14	NDB(L) LBA/DME LBF	460	460	1100
	14	NDB(L) LBA	970	970	1500
	14	RADAR (0.5 nm termination range)	330	330	800
	14	RADAR (1 nm termination range)	510	510	1200
Runway 28 LC	28	RADAR (0.5 nm termination range)	340	340	1100
	28	RADAR (1 nm termination range)	370	370	1200
Runway 32 LA	32	ILS/DME	170	250	600
	32	ILS/DME (GP inoperative)	330	330	800
	32	NDB(L) LBA/DME LF	330	330	800
	32	NDB(L) LBA	480	480	1100
	32	VDF	480	480	1100
	32	RADAR (0.5 nm termination range)	330	330	800
	32	RADAR (1 nm termination range)	330	330	800
Liverpool					
Runway 09 LA	09	LLZ/DME	320	320	800
	09	RADAR (2 nm termination range)	450	450	1000
Runway 27 LA	27	RADAR (2 nm termination range)	420	420	1000
	27	ILS/DME	160	250	600
	27	ILS/DME (GP inoperative)	320	320	800
	27	NDB(L) LPL/DME	500	500	1100
LONDON/City					
Runway 10 LB	10	ILS/DME	350	400	1000
Runway 28 LB	28	ILS/DME			
		2.5% Missed Approach climb gradient	500	550	1300
		4.5% Missed Approach climb gradient	260	310	900
	28	ILS/DME (GP inoperative)			
		2.5% Missed Approach climb gradient	550	550	1400
		3.5% Missed Approach climb gradient	470	470	1300
LONDON/Gatwick					
Runway 08R LA	08R	ILS/DME	140	250	600
	08R	ILS/DME (GP inoperative)	550	550	1200
	08R	RADAR (2 nm termination range, 1 nm MAPt)	520	520	1200
Runway 08L LC	08L	RADAR (2 nm termination range)	650	650	1500
Runway 26L LA	26L	ILS/DME	152	250	600
	26L	ILS/DME (GP inoperative)	500	500	1100
	26L	RADAR (2 nm termination range, 1 nm MAPt)	400	400	900
Runway 26R LC	26R	RADAR (2 nm termination range)	650	650	1500

Some interesting reading from the Air Pilot

Aerodrome and Approach Lighting Category	Runway	Approach Aid	OCH (ft)	Minima	
				DH/MDH (ft)	RVR (m)
1	2	3	4 Note 3	5 Note 3	6
LONDON/Heathrow					
Runway 05 LC	05	RADAR (2 nm termination range)	650	650	1500
Runway 09L LA	09L	ILS	148	250	600
	09L	ILS (GP inoperative)	380	380	900
	09L	RADAR (2 nm termination range)	650	650	1400
Runway 09R LA	09R	ILS	154	250	600
	09R	ILS (GP inoperative)	400	400	900
	09R	RADAR (2 nm termination range)	650	650	1400
Runway 23 LB	23	RADAR (2 nm termination range)	650	650	1400
Runway 27L LA	27L	ILS	151	250	600
	27L	ILS (GP inoperative)	410	410	1000
	27L	RADAR (2 nm termination range)	650	650	1400
Runway 27R LA	27R	ILS	145	250	600
	27R	ILS (GP inoperative)	380	380	900
	27R	RADAR (2 nm termination range)	650	650	1400
LONDON/Stansted					
Runway 05 LB	05	ILS/DME	157	250	700
	05	ILS/DME (GP inoperative)	350	350	1000
	05	RADAR (2 nm termination range)	650	650	1500
Runway 23 LA	23	ILS/DME	157	250	600
	23	ILS/DME (GP inoperative)	370	370	900
	23	NDB(L) SAN/DME I SX	370	370	900
	23	RADAR (2 nm termination range)	650	650	1400
LONDONDERRY/Eglinton					
Runway 26 LB	26	ILS/DME	280	330	800
	26	ILS/DME (GP inoperative)	350	350	1000
	26	NDB(L)/DME EGT	450	450	1200
	26	NDB(L) EGT	600	600	1500
Luton					
Runway 08 LB	08	ILS/DME	142	250	700
	08	ILS/DME (GP inoperative)	350	350	1000
	08	RADAR (2 nm termination range)	440	440	1200
Runway 26 LA	26	ILS/DME	146	250	600
	26	ILS/DME (GP inoperative)	330	330	800
	26	NDB(L) LUT	330	330	800
	26	RADAR (2 nm termination range)	330	350	800
Lydd					
Runway 22 LC	22	ILS/DME	320	370	1100
	22	ILS/DME (GP inoperative)	350	350	1100
	22	NDB(L) LYX/DME I LYX	380	380	1200
	Aerodrome Approach 205°MAG	NDB(L) LYY	510	510	2000
Machrihanish					
Runway 11 LC	11	VOR MAC/DME MAZ	340	340	1100
	11	VOR MAC	790	790	1500
Manchester					
Runway 06 LA	06	ILS	160	250	600
	06	ILS (GP inoperative)	360	360	900
	06	VOR/DME MCT	420	420	1000
	06	NDB(L) MCR	420	420	1000
	06	RADAR (2 nm termination range)	440	440	1000
Runway 24 LA	24	ILS	150	250	600
	24	ILS (GP inoperative)/DME I NN or MCT	320	320	800
	24	VOR/DME MCT	380	380	900
	24	NDB(L) ME/DME I NN or MCT	380	380	900
	24	RADAR (2 nm termination range)	400	400	900

Instrument Flying

Aerodrome and Approach Lighting Category	Runway	Approach Aid	OCH (ft)	Minima	
				DH/MDH (ft)	RVR (m)
1	2	3	4 Note 3	5 Note 3	6
Newcastle					
Runway 07 LA	07	ILS/DME	180	250	600
	07	ILS/DME (GP inoperative)	400	400	900
	07	ILS (GP inoperative)	550	550	1200
	07	NDB(L) WZ/DME I NC	420	420	1000
	07	NDB(L) WZ	550	550	1200
	07	VOR/DME NEW	430	430	1000
	07	RADAR (1 nm termination range)	430	430	1000
	07	RADAR (2 nm termination range)	430	430	1000
Runway 25 LA	25	ILS/DME	160	250	600
	25	ILS/DME (GP inoperative)	320	320	800
	25	NDB(L) NEW/DME I NWC	340	340	800
	25	NDB(L) NEW	340	340	800
	25	VOR/DME NEW	320	320	700
	25	RADAR (1 nm termination range)	320	320	700
	25	RADAR (2 nm termination range)	320	320	800
Norwich					
Runway 09 LC	09	NDB(L) DH	370	370	1200
	09	RADAR (1 nm termination range)	380	380	1200
Runway 27 LA	27	ILS	170	250	600
	27	ILS (GP inoperative)	320	320	800
	27	NDB(L) NH	370	370	900
	27	RADAR (1 nm termination range)	360	360	900
OXFORD/Kidlington					
Runway 02 LC	02	NDB(L) OX/DME OX	420	420	1300
Runway 09 LD	09	NDB(L) OX/DME OX	520	520	1500
	09	NDB(L) OX/MKR K	520	520	1500
	09	NDB(L) OX (MKR inoperative)	950	950	1500
PERTH/Scone					
Runway 21 LD	21	NDB(L) PTH	570	570	1500
	21	VDF/QGH	660	660	1500
	21	LLZ	350	350	1200
Plymouth					
Runway 06 LD	06	NDB(L) PY/DME PLY	450	450	1400
Runway 13 LD	13	NDB(L) PY/DME PLY	450	450	1400
	13	NDB(L) PY	910	910	1500
Runway 31 LA	31	ILS/DME	157	250	600
	31	ILS/DME (GP inoperative)	270	270	700
	31	ILS	300	350	700
	31	ILS (GP and DME inoperative)	480	480	1100
	31	NDB(L) PY/DME PLY	300	300	700
	31	NDB(L) PY	540	540	1200
	31	VDF	590	590	1300
Prestwick					
Runway 13 LA	13	ILS	180	250	600
	13	ILS (GP inoperative)	330	330	800
	13	NDB(L) PW	400	400	900
	13	RADAR (2 nm termination range)	440	440	1000
Runway 31 LA	31	ILS	170	250	600
	31	ILS (GP inoperative)	600	600	1300
	31	NDB(L) PE	600	600	1300
	31	RADAR (2 nm termination range)	680	680	1500

Some interesting reading from the Air Pilot

Aerodrome and Approach Lighting Category	Runway	Approach Aid	OCH (ft)	Minima	
				DH/MDH (ft)	RVR (m)
1	2	3	4 Note 3	5 Note 3	6
Scatsta Runway 24 LC	24	NDB(L) SS	720	720	1500
	24	RADAR (0.5 nm termination range)	490	490	1400
SCILLY ISLES/St Mary's Runway 28 LD	28	NDB(L) STM	400	400	1300
Runway 33 LD	33	NDB(L) STM	400	400	1300
Shoreham Runway 03 LD	03	NDB(L) SHM	750	750	1500
	03	VDF	850	850	1500
SOUTHAMPTON/Eastleigh Runway 02 LC	02	VOR/DME SAM	500	500	1500
	02	VOR SAM	660	660	1500
	02	RADAR (0.5 nm termination range)	480	480	1400
	02	RADAR (2 nm termination range)	500	500	1400
Runway 20 LC	20	ILS	280	330	1100
	20	ILS (GP inoperative)	600	600	1500
	20	ILS (GP inoperative)/DME SAM	350	350	1200
	20	VOR/DME SAM	470	470	1400
	20	VOR SAM	610	610	1500
	20	RADAR (0.5 nm termination range)	350	350	1100
	20	RADAR (2 nm termination range)	490	490	1400
Southend Runway 06 LC	06	NDB(L) SND/DME I ND	470	470	1400
	06	NDB(L) SND	630	630	1500
	06	RADAR (0.5 nm termination range)	390	390	1200
	06	RADAR (2 nm termination range)	600	600	1500
Runway 24 LC	24	ILS/DME	280	330	1000
	24	ILS/DME (GP inoperative)	350	350	1100
	24	ILS (GP and DME inoperative)	400	400	1200
	24	RADAR (0.5 nm termination range)	350	350	1100
	24	RADAR (2 nm termination range)	600	600	1500
Aerodrome Approach 230°MAG		NDB(L) SND/DME I ND FAT 230° MAG	550	550	1500
		NDB(L) SND FAT 230° MAG	610	610	1500
Stornoway Runway 18 LC	18	LLZ I SV	300	300	1000
	18	NDB(L) SWY	460	460	1400
	18	NDB(L) SWY/DME STZ	330	330	1100
Runway 36 LC	36	NDB(L) SWY/DME STZ	410	410	1300
Aerodrome Approach 285°MAG		VOR STN	550	550	2000

Instrument Flying

Aerodrome and Approach Lighting Category	Runway	Approach Aid	OCH (ft)	Minima	
				DH/MDH (ft)	RVR (m)
1	2	3	4 Note 3	5 Note 3	6
Sumburgh					
Runway 09 LD	09	NDB(L) SBH/LLZ/DME SUB	300	300	1100 ←
	09	LLZ/DME SUB/VOR SUM	300	300	1100
	09	VOR/DME SUM	820	820	1500
	09	VOR SUM	820	820	1500
	09	RADAR (2 nm termination range)	410	410	1400
Runway 15 LC	15	VOR/DME SUM	700	700	1500
	15	VOR SUM	1100	1100	1500
Runway 27 LD	27	ILS/DME/VOR SUM	250	300	1000
	27	ILS/DME (GP inoperative)/VOR SUM	310	310	1200
	27	VOR/DME SUM	460	460	1500
	27	VOR SUM	570	570	1500
	27	NDB(L) SBH/ILS/DME I SG	250	300	1100
	27	NDB(L) SBH/ILS/DME I SG (GP inoperative)	310	310	1200
	27	RADAR (2 nm termination range with VOR SUM)	550	550	1500
	27	RADAR (2 nm termination range without VOR SUM)	650	650	1500
	Aerodrome Approach 005°MAG	VOR/DME SUM	700	700	2000
Swansea					
Runway 04 LC	04	NDB(L) SWN/DME SWZ	350	350	1100
	04	NDB(L) SWN	600	600	1500
	04	VDF 045°	650	650	1500
Runway 22 LC	22	NDB(L) SWN/DME SWZ	480	480	1400
Teesside					
Runway 05 LB	05	ILS/DME	145	250	700
	05	ILS/DME (GP inoperative)	320	320	1000
	05	NDB(L) TD/DME I TSE	360	360	1100
	05	RADAR (1 nm termination range)	360	360	1100
Runway 23 LA	23	ILS/DME	140	250	600
	23	ILS/DME (GP inoperative)	390	390	900
	23	NDB(L) TD	390	390	900
	23	VDF	620	620	1400
	23	RADAR (1 nm termination range)	400	400	900
Tiree					
Runway 06 LD	06	VOR/DME TIR	720	720	1500
Runway 24 LD	24	VOR/DME TIR	360	360	1300
	24	VOR TIR	630	630	1500
Unst					
Runway 30 LD	30	NDB(L) UT	410	410	1400
	30	NDB(L) UT/DME VFD	360	360	1300
Wick					
Runway 13 LC	13	VOR WIK/DME WIZ	320	320	1100
	13	VOR WIK	740	740	1500
	13	NDB(L) WIK/DME WIZ	350	350	1100
Runway 26 LD	26	VOR WIK/DME WIZ	400	400	1300
	26	VOR WIK	400	400	1300
Runway 31 LC	31	VOR WIK/DME WIZ	330	330	1100
	31	VOR WIK	380	380	1200
	31	NDB(L) WIK	300	300	1000

Some interesting reading from the Air Pilot

Aerodrome and Approach Lighting Category	Runway	Approach Aid	OCH (ft)	Minima	
				DH/MDH (ft)	RVR (m)
1	2	3	4 Note 3	5 Note 3	6
Woodford					
Runway 07 LD	07	NDB(L) WFD/DME I WU	400	400	1300
	07	RADAR (2 nm termination range)	670	670	1500
Runway 25 LC	25	ILS/DME	400	450	1200
	25	ILS/DME (GP inoperative)	600	600	1500
	25	NDB(L) WFD/DME I WU	670	670	1500
	25	RADAR (2 nm termination range)	830	830	1500
Yeovil					
Runway 10 LD	10	NDB(L) YVL/DME YVL	480	480	1500
	10	NDB(L) YVL	590	590	1500
	10	RADAR (0.5 nm termination range)	400	400	1300
	10	RADAR (2 nm termination range)	600	600	1500
Runway 28 LD	28	NDB(L) YVL/DME YVL	480	480	1500
	28	NDB(L) YVL	700	700	1500
	28	RADAR (0.5 nm termination range)	400	400	1300
	28	RADAR (2 nm termination range)	600	600	1500

Index